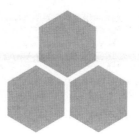

WRITER: **JONATHAN HICKMAN**

ARTISTS: **STEVE EPTING** [ISSUES 1-3] **AND BARRY KITSON** [ISSUES 4-5]

INKERS: **STEVE EPTING, RICK MAGYAR & BUTCH GUICE** [ISSUES 1-3]; **AND BARRY KITSON** [ISSUES 4-5]

COLOR ARTIST: **PAUL MOUNTS**

LETTERERS: **VIRTUAL CALLIGRAPHY'S RUS WOOTON** [ISSUES 1-2] **AND CLAYTON COWLES** [ISSUES 3-5]

COVER ARTISTS: **STEVE EPTING; DANIEL ACUÑA; AND MARK BAGLEY, ANDY LANNING & PAUL MOUNTS**

ASSOCIATE EDITOR: **LAUREN SANKOVITCH**

EDITOR: **TOM BREVOORT**

COLLECTION EDITOR: **JENNIFER GRÜNWALD**
EDITORIAL ASSISTANTS: **JAMES EMMETT & JOE HOCHSTEIN**
ASSISTANT EDITORS: **ALEX STARBUCK & NELSON RIBEIRO**
EDITOR, SPECIAL PROJECTS: **MARK D. BEAZLEY**
SENIOR EDITOR, SPECIAL PROJECTS: **JEFF YOUNGQUIST**
SENIOR VICE PRESIDENT OF SALES: **DAVID GABRIEL**
SVP OF BRAND PLANNING & COMMUNICATIONS: **MICHAEL PASCIULLO**

EDITOR IN CHIEF: **AXEL ALONSO**
CHIEF CREATIVE OFFICER: **JOE QUESADA**
PUBLISHER: **DAN BUCKLEY**
EXECUTIVE PRODUCER: **ALAN FINE**

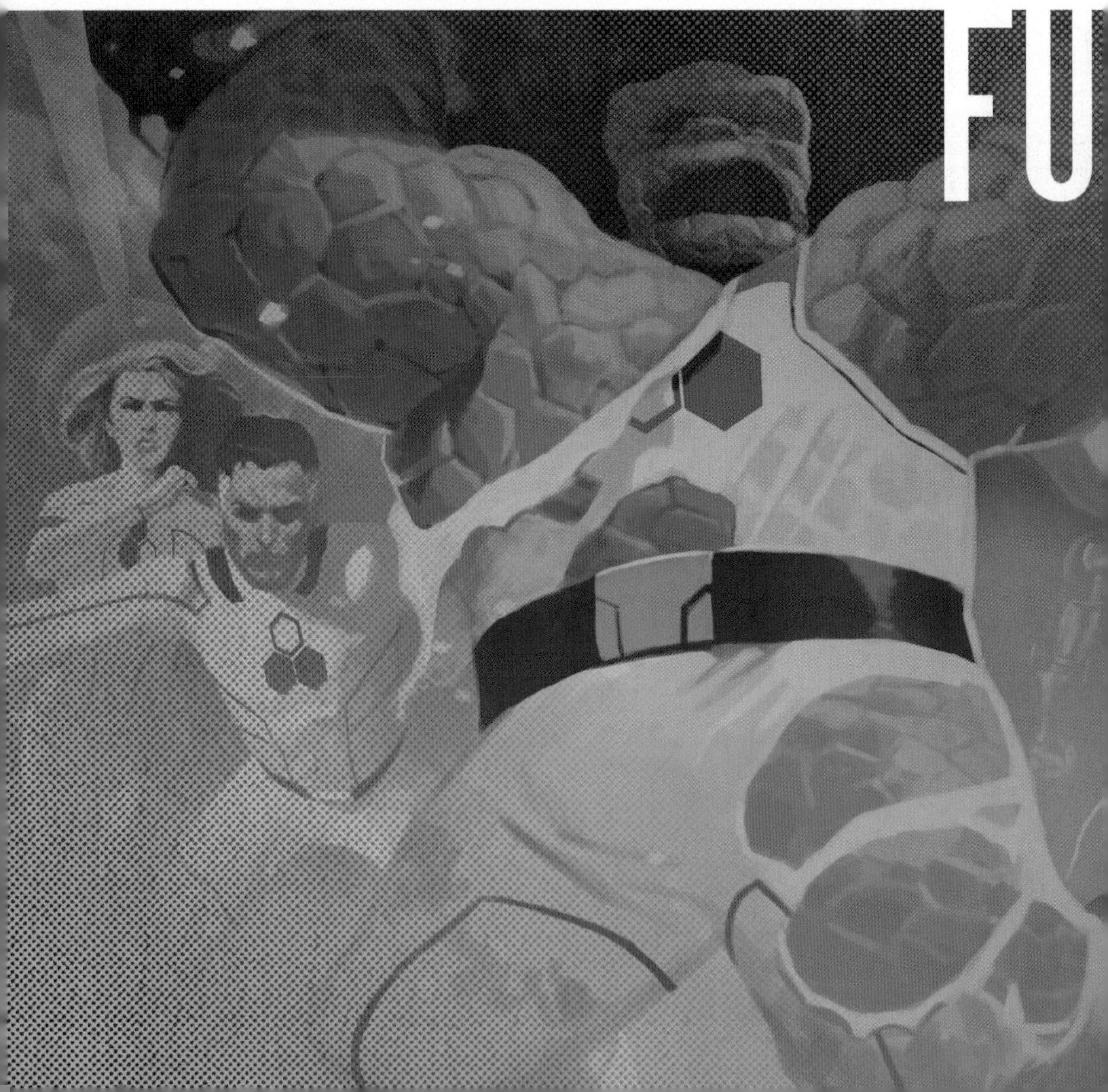
FU

URE FOUNDATION

UNIFIED FIELD THEORY: STAN LEE & JACK KIRBY

FF BY JONATHAN HICKMAN VOL. 1. Contains material originally published in magazine form as FF #1-5. First printing 2012. ISBN# 978-0-7851-5145-6. Published by MARVEL WORLDWIDE, INC., a subsidiary of MARVEL ENTERTAINMENT, LLC. OFFICE OF PUBLICATION: 135 West 50th Street, New York, NY 10020. Copyright © 2011 and 2012 Marvel Characters, Inc. All rights reserved. $15.99 per copy in the U.S. and $17.99 in Canada (GST #R127032852); Canadian Agreement #40668537. All characters featured in this issue and the distinctive names and likenesses thereof, and all related indicia are trademarks of Marvel Characters, Inc. No similarity between any of the names, characters, persons, and/or institutions in this magazine with those of any living or dead person or institution is intended, and any such similarity which may exist is purely coincidental. **Printed in the U.S.A.** ALAN FINE, EVP - Office of the President, Marvel Worldwide, Inc. and EVP & CMO Marvel Characters B.V.; DAN BUCKLEY, Publisher & President - Print, Animation & Digital Divisions; JOE QUESADA, Chief Creative Officer; DAVID BOGART, SVP of Business Affairs & Talent Management; TOM BREVOORT, SVP of Publishing; C.B. CEBULSKI, SVP of Creator & Content Development; DAVID GABRIEL, SVP of Publishing Sales & Circulation; MICHAEL PASCIULLO, SVP of Brand Planning & Communications; JIM O'KEEFE, VP of Operations & Logistics; DAN CARR, Executive Director of Publishing Technology; SUSAN CRESPI, Editorial Operations Manager; ALEX MORALES, Publishing Operations Manager; STAN LEE, Chairman Emeritus. For information regarding advertising in Marvel Comics or on Marvel.com, please contact John Dokes, SVP Integrated Sales and Marketing, at jdokes@marvel.com. For Marvel subscription inquiries, please call 800-217-9158. **Manufactured between 1/25/2012 and 2/13/2012 by R.R. DONNELLEY, INC., SALEM, VA, USA.**

10 9 8 7 6 5 4 3 2 1

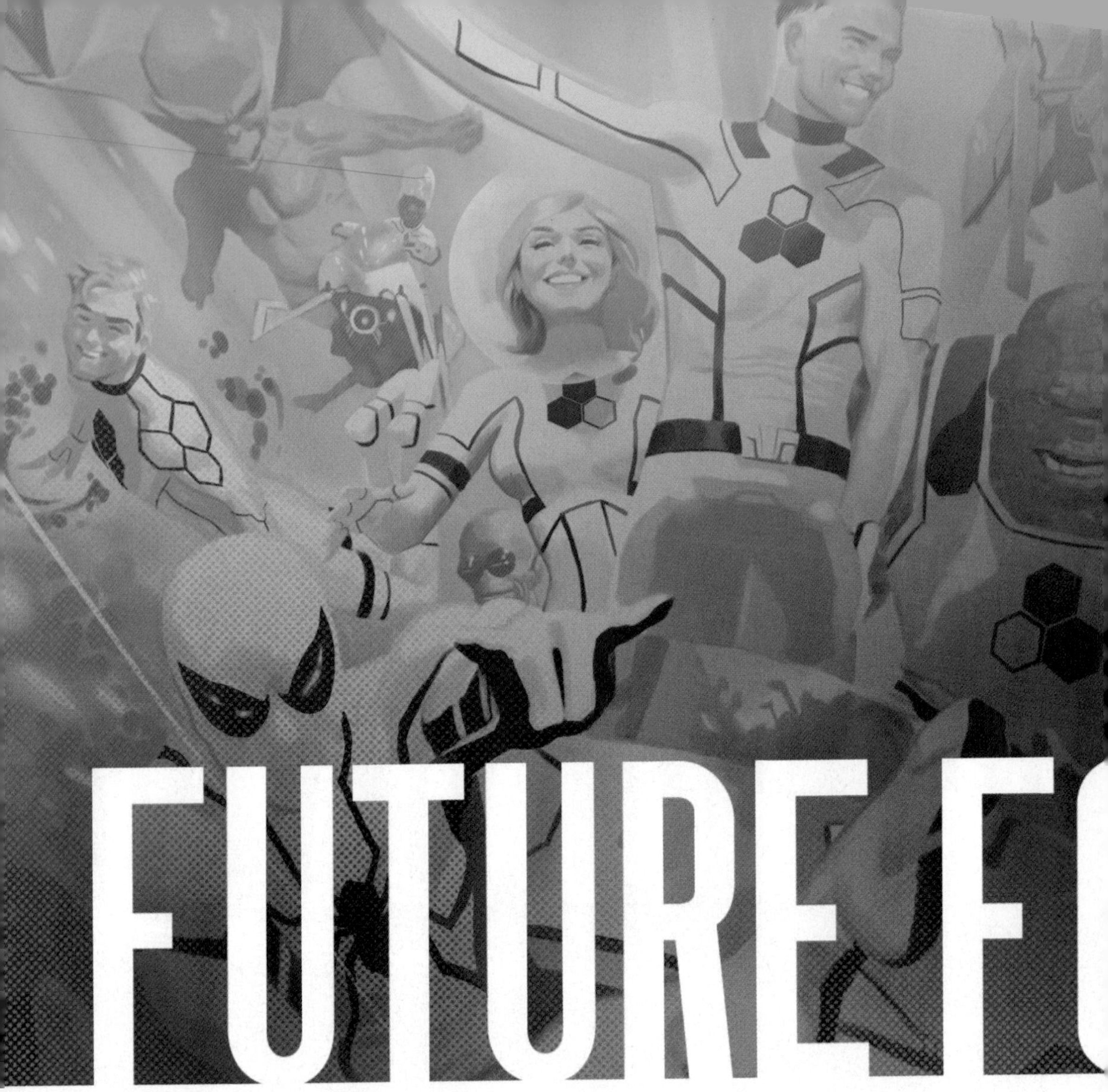
FUTURE FO

OUNDATION

VOL **ONE** **TOMORROW**

SO THIS IS TOMORROW

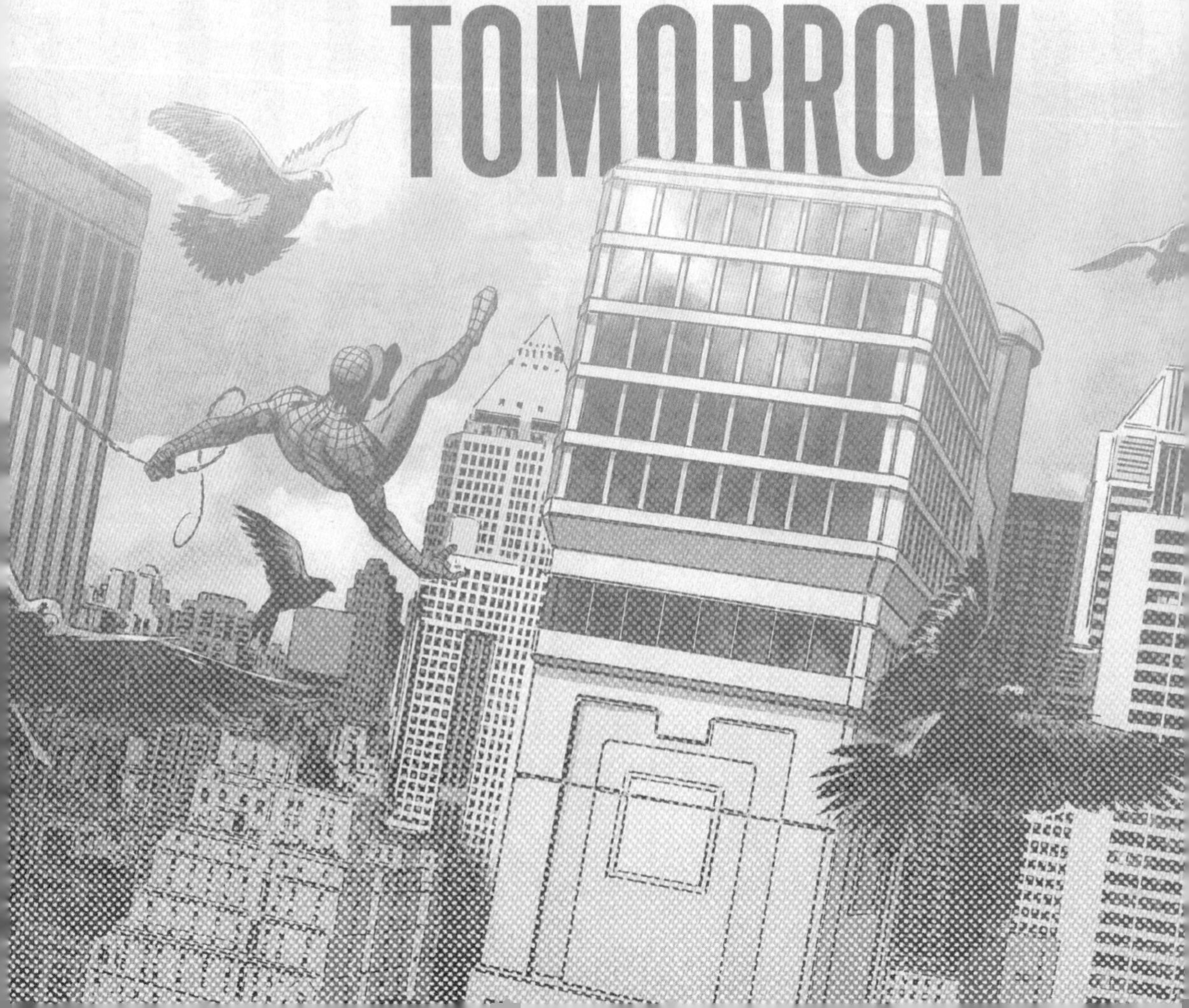

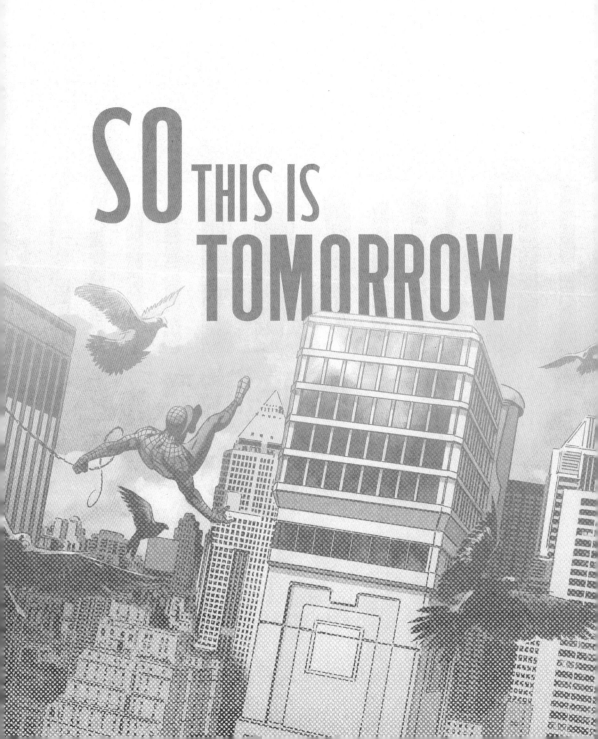

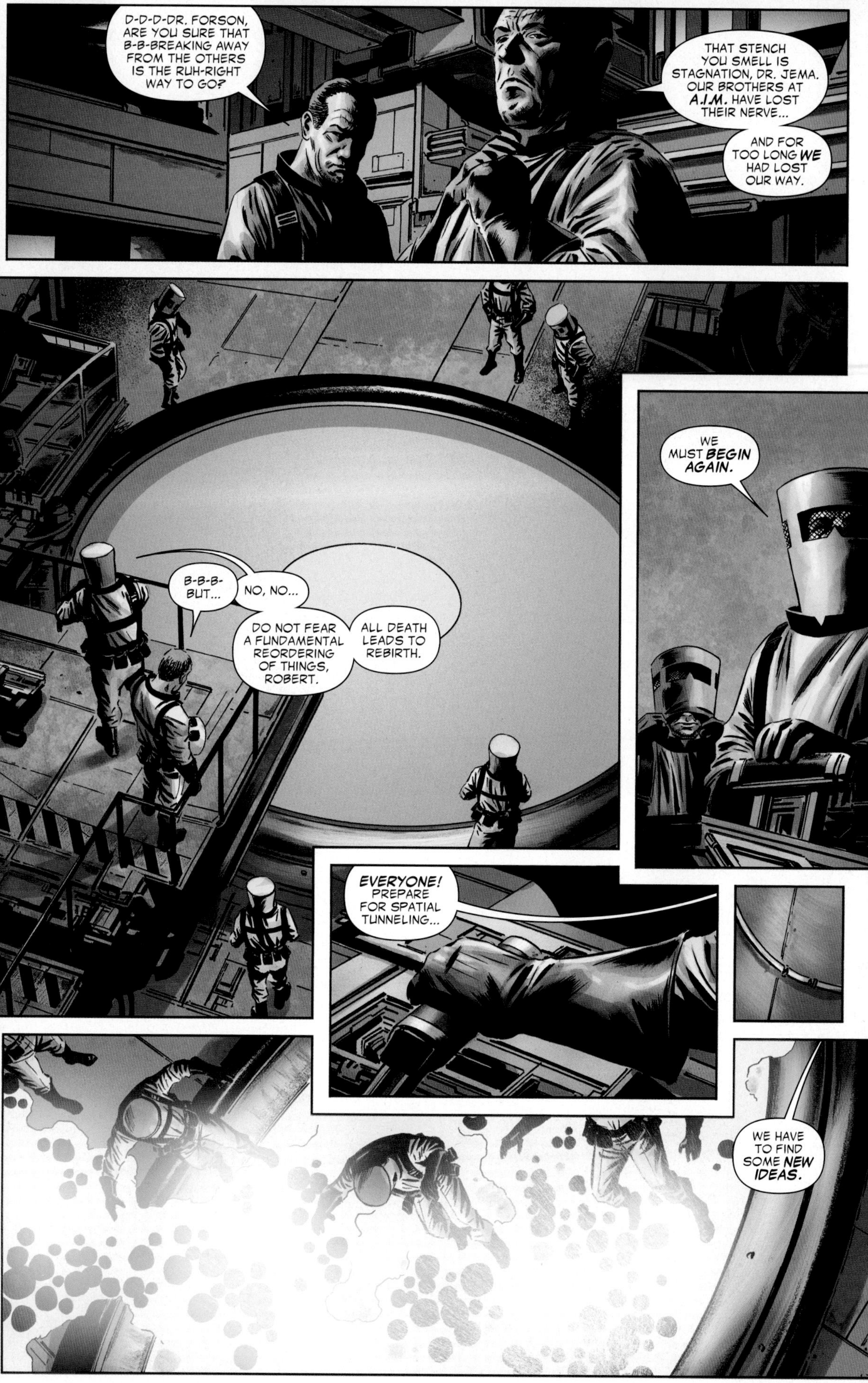
D-D-D-DR. FORSON, ARE YOU SURE THAT B-B-BREAKING AWAY FROM THE OTHERS IS THE RUH-RIGHT WAY TO GO?
THAT STENCH YOU SMELL IS STAGNATION, DR. JEMA. OUR BROTHERS AT A.I.M. HAVE LOST THEIR NERVE...
AND FOR TOO LONG WE HAD LOST OUR WAY.
WE MUST BEGIN AGAIN.
B-B-B-BUT...
NO, NO...
DO NOT FEAR A FUNDAMENTAL REORDERING OF THINGS, ROBERT.
ALL DEATH LEADS TO REBIRTH.
EVERYONE! PREPARE FOR SPATIAL TUNNELING...
WE HAVE TO FIND SOME NEW IDEAS.

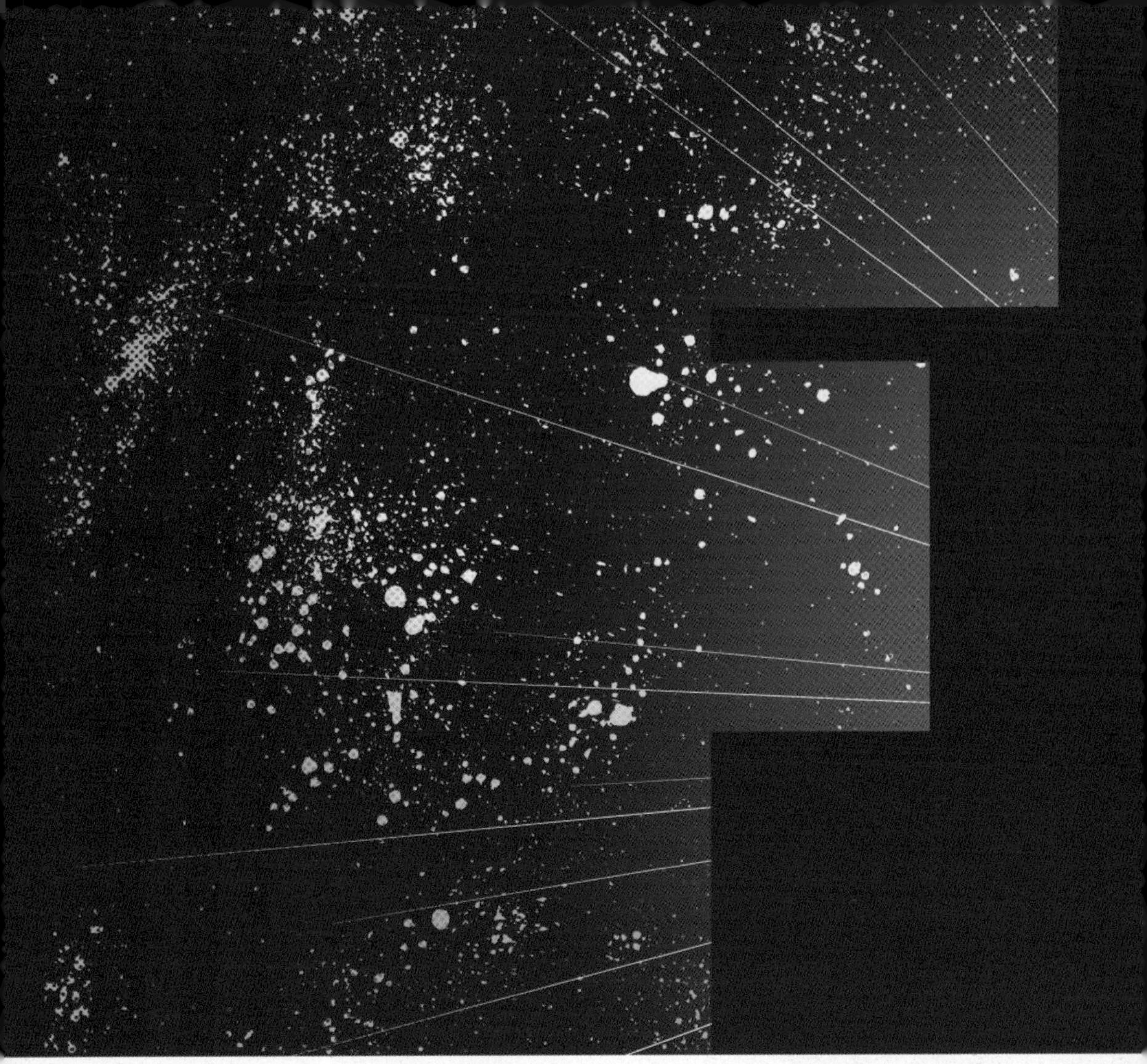

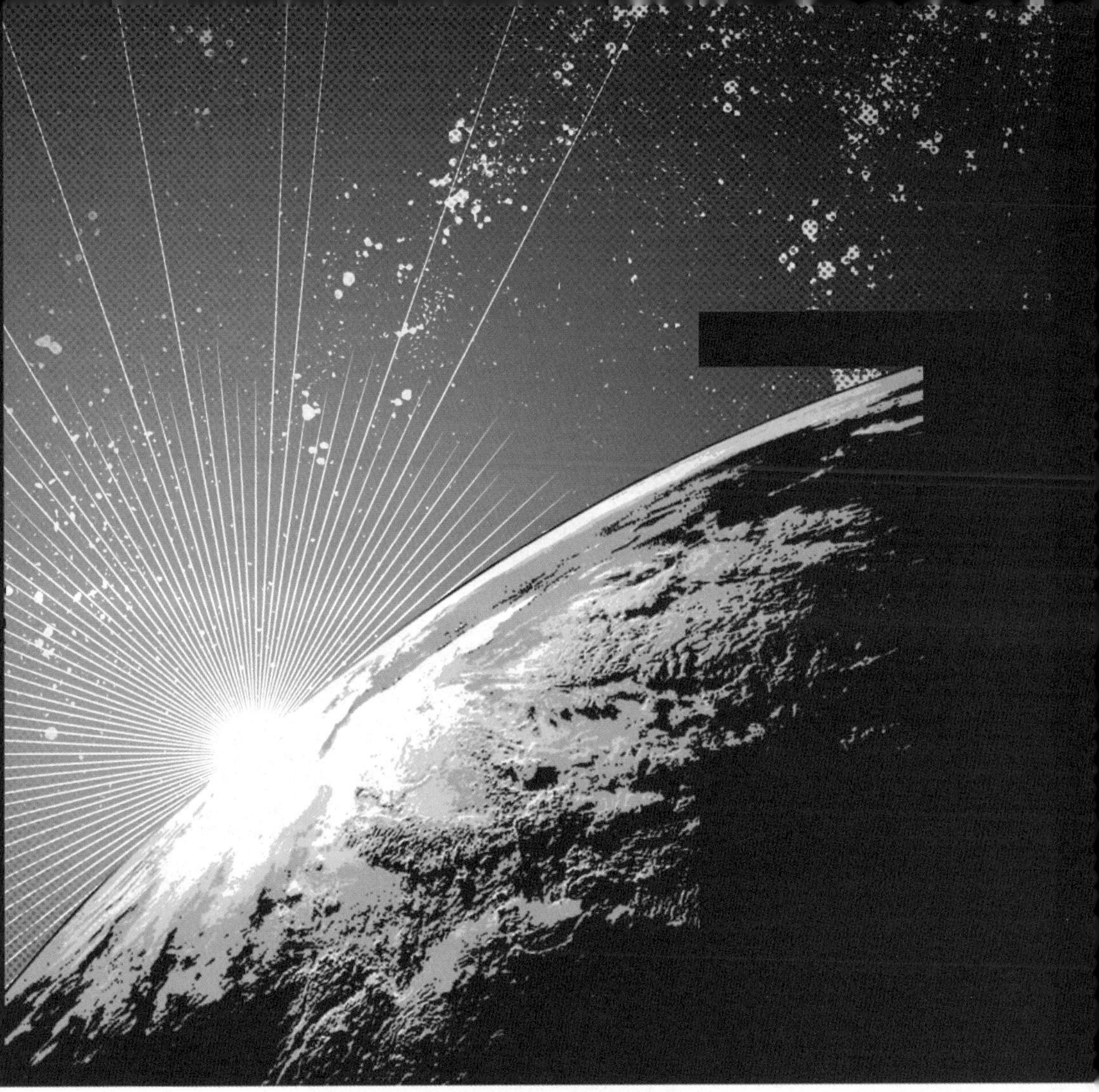

THE HUMAN TORCH HAS DIED.
THE FANTASTIC FOUR IS NO MORE.
WELCOME TO TOMORROW.
WELCOME TO THE FUTURE FOUNDATION.

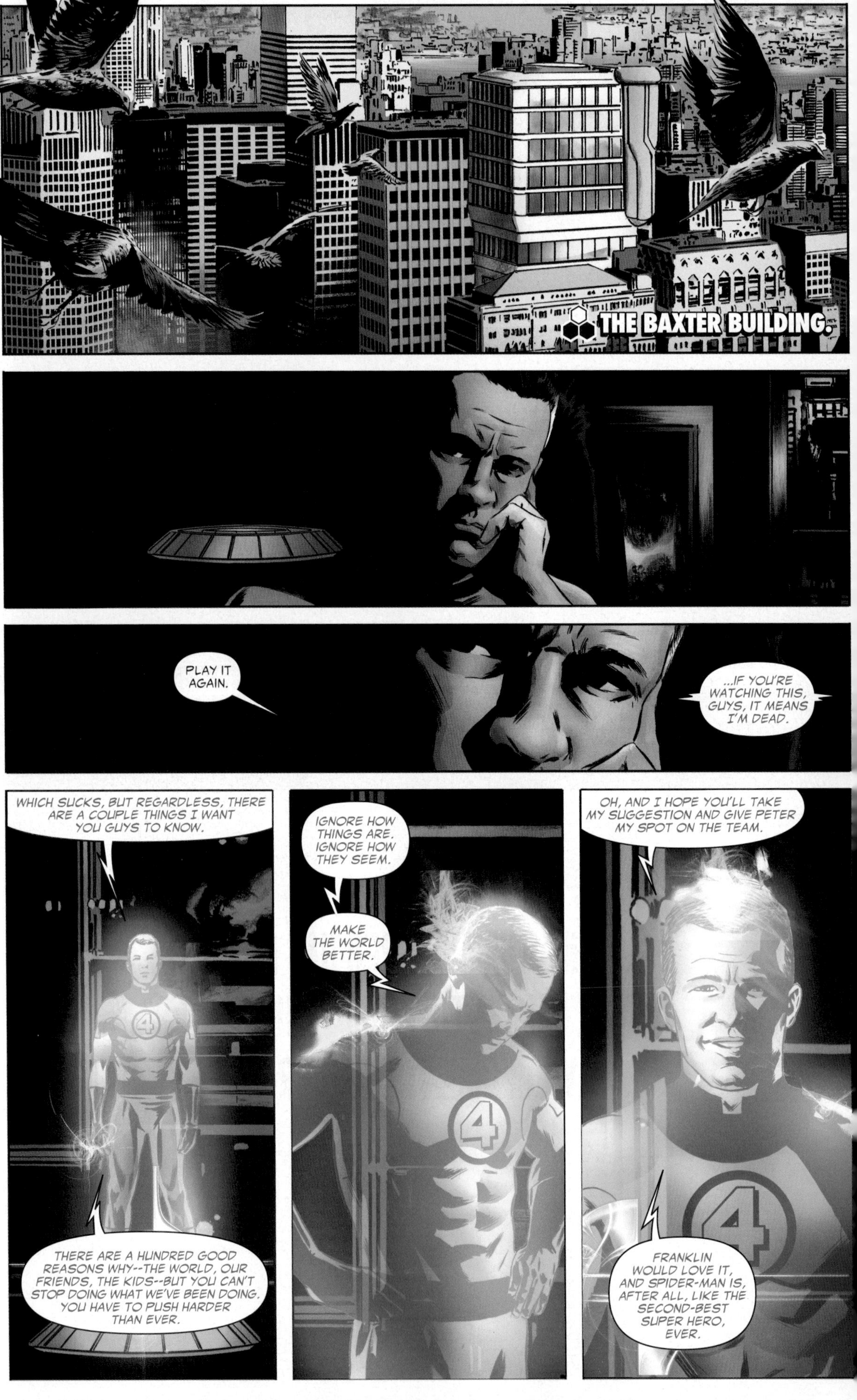
THE BAXTER BUILDING.
PLAY IT AGAIN.
...IF YOU'RE WATCHING THIS, GUYS, IT MEANS I'M DEAD.
WHICH SUCKS, BUT REGARDLESS, THERE ARE A COUPLE THINGS I WANT YOU GUYS TO KNOW.
THERE ARE A HUNDRED GOOD REASONS WHY--THE WORLD, OUR FRIENDS, THE KIDS--BUT YOU CAN'T STOP DOING WHAT WE'VE BEEN DOING. YOU HAVE TO PUSH HARDER THAN EVER.
IGNORE HOW THINGS ARE. IGNORE HOW THEY SEEM.
MAKE THE WORLD BETTER.
OH, AND I HOPE YOU'LL TAKE MY SUGGESTION AND GIVE PETER MY SPOT ON THE TEAM.
FRANKLIN WOULD LOVE IT, AND SPIDER-MAN IS, AFTER ALL, LIKE THE SECOND-BEST SUPER HERO, EVER.

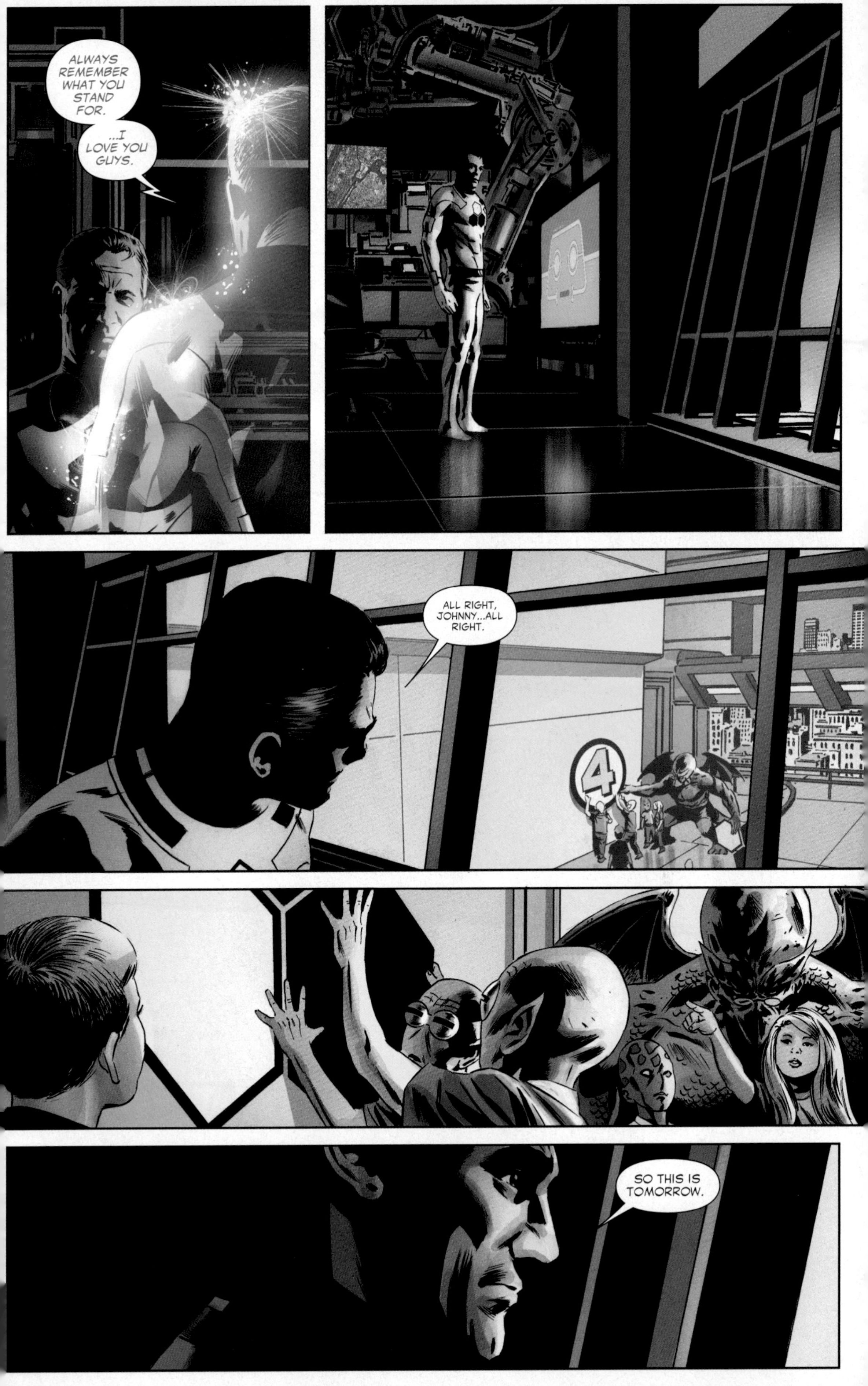
ALWAYS REMEMBER WHAT YOU STAND FOR.
...I LOVE YOU GUYS.
ALL RIGHT, JOHNNY...ALL RIGHT.
SO THIS IS TOMORROW.

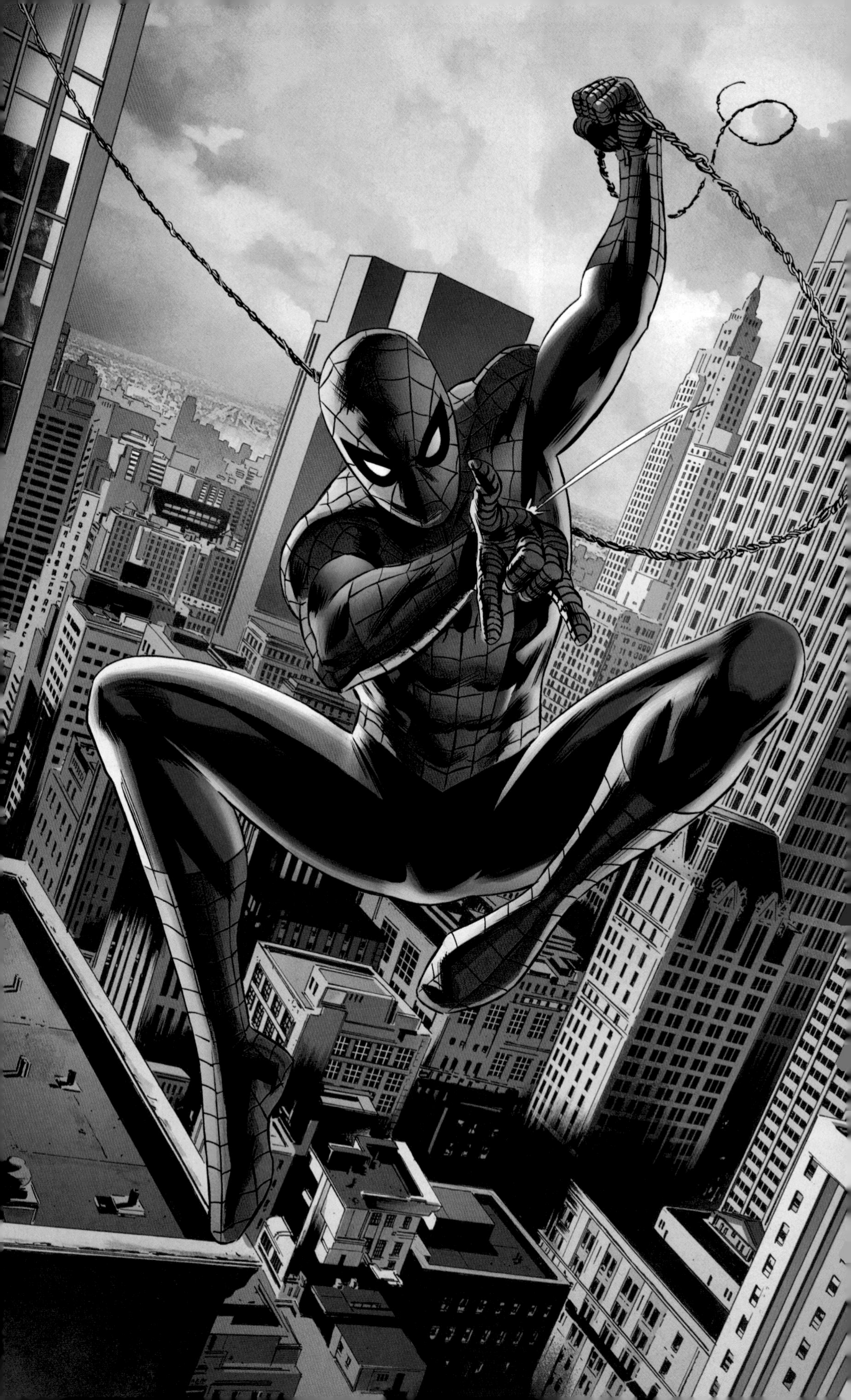

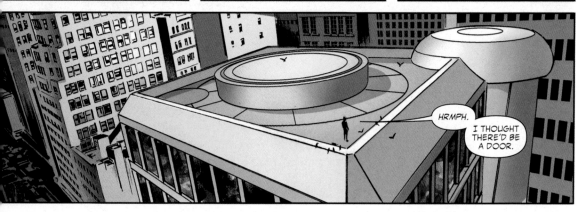

HRMPH.

I THOUGHT THERE'D BE A DOOR.

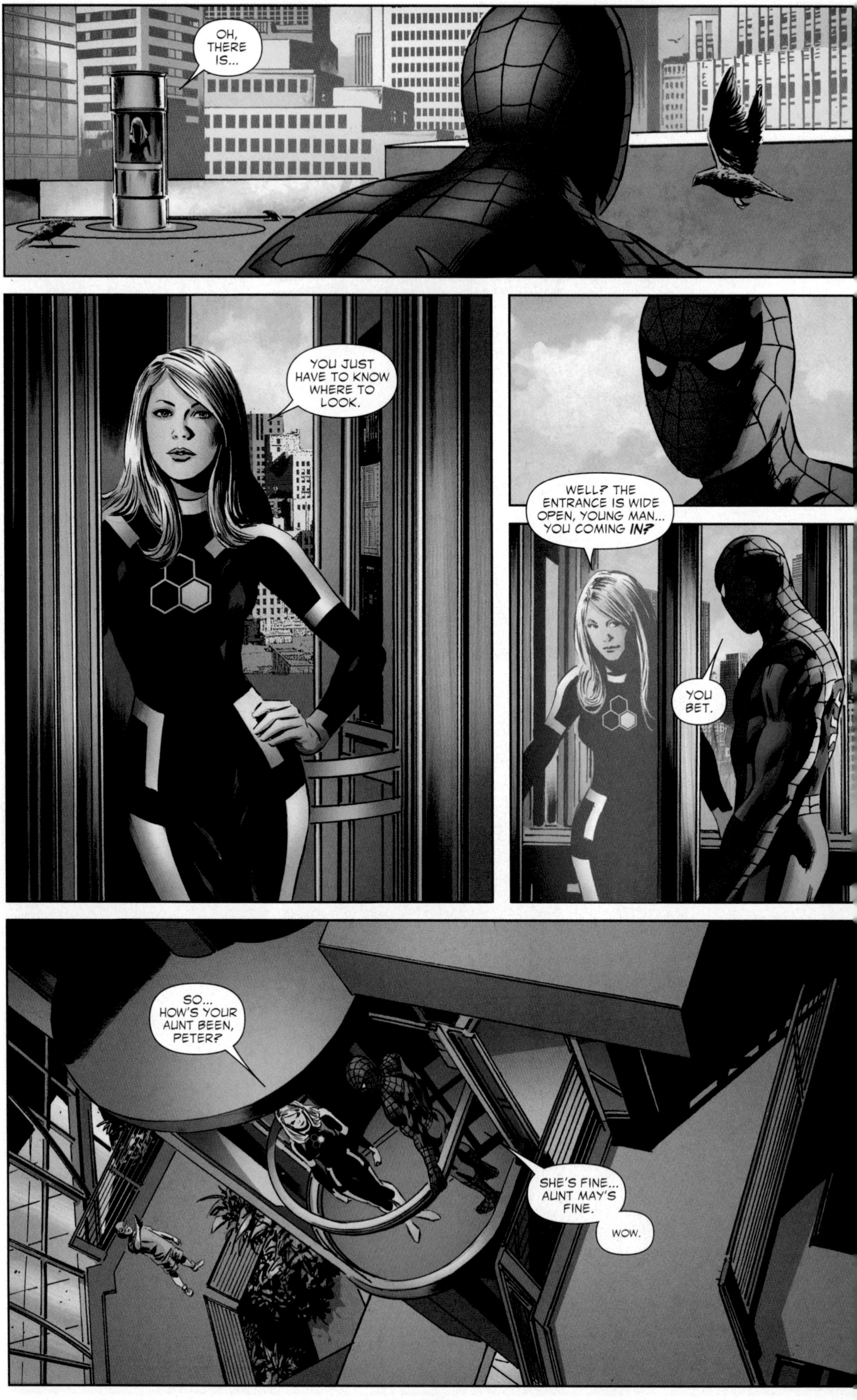
OH, THERE IS...
YOU JUST HAVE TO KNOW WHERE TO LOOK.
WELL? THE ENTRANCE IS WIDE OPEN, YOUNG MAN... YOU COMING IN?
YOU BET.
SO... HOW'S YOUR AUNT BEEN, PETER?
SHE'S FINE... AUNT MAY'S FINE.
WOW.

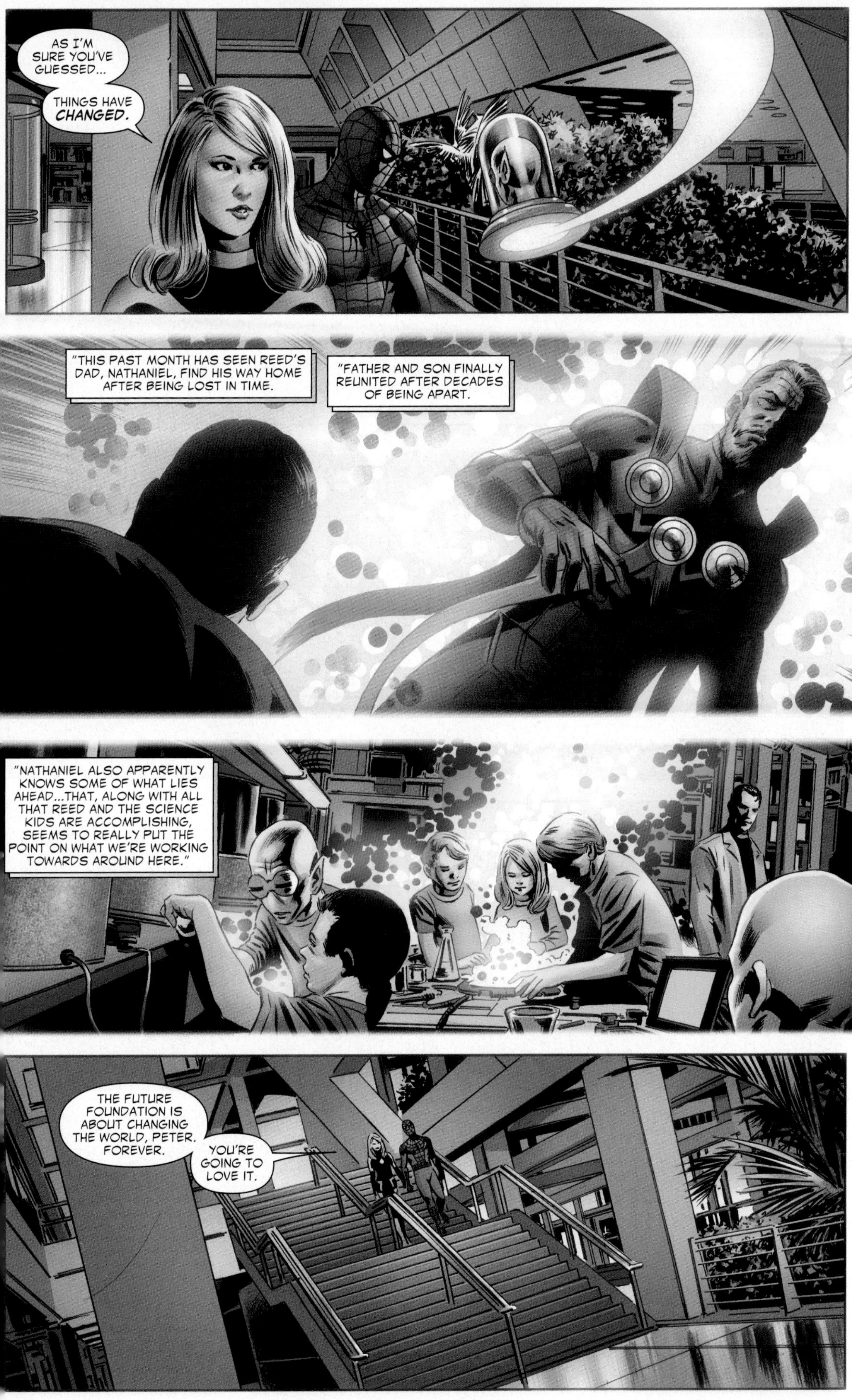

AS I'M SURE YOU'VE GUESSED...
THINGS HAVE CHANGED.
"THIS PAST MONTH HAS SEEN REED'S DAD, NATHANIEL, FIND HIS WAY HOME AFTER BEING LOST IN TIME.
"FATHER AND SON FINALLY REUNITED AFTER DECADES OF BEING APART.
"NATHANIEL ALSO APPARENTLY KNOWS SOME OF WHAT LIES AHEAD...THAT, ALONG WITH ALL THAT REED AND THE SCIENCE KIDS ARE ACCOMPLISHING, SEEMS TO REALLY PUT THE POINT ON WHAT WE'RE WORKING TOWARDS AROUND HERE."
THE FUTURE FOUNDATION IS ABOUT CHANGING THE WORLD, PETER. FOREVER.
YOU'RE GOING TO LOVE IT.

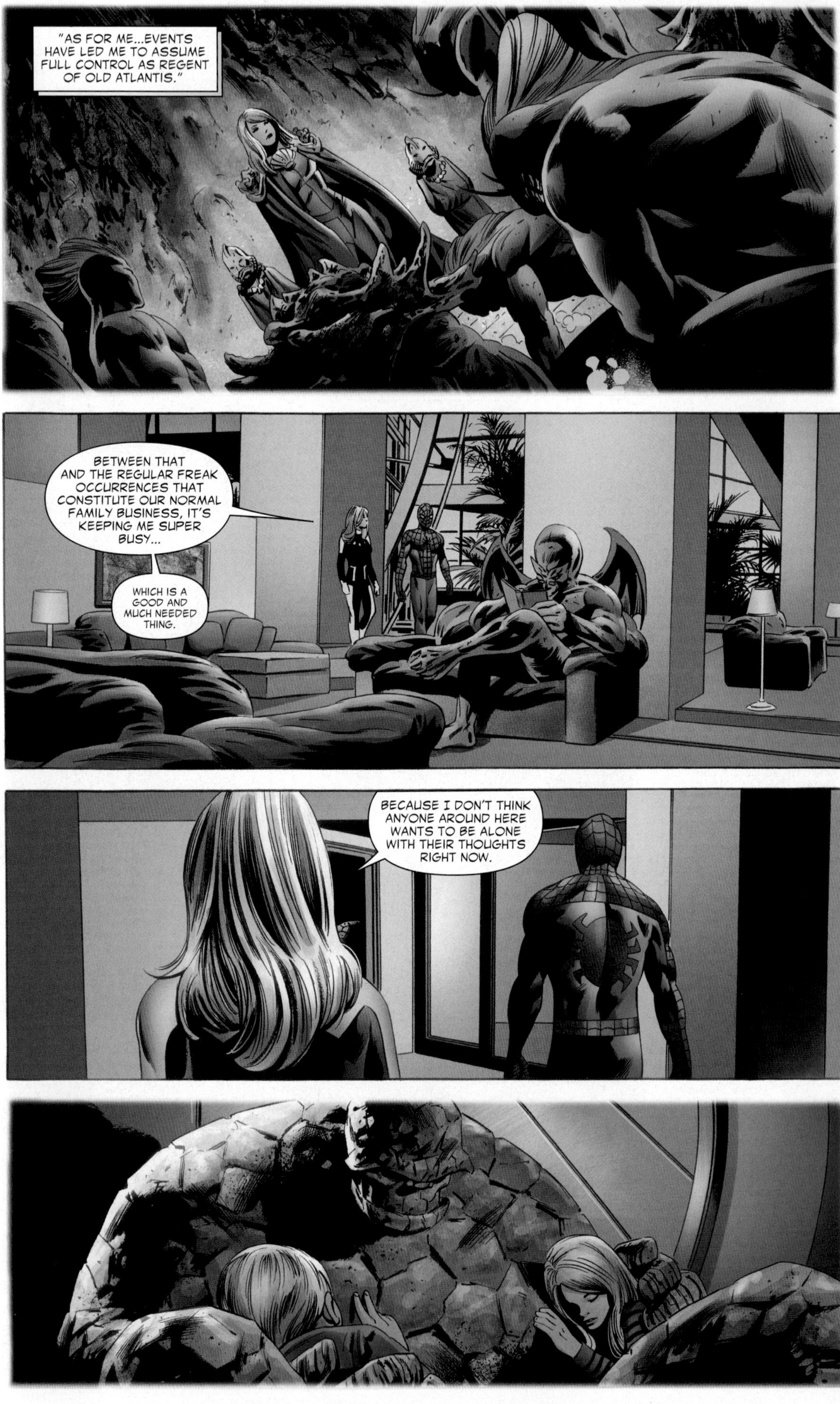
"AS FOR ME...EVENTS HAVE LED ME TO ASSUME FULL CONTROL AS REGENT OF OLD ATLANTIS."
BETWEEN THAT AND THE REGULAR FREAK OCCURRENCES THAT CONSTITUTE OUR NORMAL FAMILY BUSINESS, IT'S KEEPING ME SUPER BUSY...
WHICH IS A GOOD AND MUCH NEEDED THING.
BECAUSE I DON'T THINK ANYONE AROUND HERE WANTS TO BE ALONE WITH THEIR THOUGHTS RIGHT NOW.

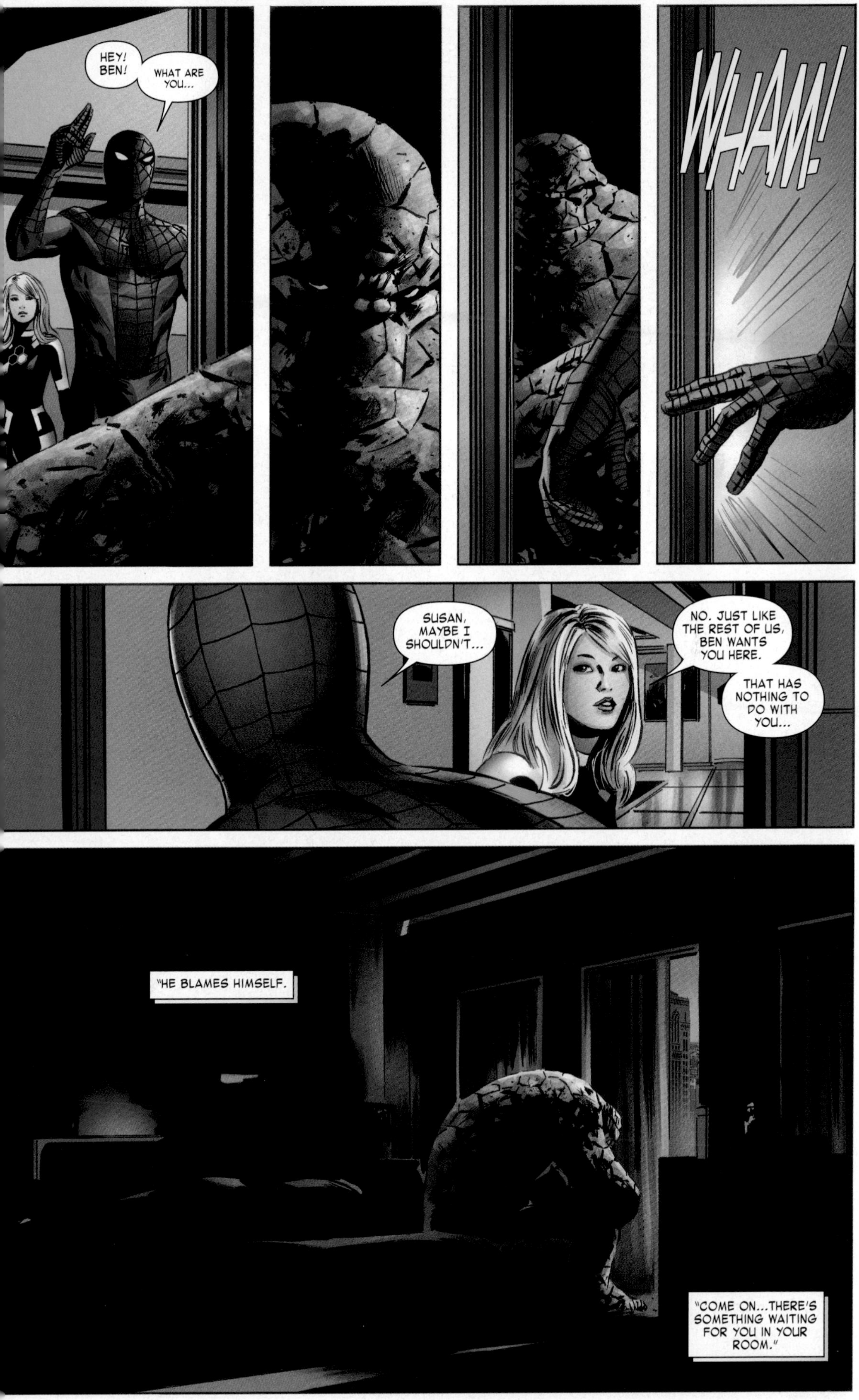

HEY! BEN!
WHAT ARE YOU...
WHAM!
SUSAN, MAYBE I SHOULDN'T...
NO. JUST LIKE THE REST OF US, BEN WANTS YOU HERE.
THAT HAS NOTHING TO DO WITH YOU...
"HE BLAMES HIMSELF.
"COME ON...THERE'S SOMETHING WAITING FOR YOU IN YOUR ROOM."

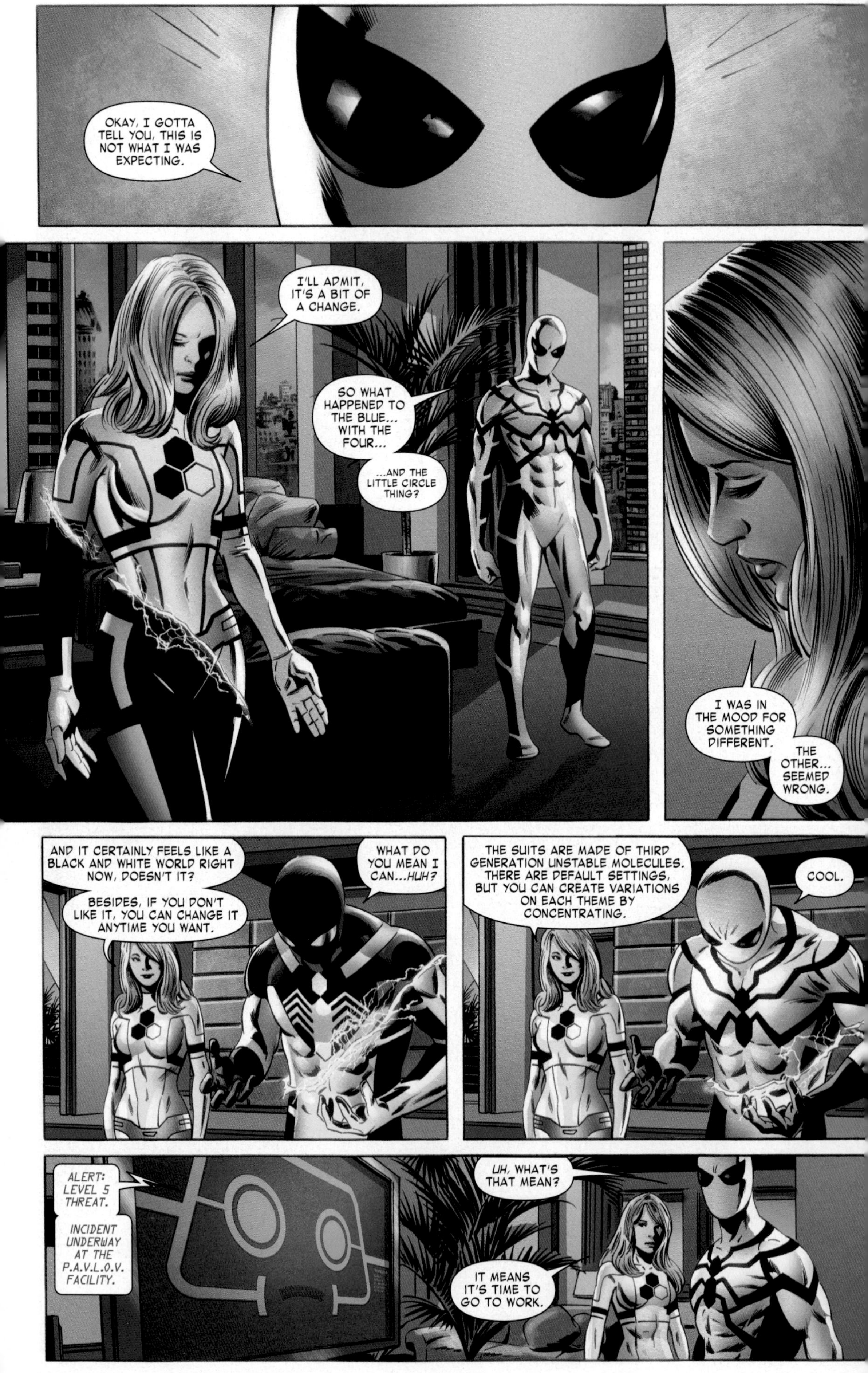

OKAY, I GOTTA TELL YOU, THIS IS NOT WHAT I WAS EXPECTING.
I'LL ADMIT, IT'S A BIT OF A CHANGE.
SO WHAT HAPPENED TO THE BLUE... WITH THE FOUR...
...AND THE LITTLE CIRCLE THING?
I WAS IN THE MOOD FOR SOMETHING DIFFERENT.
THE OTHER... SEEMED WRONG.
AND IT CERTAINLY FEELS LIKE A BLACK AND WHITE WORLD RIGHT NOW, DOESN'T IT?
BESIDES, IF YOU DON'T LIKE IT, YOU CAN CHANGE IT ANYTIME YOU WANT.
WHAT DO YOU MEAN I CAN...*HUH?*
THE SUITS ARE MADE OF THIRD GENERATION UNSTABLE MOLECULES. THERE ARE DEFAULT SETTINGS, BUT YOU CAN CREATE VARIATIONS ON EACH THEME BY CONCENTRATING.
COOL.
ALERT: LEVEL 5 THREAT.
INCIDENT UNDERWAY AT THE P.A.V.L.O.V. FACILITY.
UH, WHAT'S THAT MEAN?
IT MEANS IT'S TIME TO GO TO WORK.

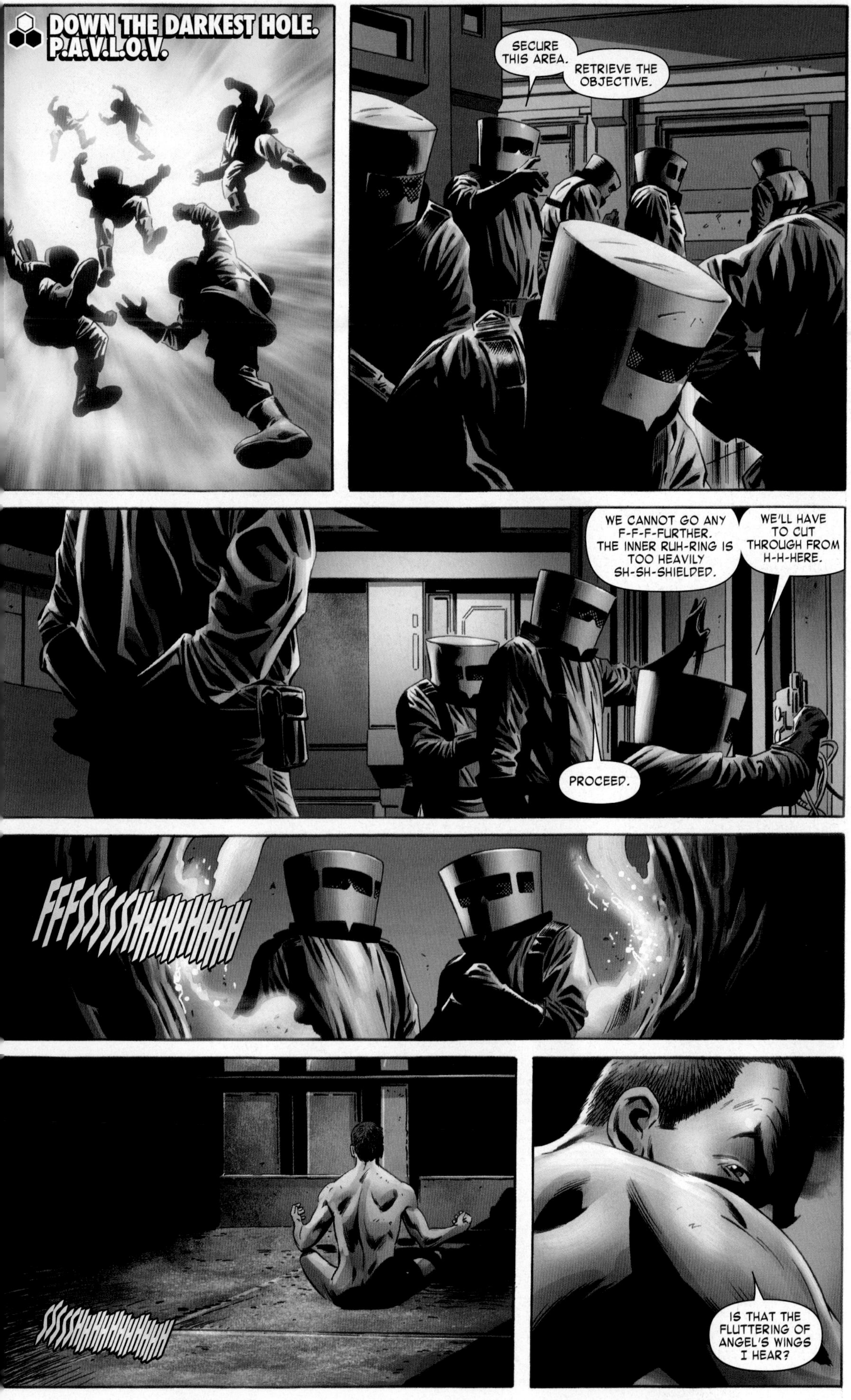
DOWN THE DARKEST HOLE.
P.A.V.L.O.V.
SECURE THIS AREA.
RETRIEVE THE OBJECTIVE.
WE CANNOT GO ANY F-F-F-FURTHER. THE INNER RUH-RING IS TOO HEAVILY SH-SH-SHIELDED.
WE'LL HAVE TO CUT THROUGH FROM H-H-HERE.
PROCEED.
FFFSSSSSHHHHHHHH
SSSSSHHHHHHHHHH
IS THAT THE FLUTTERING OF ANGEL'S WINGS I HEAR?

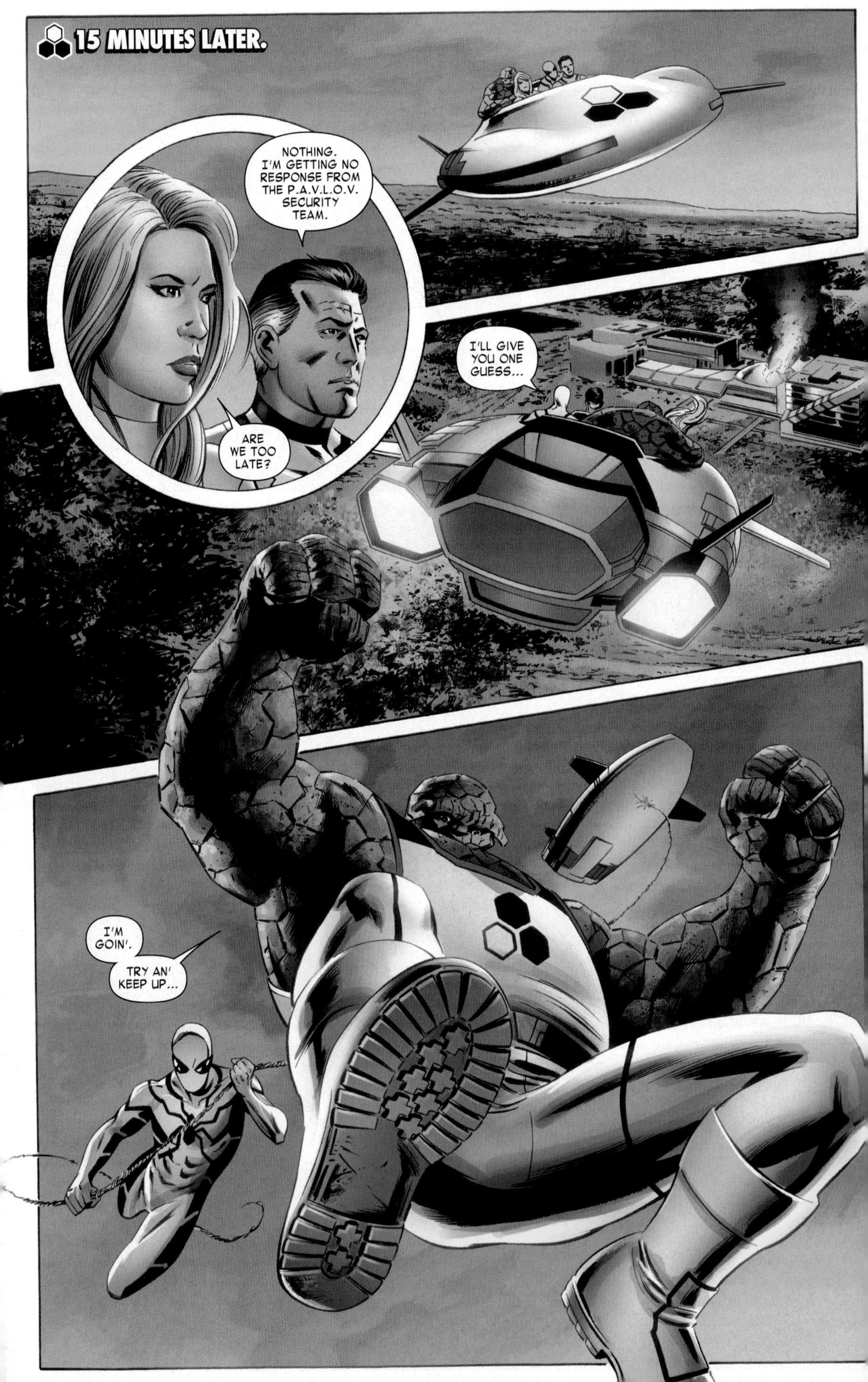
15 MINUTES LATER.
NOTHING. I'M GETTING NO RESPONSE FROM THE P.A.V.L.O.V. SECURITY TEAM.
ARE WE TOO LATE?
I'LL GIVE YOU ONE GUESS...
I'M GOIN'.
TRY AN' KEEP UP...

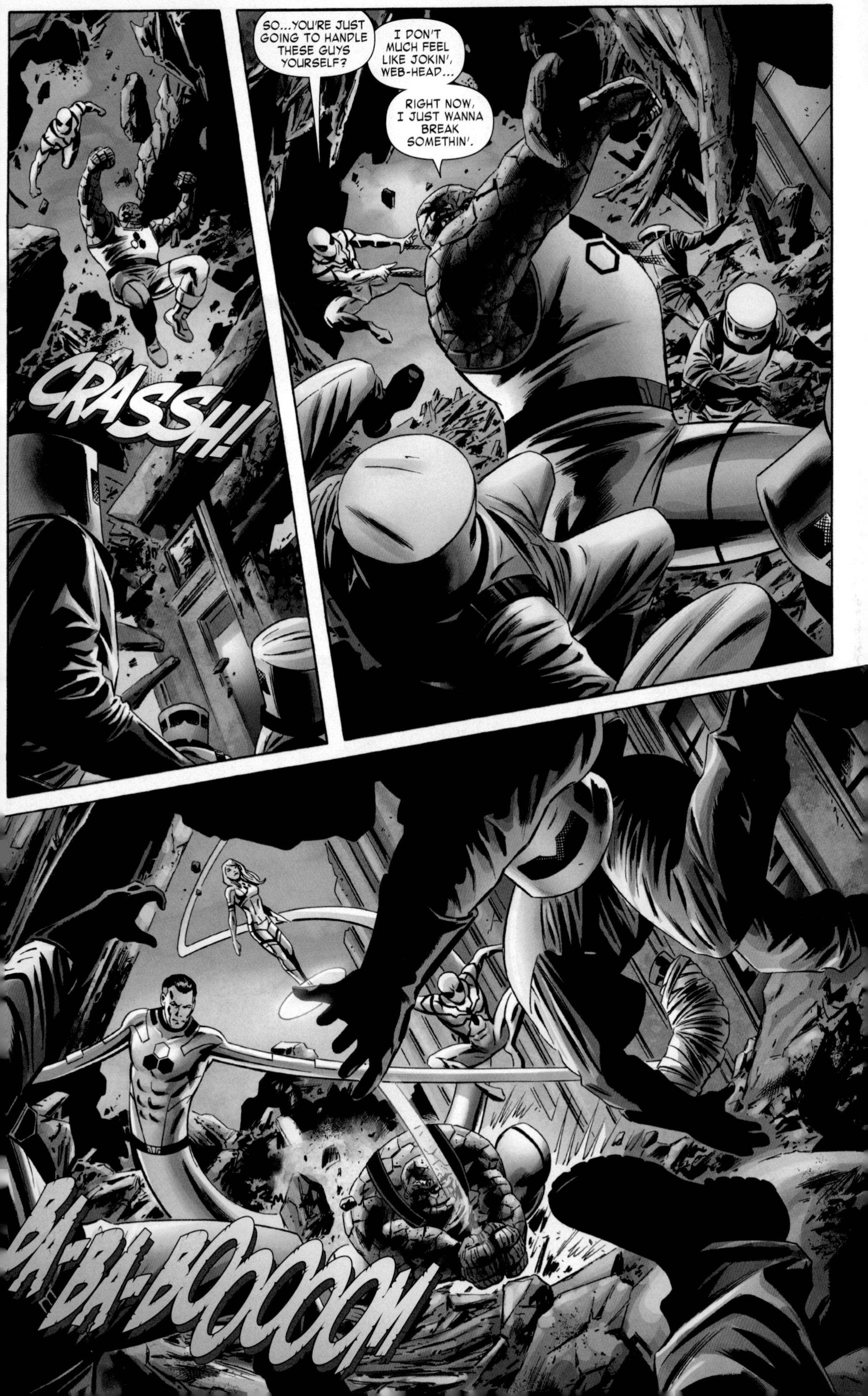
CRASSH!!
SO...YOU'RE JUST GOING TO HANDLE THESE GUYS YOURSELF?
I DON'T MUCH FEEL LIKE JOKIN', WEB-HEAD...
RIGHT NOW, I JUST WANNA BREAK SOMETHIN'.
BA-BA-BOOOOOM

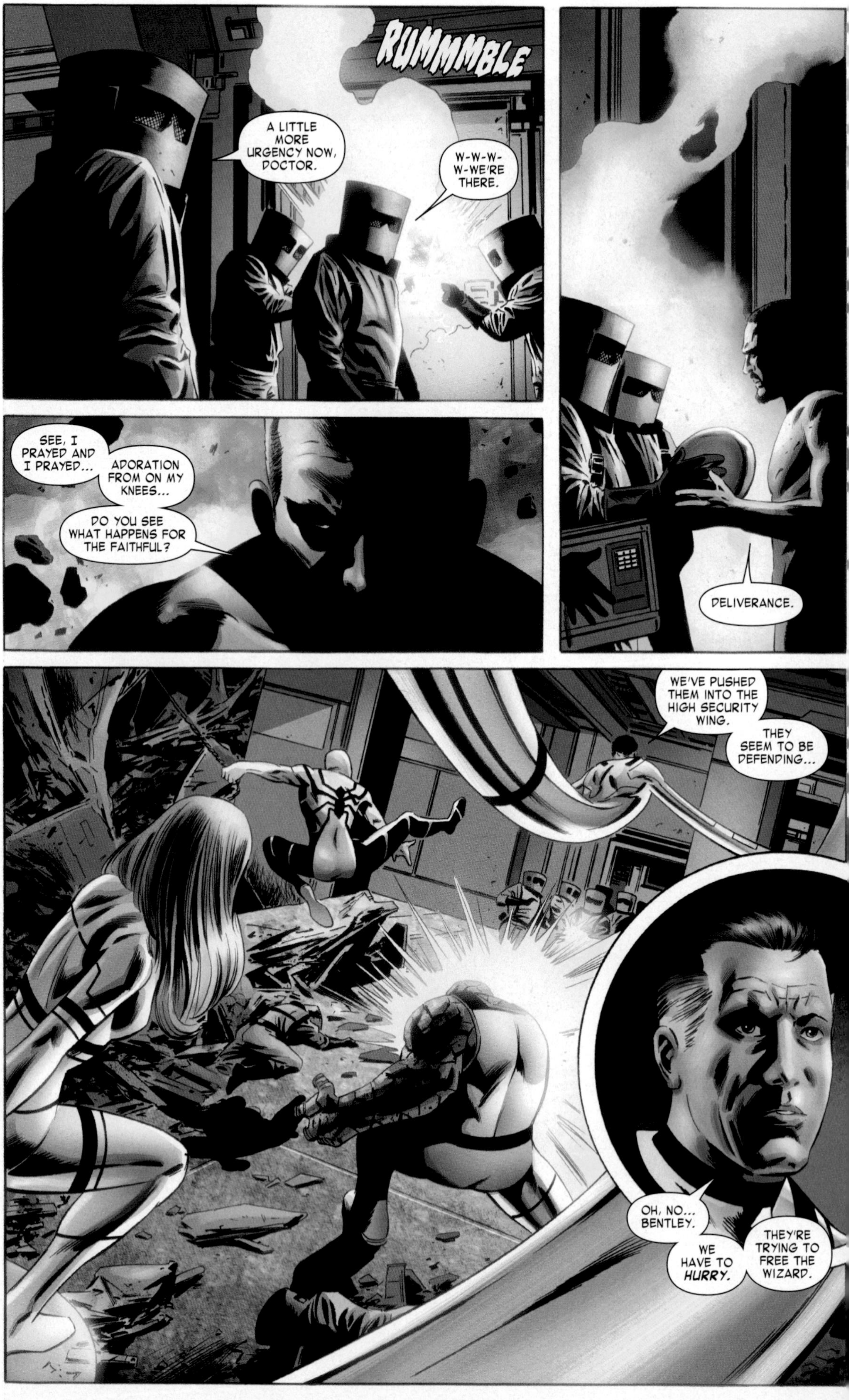
RUMMMBLE
A LITTLE MORE URGENCY NOW, DOCTOR.
W-W-W-W-WE'RE THERE.
DELIVERANCE.
SEE, I PRAYED AND I PRAYED...
ADORATION FROM ON MY KNEES...
DO YOU SEE WHAT HAPPENS FOR THE FAITHFUL?
WE'VE PUSHED THEM INTO THE HIGH SECURITY WING.
THEY SEEM TO BE DEFENDING...
OH, NO... BENTLEY.
THEY'RE TRYING TO FREE THE WIZARD.
WE HAVE TO HURRY.

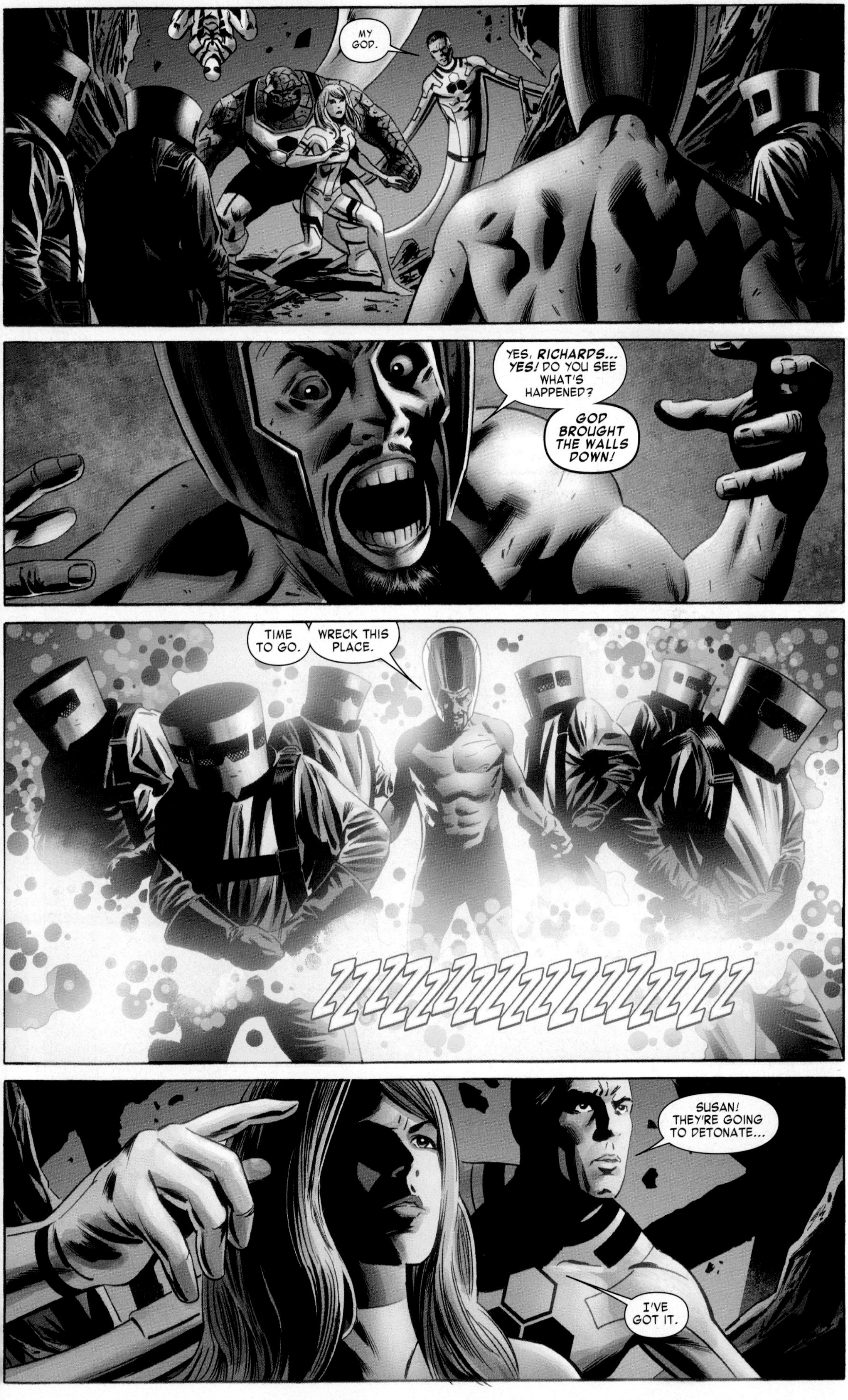
MY GOD.
YES, RICHARDS... YES! DO YOU SEE WHAT'S HAPPENED?
GOD BROUGHT THE WALLS DOWN!
TIME TO GO.
WRECK THIS PLACE.
ZZZZZZZZZZZZZZZZZZZ
SUSAN! THEY'RE GOING TO DETONATE...
I'VE GOT IT.

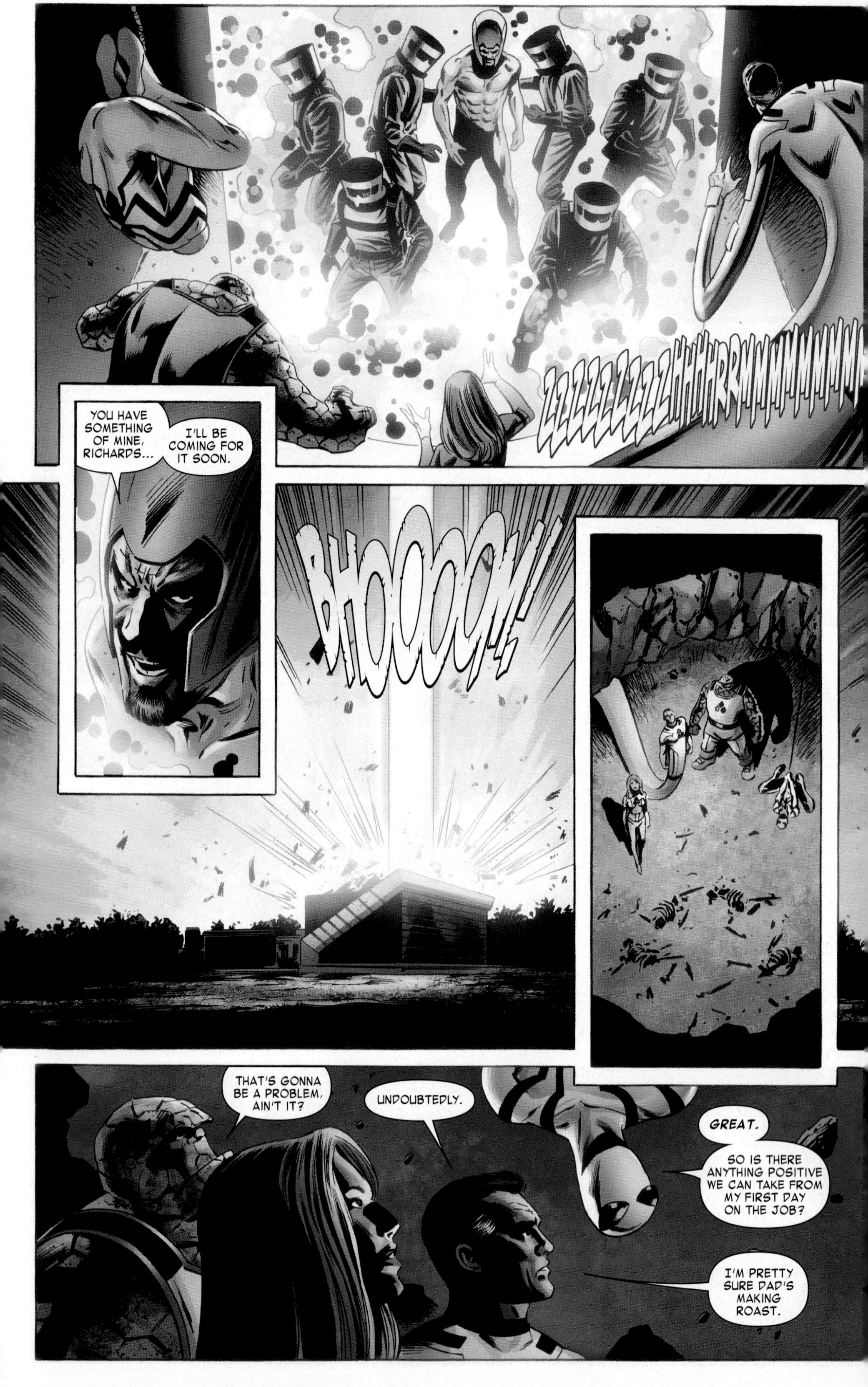

ZZZZZZZZZZHHHHRRMMMMMMMMM
YOU HAVE SOMETHING OF MINE, RICHARDS...
I'LL BE COMING FOR IT SOON.
BHOOOOM!
THAT'S GONNA BE A PROBLEM, AIN'T IT?
UNDOUBTEDLY.
GREAT.
SO IS THERE ANYTHING POSITIVE WE CAN TAKE FROM MY FIRST DAY ON THE JOB?
I'M PRETTY SURE DAD'S MAKING ROAST.

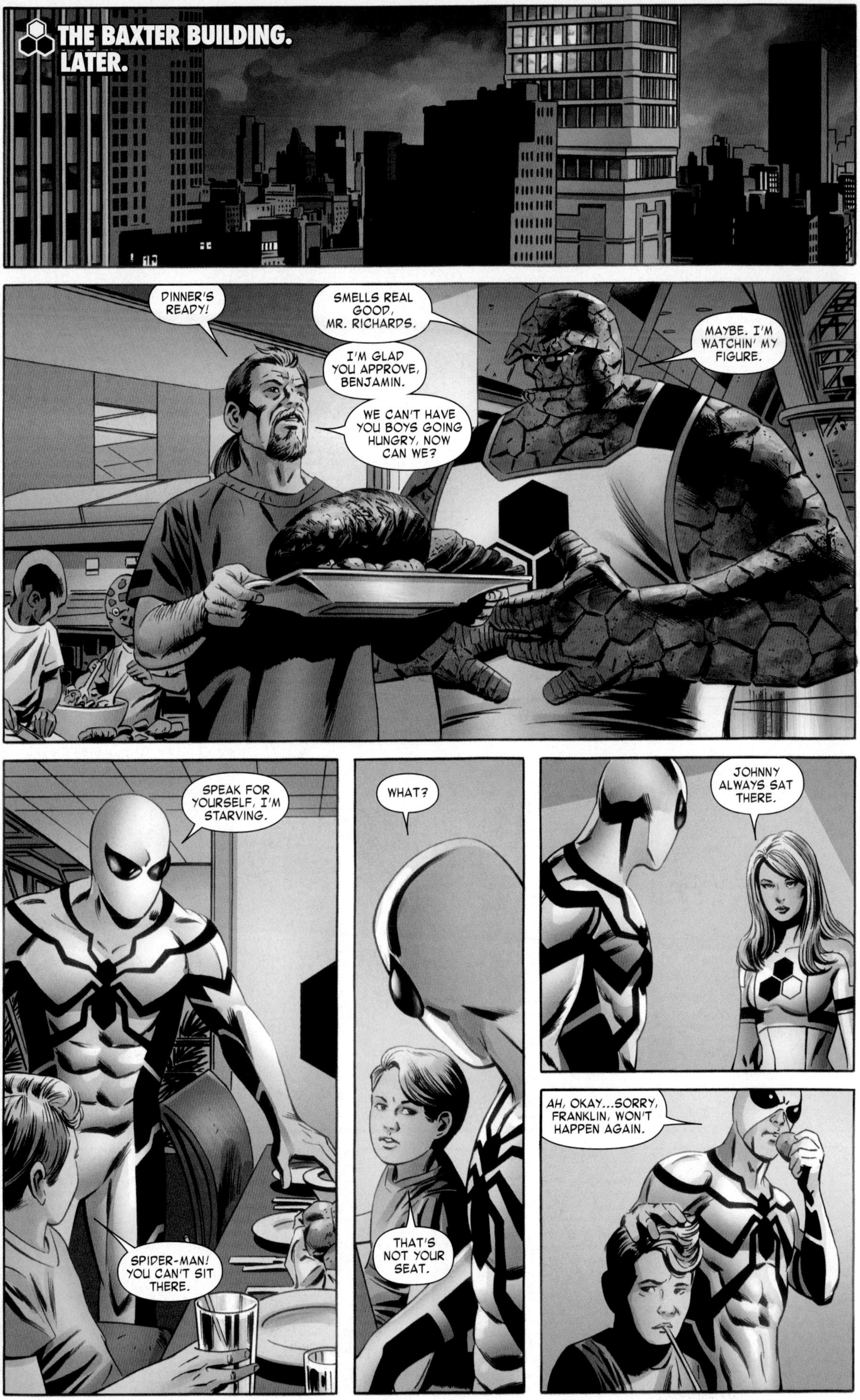
THE BAXTER BUILDING. LATER.
DINNER'S READY!
SMELLS REAL GOOD, MR. RICHARDS.
I'M GLAD YOU APPROVE, BENJAMIN.
WE CAN'T HAVE YOU BOYS GOING HUNGRY, NOW CAN WE?
MAYBE. I'M WATCHIN' MY FIGURE.
SPEAK FOR YOURSELF, I'M STARVING.
SPIDER-MAN! YOU CAN'T SIT THERE.
WHAT?
THAT'S NOT YOUR SEAT.
JOHNNY ALWAYS SAT THERE.
AH, OKAY...SORRY, FRANKLIN, WON'T HAPPEN AGAIN.

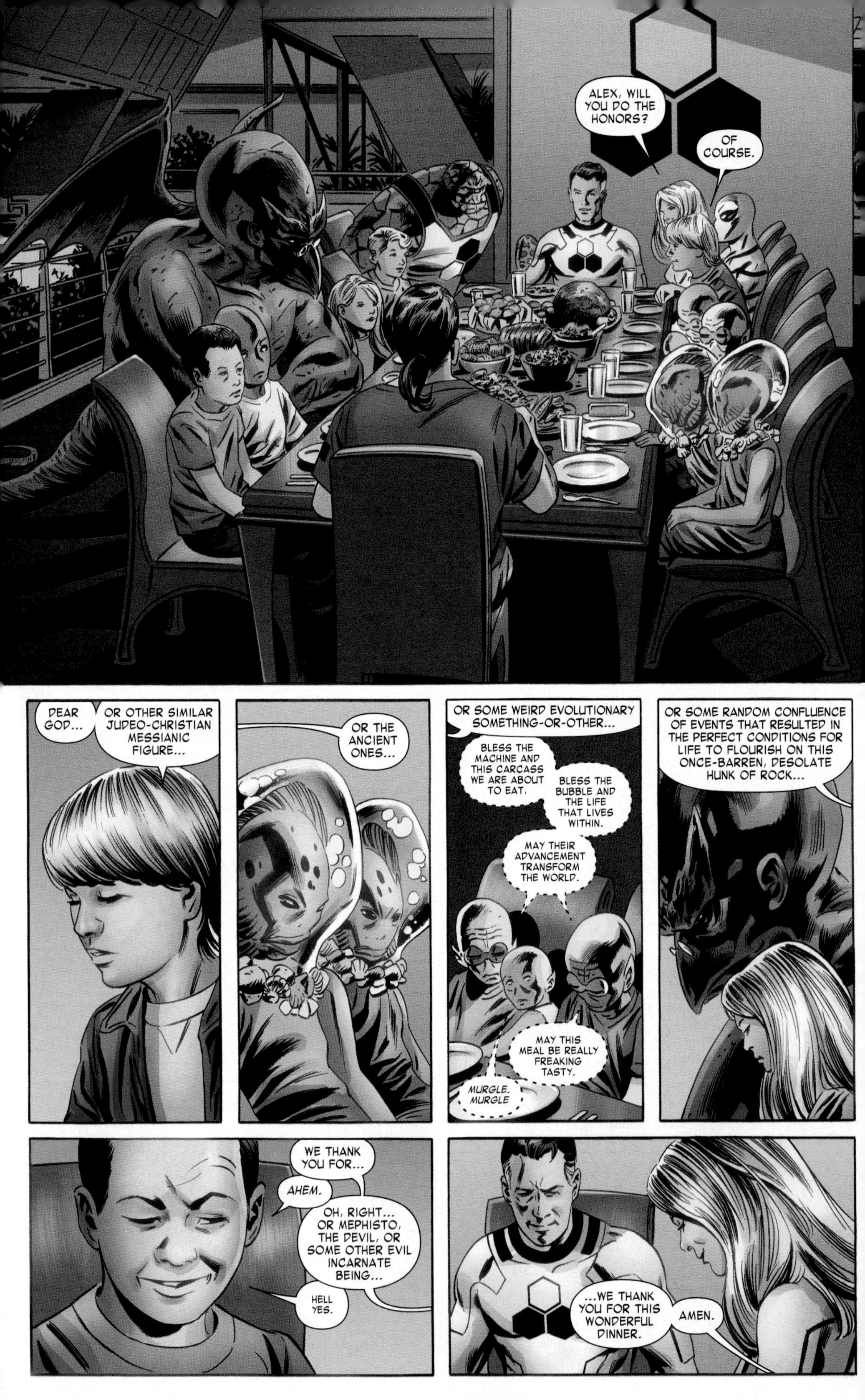
ALEX, WILL YOU DO THE HONORS?
OF COURSE.
DEAR GOD...
OR OTHER SIMILAR JUDEO-CHRISTIAN MESSIANIC FIGURE...
OR THE ANCIENT ONES...
OR SOME WEIRD EVOLUTIONARY SOMETHING-OR-OTHER...
BLESS THE MACHINE AND THIS CARCASS WE ARE ABOUT TO EAT.
BLESS THE BUBBLE AND THE LIFE THAT LIVES WITHIN.
MAY THEIR ADVANCEMENT TRANSFORM THE WORLD.
MAY THIS MEAL BE REALLY FREAKING TASTY.
MURGLE. MURGLE
OR SOME RANDOM CONFLUENCE OF EVENTS THAT RESULTED IN THE PERFECT CONDITIONS FOR LIFE TO FLOURISH ON THIS ONCE-BARREN, DESOLATE HUNK OF ROCK...
WE THANK YOU FOR...
AHEM.
OH, RIGHT... OR MEPHISTO, THE DEVIL, OR SOME OTHER EVIL INCARNATE BEING...
HELL YES.
...WE THANK YOU FOR THIS WONDERFUL DINNER.
AMEN.

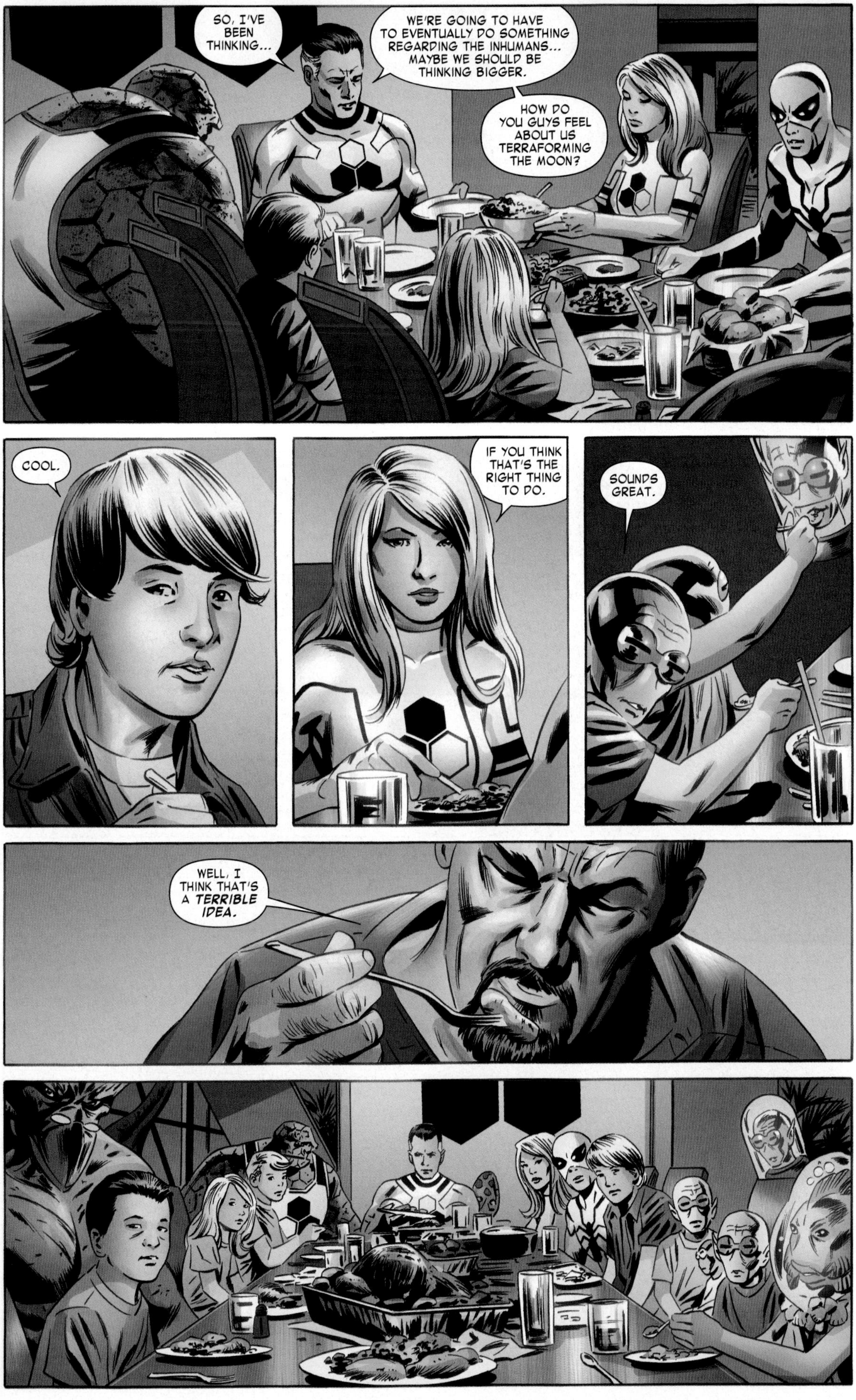
SO, I'VE BEEN THINKING...
WE'RE GOING TO HAVE TO EVENTUALLY DO SOMETHING REGARDING THE INHUMANS... MAYBE WE SHOULD BE THINKING BIGGER.
HOW DO YOU GUYS FEEL ABOUT US TERRAFORMING THE MOON?
COOL.
IF YOU THINK THAT'S THE RIGHT THING TO DO.
SOUNDS GREAT.
WELL, I THINK THAT'S A *TERRIBLE IDEA.*

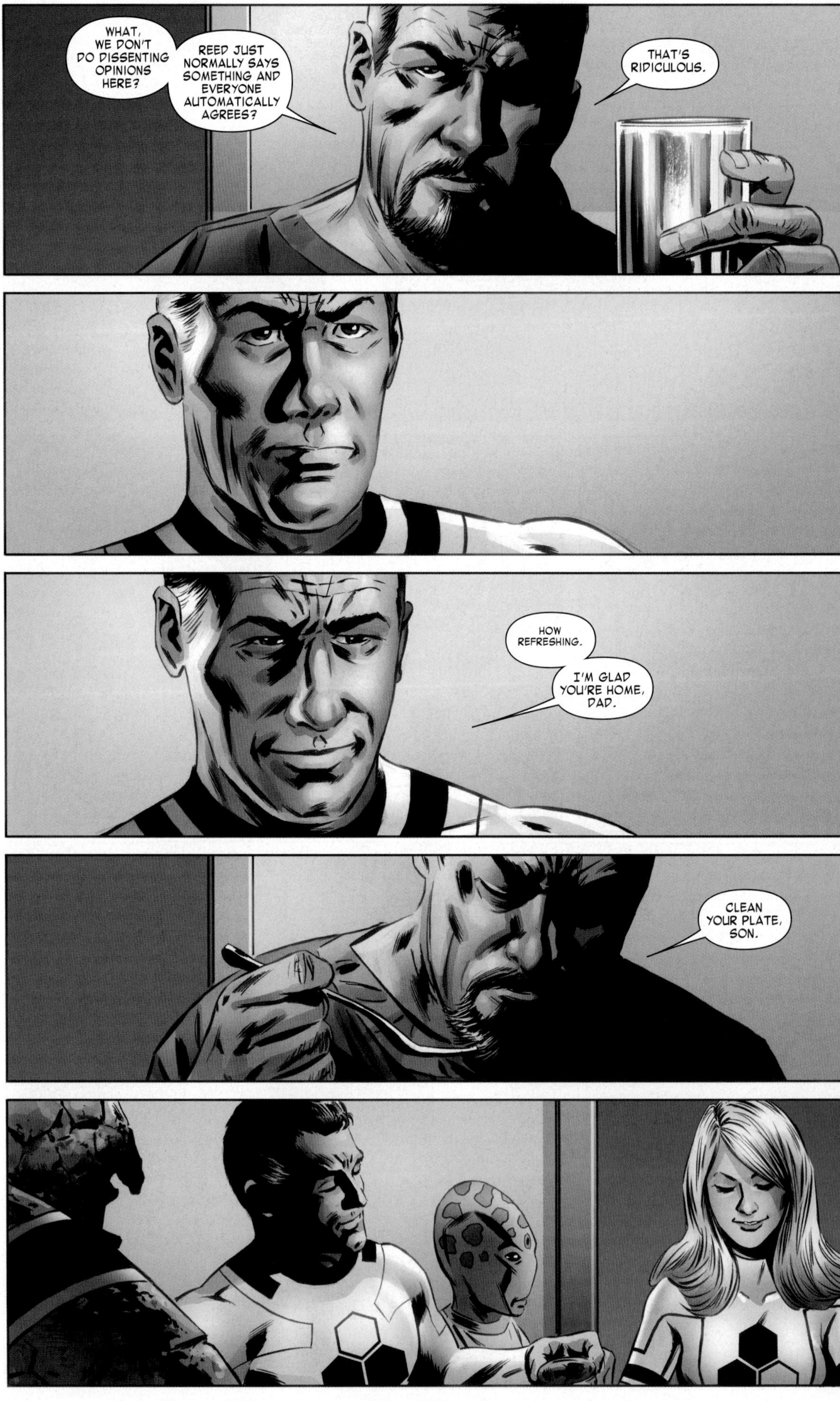

WHAT, WE DON'T DO DISSENTING OPINIONS HERE?
REED JUST NORMALLY SAYS SOMETHING AND EVERYONE AUTOMATICALLY AGREES?
THAT'S RIDICULOUS.
HOW REFRESHING.
I'M GLAD YOU'RE HOME, DAD.
CLEAN YOUR PLATE, SON.

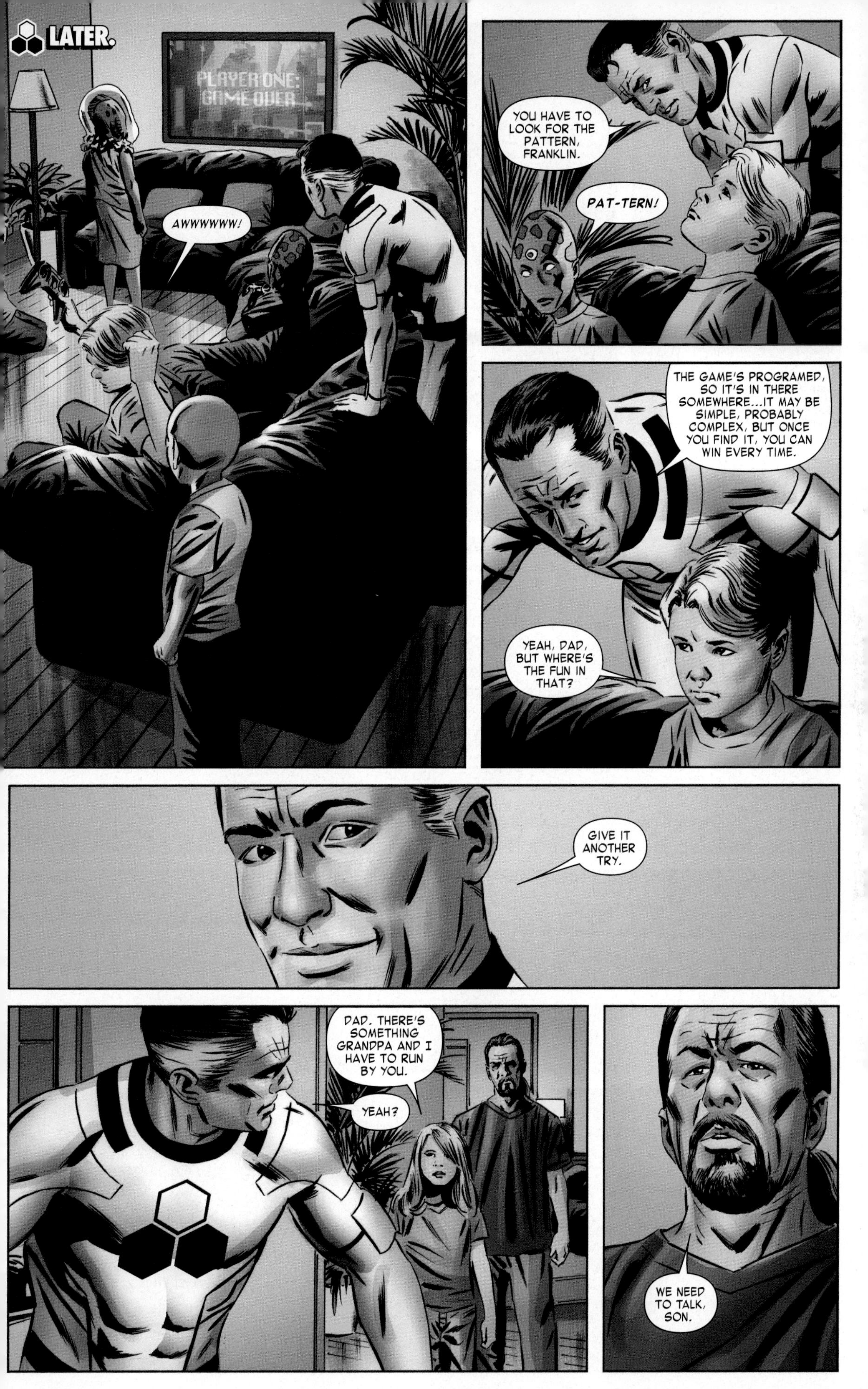
LATER.
PLAYER ONE: GAME OVER
AWWWWWW!
YOU HAVE TO LOOK FOR THE PATTERN, FRANKLIN.
PAT-TERN!
THE GAME'S PROGRAMED, SO IT'S IN THERE SOMEWHERE...IT MAY BE SIMPLE, PROBABLY COMPLEX, BUT ONCE YOU FIND IT, YOU CAN WIN EVERY TIME.
YEAH, DAD, BUT WHERE'S THE FUN IN THAT?
GIVE IT ANOTHER TRY.
DAD. THERE'S SOMETHING GRANDPA AND I HAVE TO RUN BY YOU.
YEAH?
WE NEED TO TALK, SON.

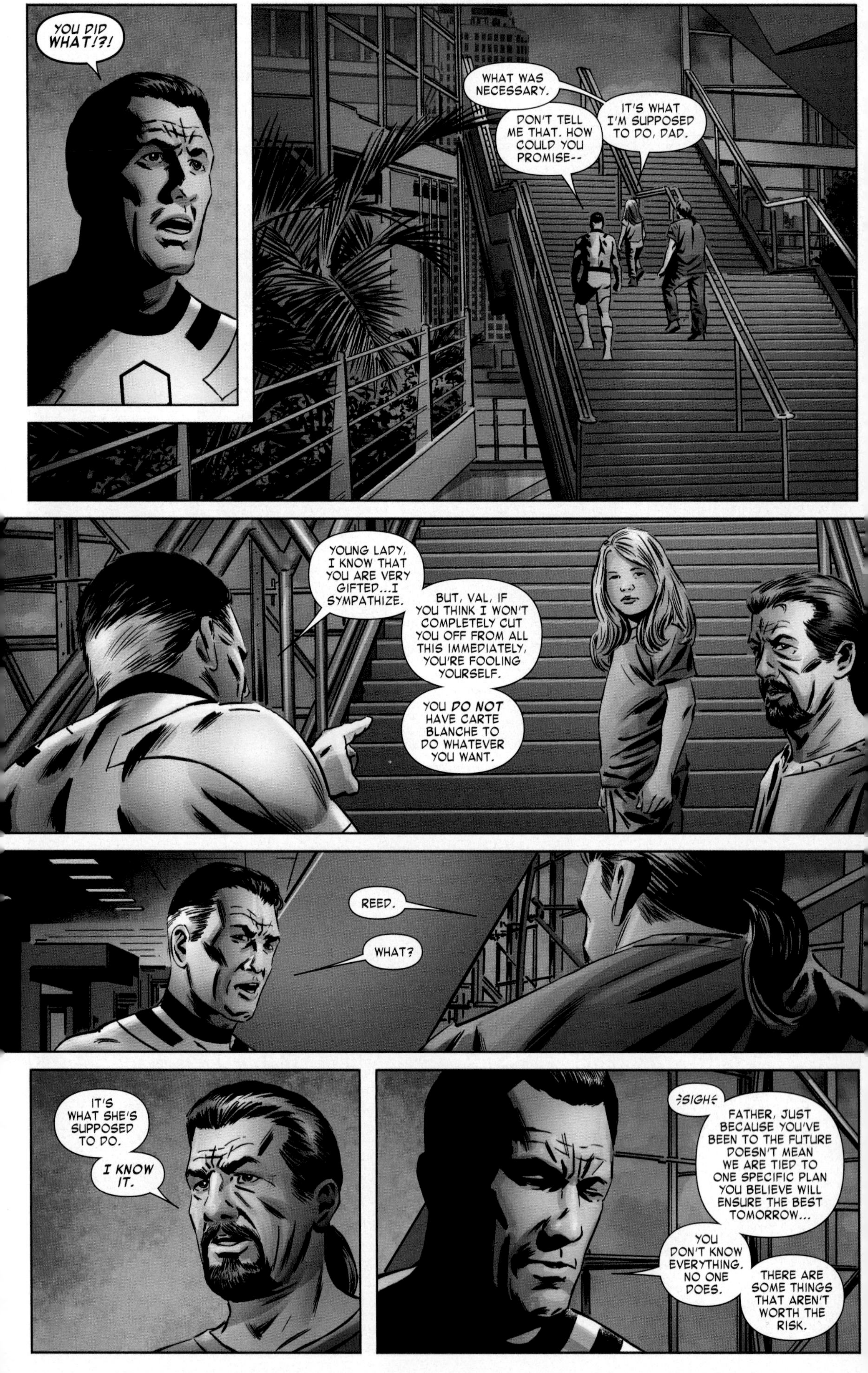
YOU DID WHAT!?!
WHAT WAS NECESSARY.
DON'T TELL ME THAT. HOW COULD YOU PROMISE--
IT'S WHAT I'M SUPPOSED TO DO, DAD.
YOUNG LADY, I KNOW THAT YOU ARE VERY GIFTED...I SYMPATHIZE.
BUT, VAL, IF YOU THINK I WON'T COMPLETELY CUT YOU OFF FROM ALL THIS IMMEDIATELY, YOU'RE FOOLING YOURSELF.
YOU DO NOT HAVE CARTE BLANCHE TO DO WHATEVER YOU WANT.
REED.
WHAT?
IT'S WHAT SHE'S SUPPOSED TO DO.
I KNOW IT.
SIGH
FATHER, JUST BECAUSE YOU'VE BEEN TO THE FUTURE DOESN'T MEAN WE ARE TIED TO ONE SPECIFIC PLAN YOU BELIEVE WILL ENSURE THE BEST TOMORROW...
YOU DON'T KNOW EVERYTHING. NO ONE DOES.
THERE ARE SOME THINGS THAT AREN'T WORTH THE RISK.

"BETTER SAFE THAN SORRY."

WHO LIVES LIKE THAT?

WHEN I WAS HER AGE, WAS I...

EVEN WORSE.

SORRY ABOUT THAT.

DON'T WORRY ABOUT IT.

BUT, DAD, THIS--

I KNOW... I KNOW--BUT WE'RE GOING TO NEED HIM.

THE OTHERS WILL LOOK TO YOU. THEY'LL WANT TO SEE HOW YOU HANDLE IT. THEY'LL NEED TO SEE THAT YOU'RE FINE WITH THIS.

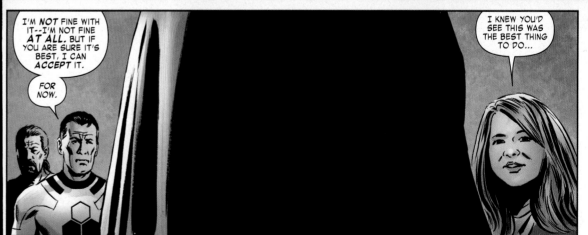

I'M NOT FINE WITH IT--I'M NOT FINE AT ALL. BUT IF YOU ARE SURE IT'S BEST, I CAN ACCEPT IT.

FOR NOW.

I KNEW YOU'D SEE THIS WAS THE BEST THING TO DO...

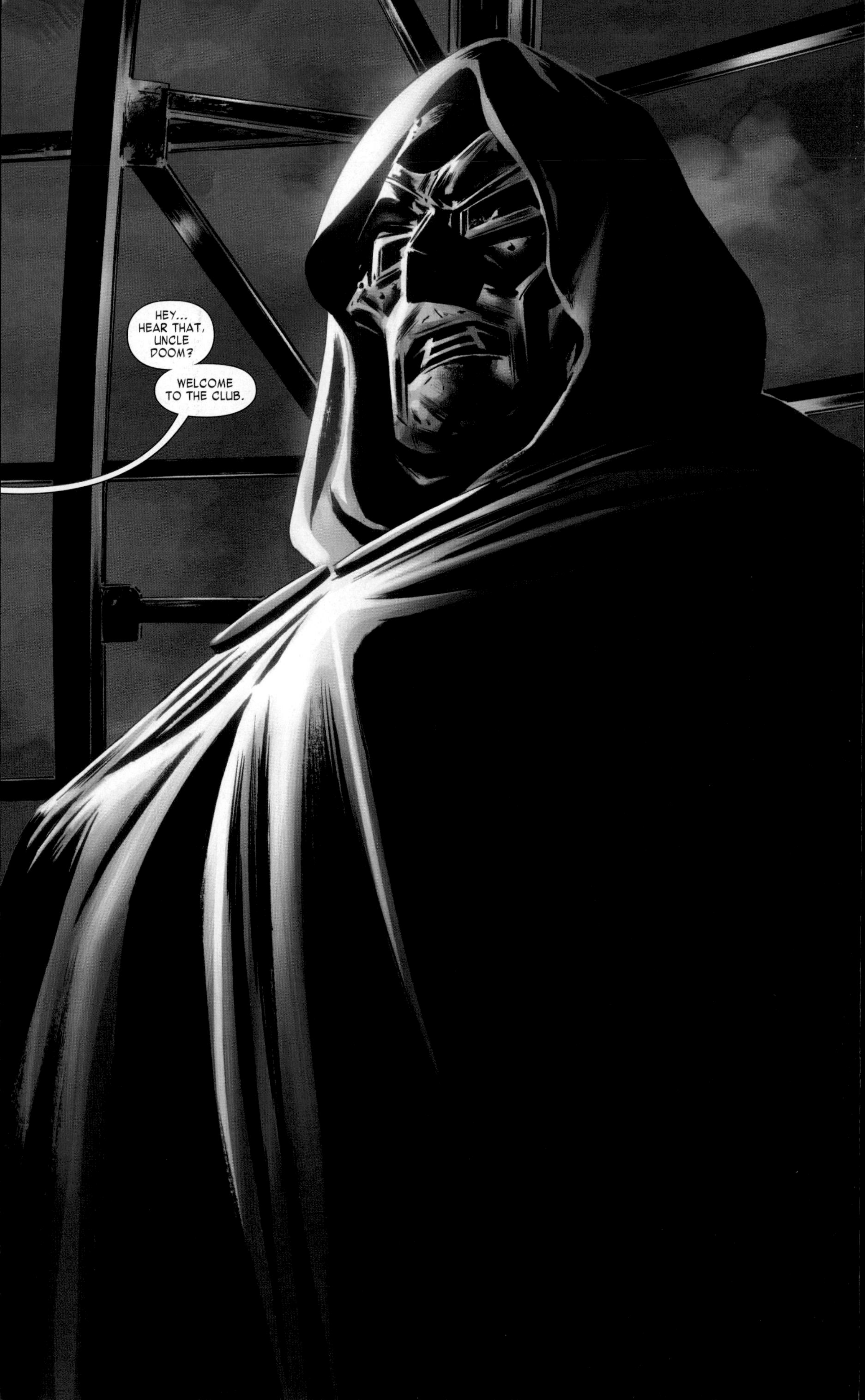
HEY... HEAR THAT, UNCLE DOOM?
WELCOME TO THE CLUB.

THE FIRST FAMILY

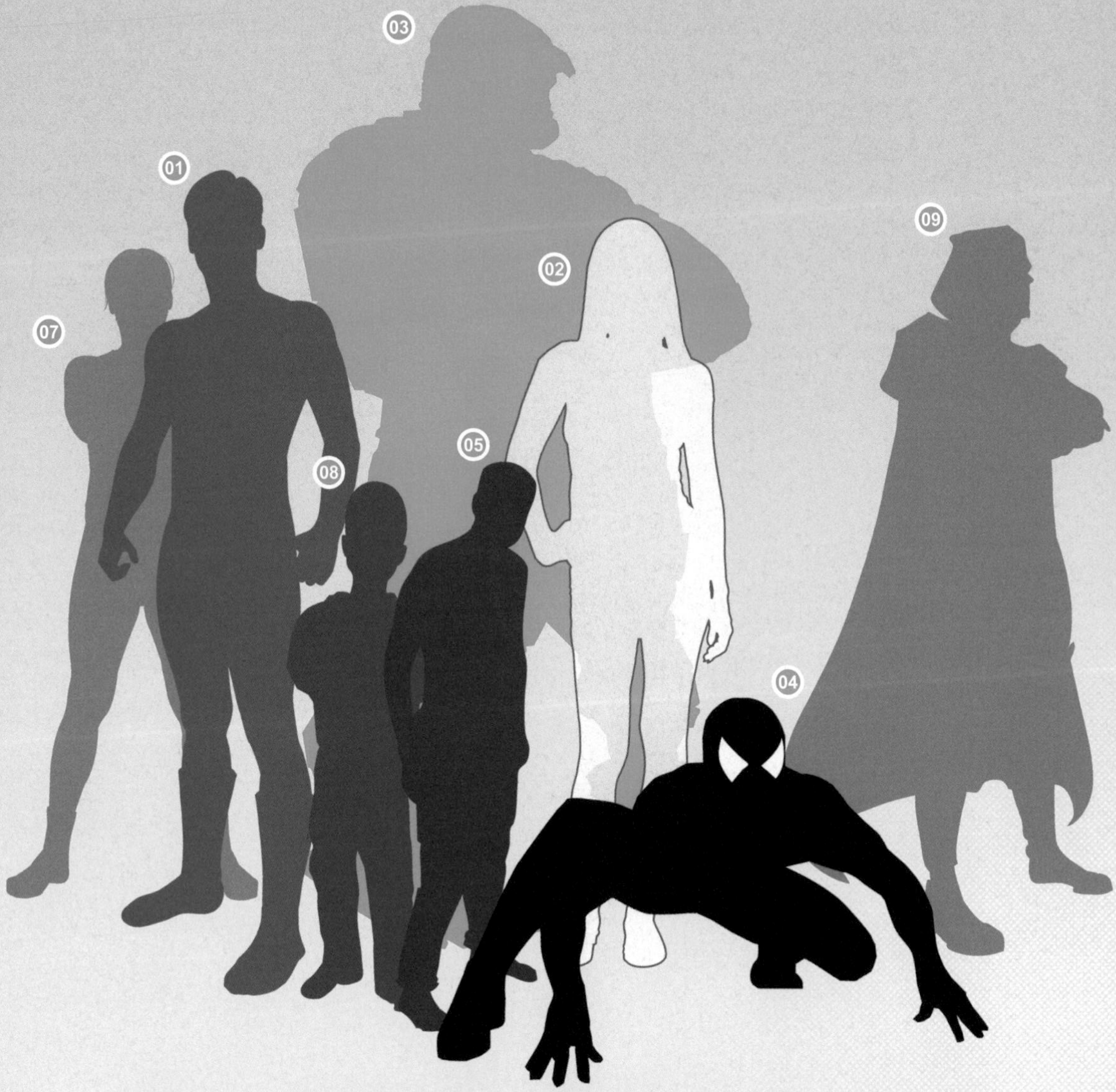
03
01
09
02
07
05
08
04

	Name:	Description:
01.	Reed Richards	Mister Fantastic. The head of the family.
02.	Susan Richards	The Invisible Woman. Force-field projection. Sister to the fallen Johnny Storm.
03.	Ben Grimm	The Thing. Reed's best friend since college. A man trapped in a monster's body.
04.	Peter Parker	The Amazing Spider-Man. Super hero.
05.	Franklin Richards	The son of Reed and Susan. Will one day be the most powerful mutant on Earth.
06.	Valeria Richards	The daughter of Reed and Susan. Super-intellect.
07.	Nathaniel Richards	Reed's long-lost father now returned home. A time traveller, and the only Nathaniel remaining in the multiverse.
08.	Leech	The best friend and roommate of Franklin Richards. A mutant with the power to negate another mutant's power.
09.	Victor Von Doom	Doctor Doom. Super villain and long-time foe of the Fantastic Four.

THE FUTURE FOUNDATION

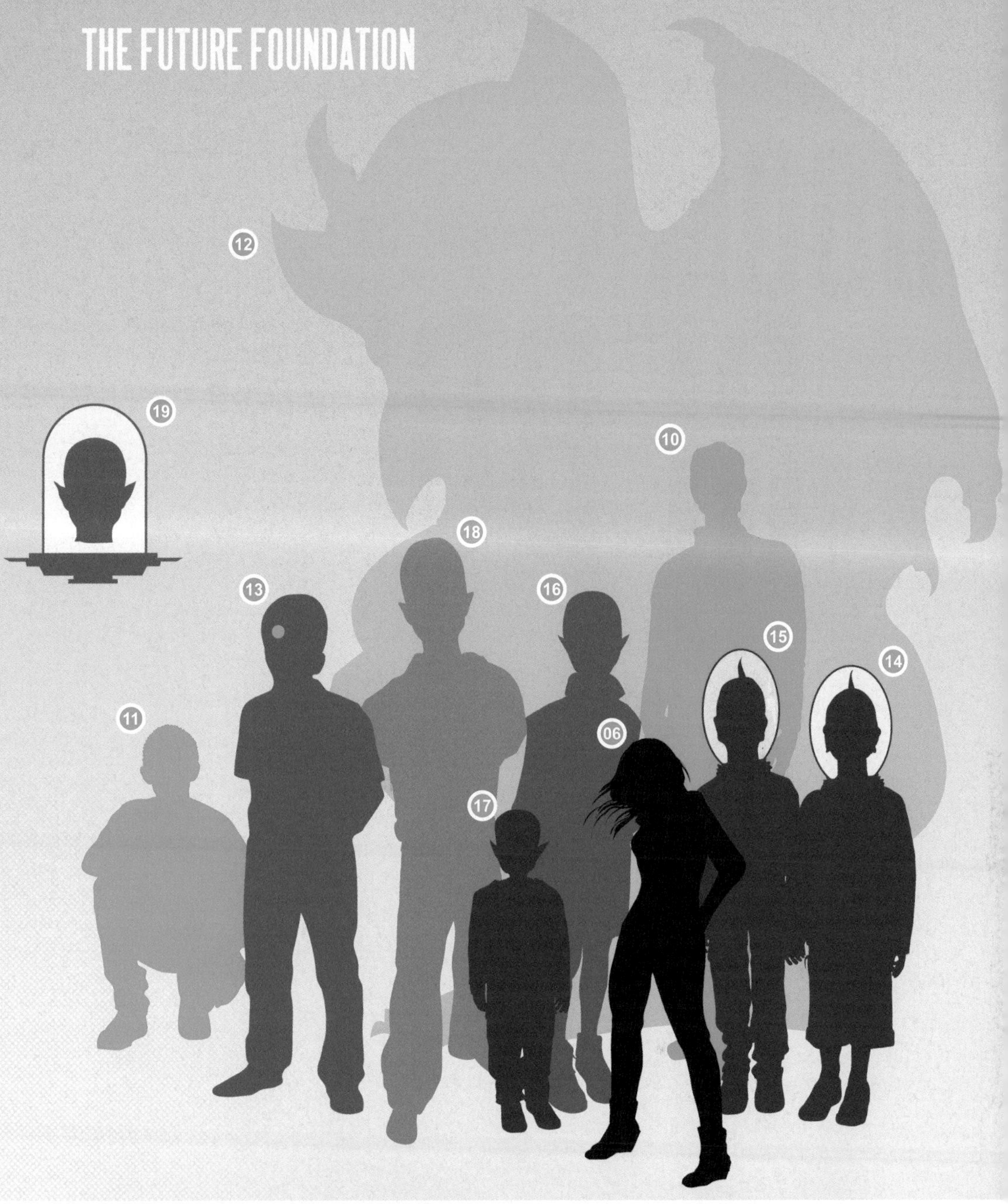
12
19
10
18
13
16
15
14
11
06
17

	Name:	Description:
01.	Reed Richards	Mister Fantastic. Headmaster and creator of the Future Foundation.
04.	Peter Parker	The Spectacular Spider-Man. Super-scientist.
06.	Valeria Richards	The daughter of Reed and Susan. Trouble.
10.	Alex Power	Eldest of the Power clan known as Power Pack. Has the ability to control gravity.
11.	Bentley 23	A child clone of Bentley Wittman, the Wizard. Genius, and ward of Reed Richards.
12.	Dragon Man	An android brought to life by the villain Diablo, now reprogrammed for peace.
13.	Artie Maddicks	A problem-solver. Has the ability to holographically project his thoughts.
14.	Wu	Male co-heir to the Ul-Uhari throne at the Peak. Ward of Susan Richards.
15.	Vii	Female co-heir to the Ul-Uhari throne at the Peak. Ward of Susan Richards.
16.	Mik	The smartest Moloid survivor from the Forever City of the High Evolutionary.
17.	Korr	The youngest Moloid survivor from the Forever City of the High Evolutionary.
18.	Turg	The oldest Moloid survivor from the Forever City of the High Evolutionary.
19.	Tong	A floating head, former herald to long-term foe of the Fantastic Four, the Mole Man.

DOOM IS REBORN

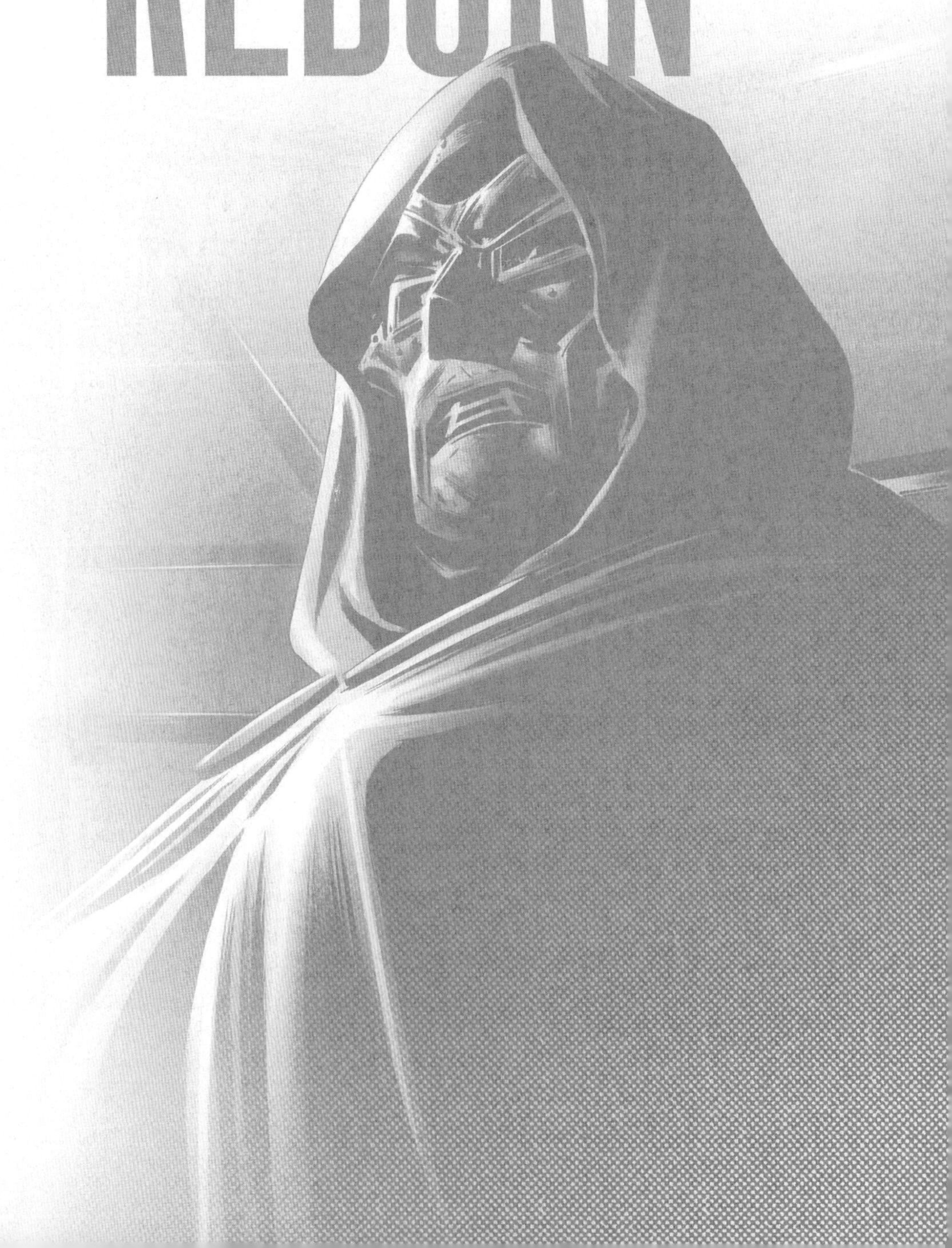

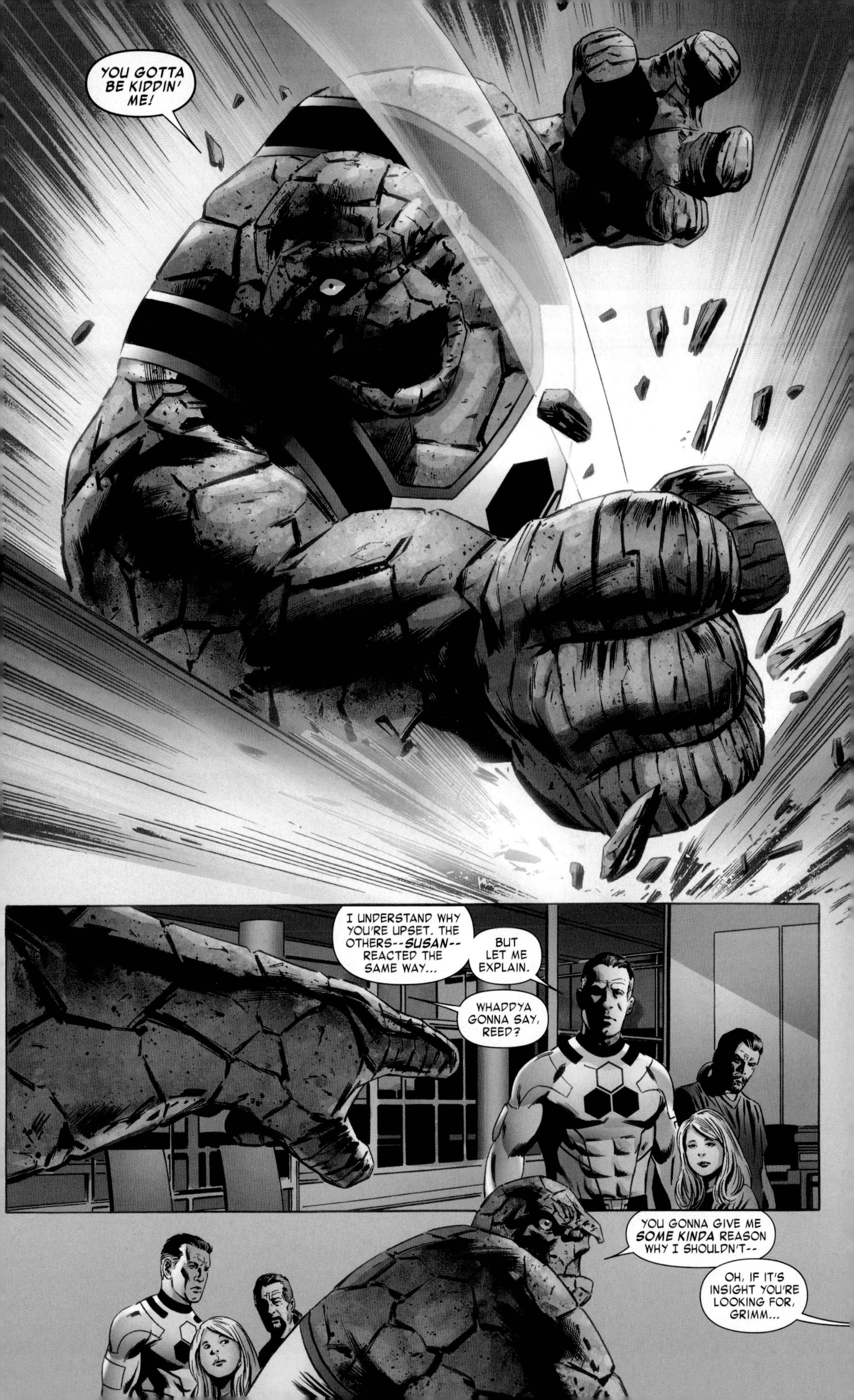

YOU GOTTA BE KIDDIN' ME!
I UNDERSTAND WHY YOU'RE UPSET. THE OTHERS--SUSAN--REACTED THE SAME WAY...
BUT LET ME EXPLAIN.
WHADDYA GONNA SAY, REED?
YOU GONNA GIVE ME SOME KINDA REASON WHY I SHOULDN'T--
OH, IF IT'S INSIGHT YOU'RE LOOKING FOR, GRIMM...

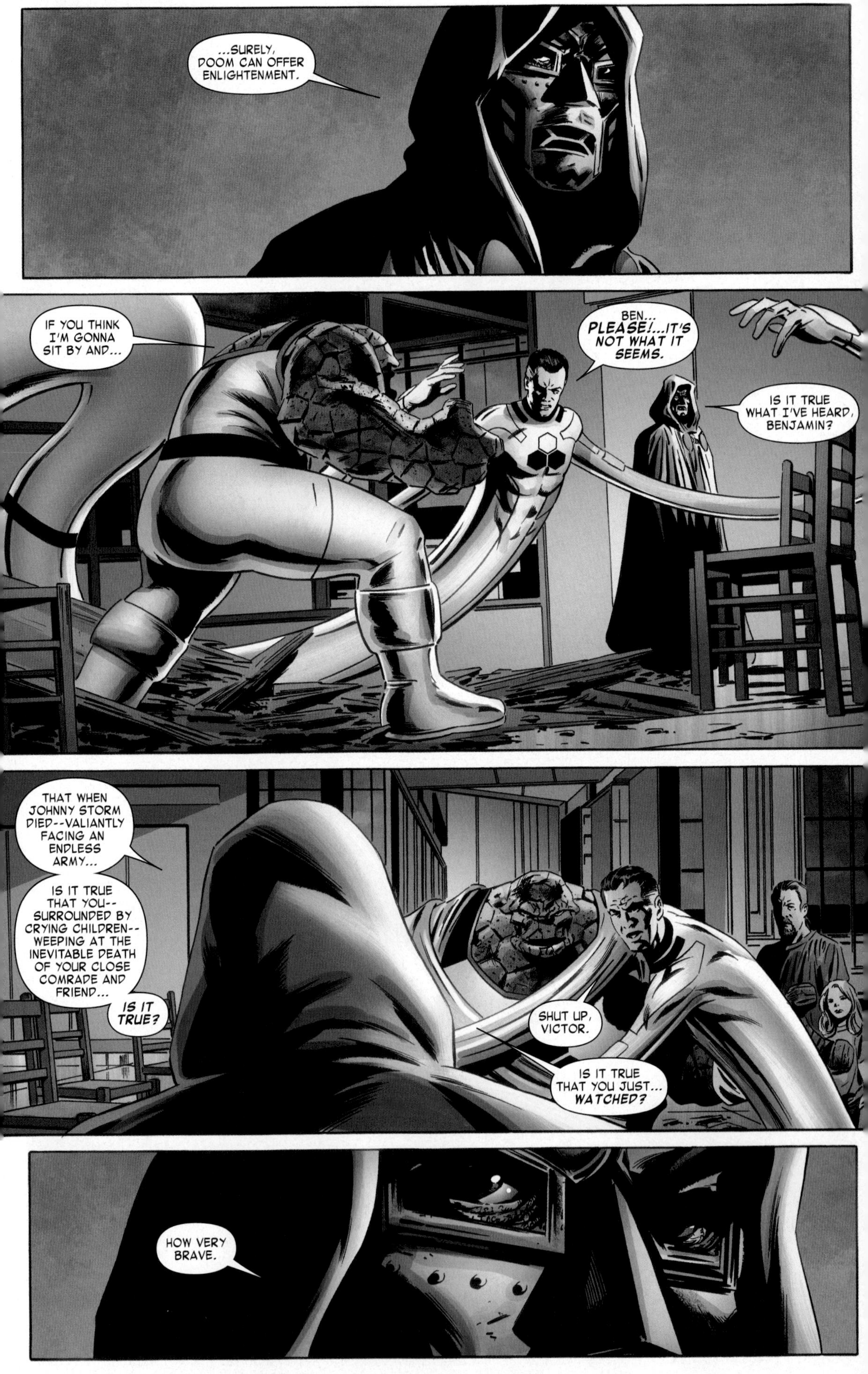
...SURELY, DOOM CAN OFFER ENLIGHTENMENT.
IF YOU THINK I'M GONNA SIT BY AND...
BEN... PLEASE!...IT'S NOT WHAT IT SEEMS.
IS IT TRUE WHAT I'VE HEARD, BENJAMIN?
THAT WHEN JOHNNY STORM DIED--VALIANTLY FACING AN ENDLESS ARMY...
IS IT TRUE THAT YOU--SURROUNDED BY CRYING CHILDREN--WEEPING AT THE INEVITABLE DEATH OF YOUR CLOSE COMRADE AND FRIEND... IS IT TRUE?
SHUT UP, VICTOR.
IS IT TRUE THAT YOU JUST... WATCHED?
HOW VERY BRAVE.

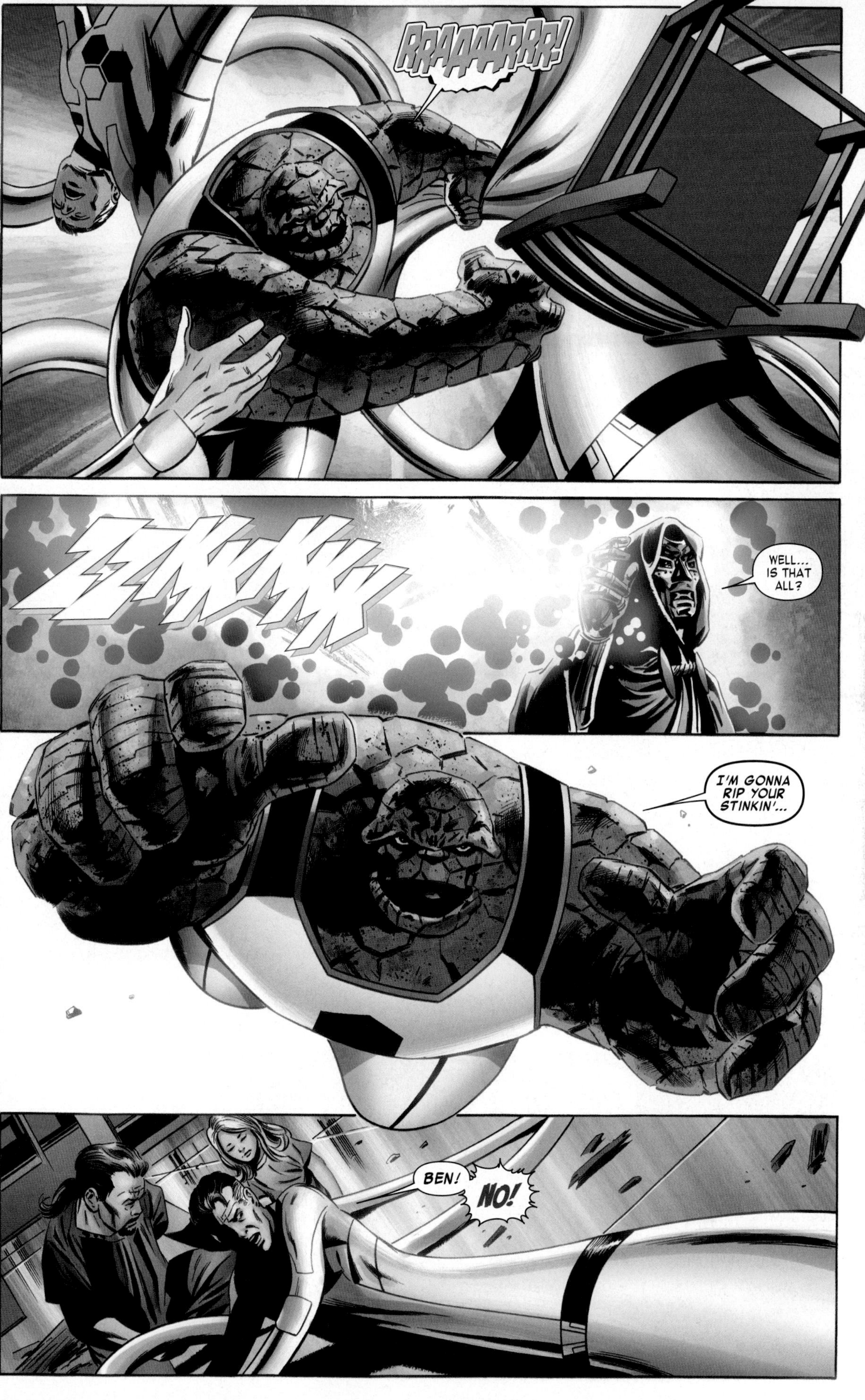
RRAAAARRR!
ZZKKKKK
WELL... IS THAT ALL?
I'M GONNA RIP YOUR STINKIN'...
BEN!
NO!

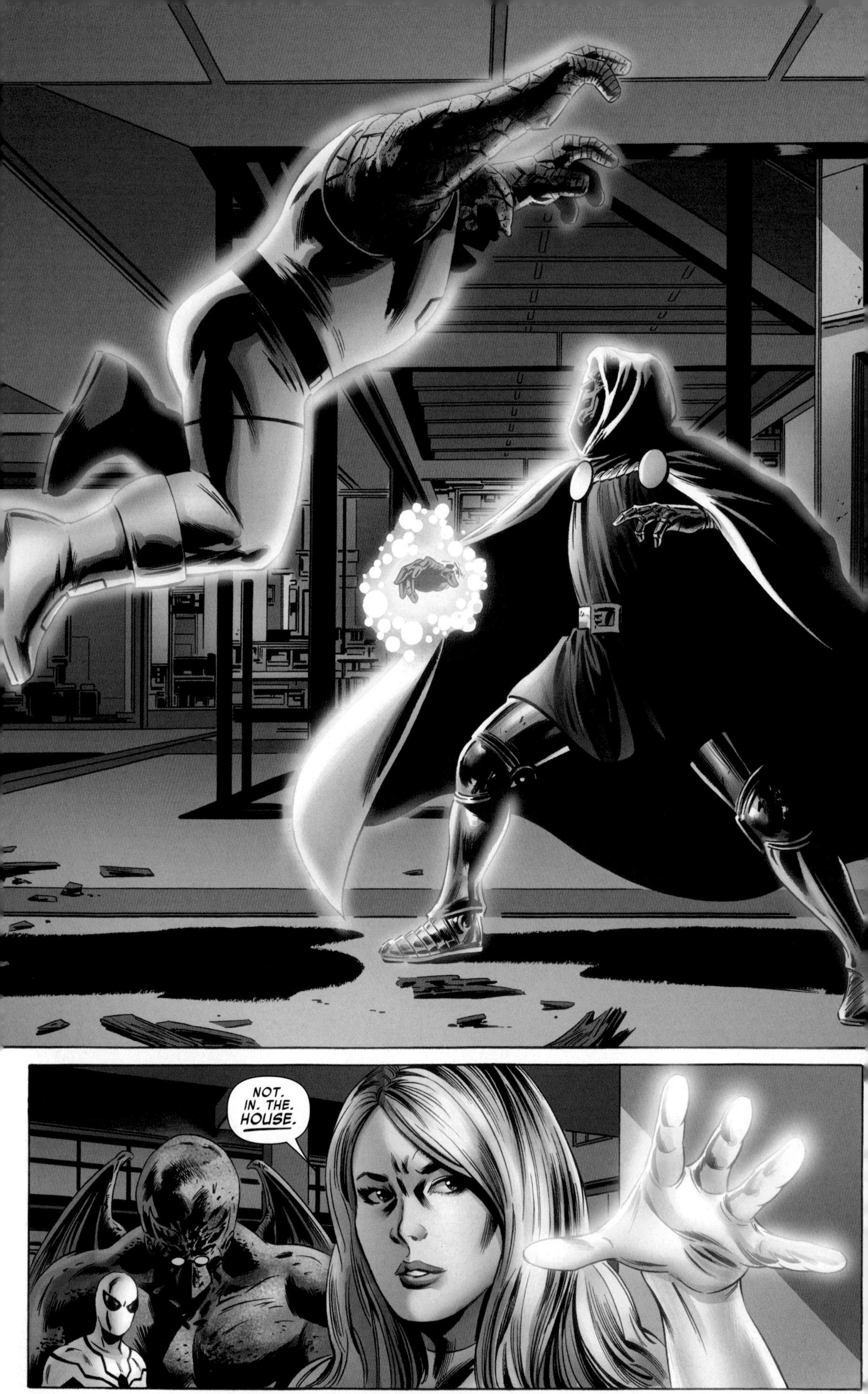
NOT. IN. THE. HOUSE.

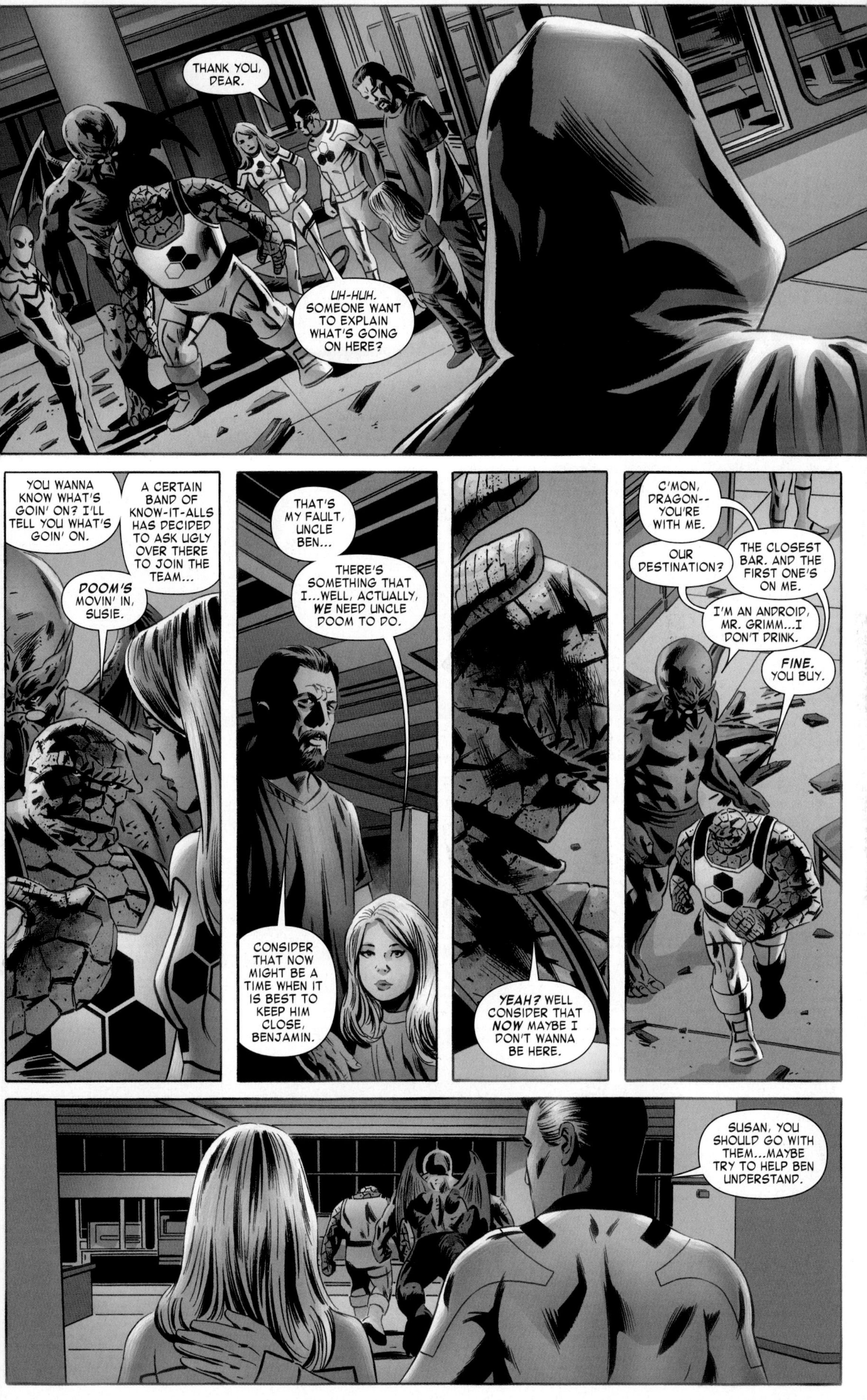
THANK YOU, DEAR.
UH-HUH. SOMEONE WANT TO EXPLAIN WHAT'S GOING ON HERE?
YOU WANNA KNOW WHAT'S GOIN' ON? I'LL TELL YOU WHAT'S GOIN' ON.
A CERTAIN BAND OF KNOW-IT-ALLS HAS DECIDED TO ASK UGLY OVER THERE TO JOIN THE TEAM...
DOOM'S MOVIN' IN, SUSIE.
THAT'S MY FAULT, UNCLE BEN...
THERE'S SOMETHING THAT I...WELL, ACTUALLY, WE NEED UNCLE DOOM TO DO.
CONSIDER THAT NOW MIGHT BE A TIME WHEN IT IS BEST TO KEEP HIM CLOSE, BENJAMIN.
YEAH? WELL CONSIDER THAT NOW MAYBE I DON'T WANNA BE HERE.
C'MON, DRAGON--YOU'RE WITH ME.
OUR DESTINATION?
THE CLOSEST BAR. AND THE FIRST ONE'S ON ME.
I'M AN ANDROID, MR. GRIMM...I DON'T DRINK.
FINE. YOU BUY.
SUSAN, YOU SHOULD GO WITH THEM...MAYBE TRY TO HELP BEN UNDERSTAND.

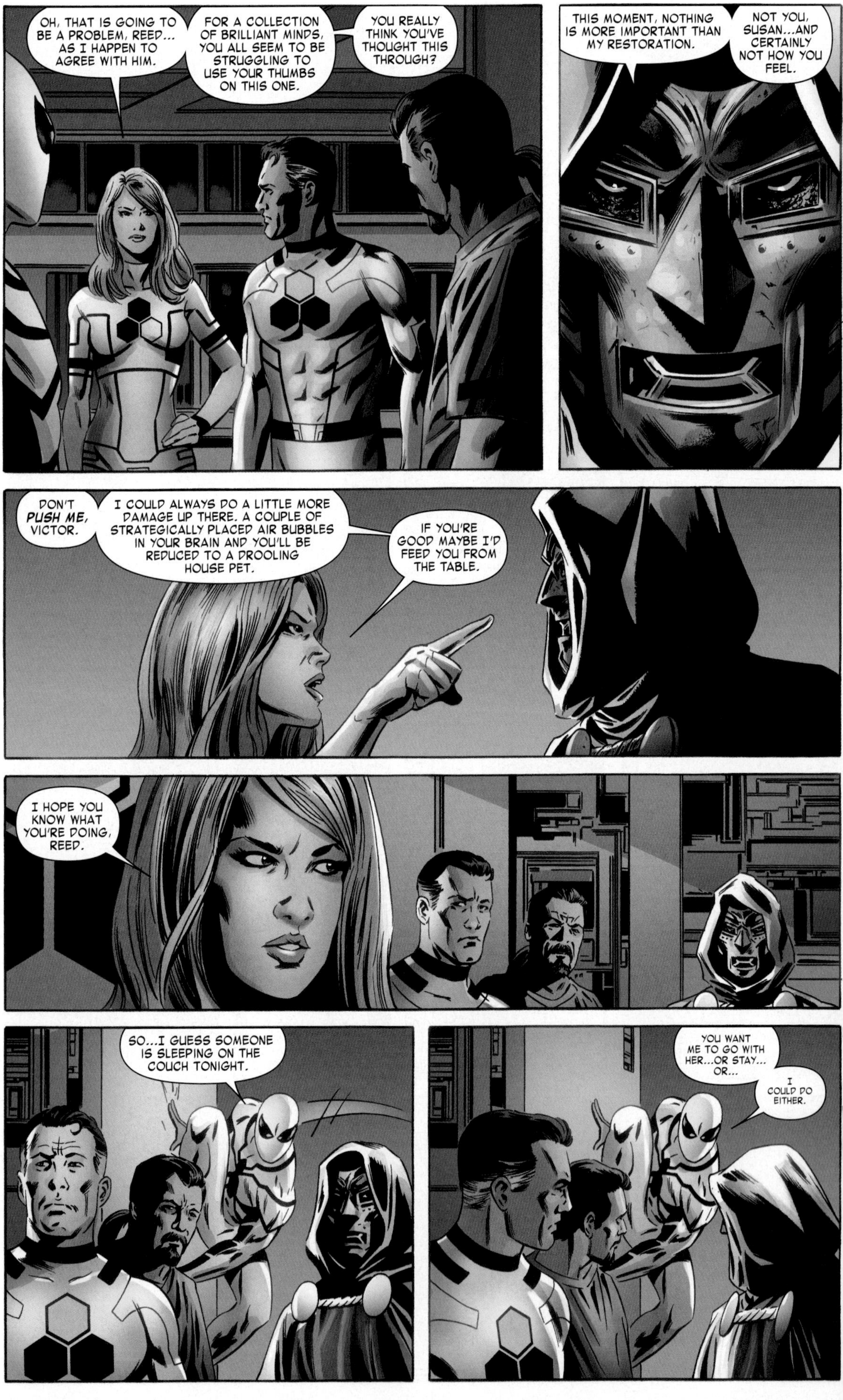

OH, THAT IS GOING TO BE A PROBLEM, REED... AS I HAPPEN TO AGREE WITH HIM.
FOR A COLLECTION OF BRILLIANT MINDS, YOU ALL SEEM TO BE STRUGGLING TO USE YOUR THUMBS ON THIS ONE.
YOU REALLY THINK YOU'VE THOUGHT THIS THROUGH?
THIS MOMENT, NOTHING IS MORE IMPORTANT THAN MY RESTORATION.
NOT YOU, SUSAN...AND CERTAINLY NOT HOW YOU FEEL.
DON'T *PUSH ME,* VICTOR.
I COULD ALWAYS DO A LITTLE MORE DAMAGE UP THERE. A COUPLE OF STRATEGICALLY PLACED AIR BUBBLES IN YOUR BRAIN AND YOU'LL BE REDUCED TO A DROOLING HOUSE PET.
IF YOU'RE GOOD MAYBE I'D FEED YOU FROM THE TABLE.
I HOPE YOU KNOW WHAT YOU'RE DOING, REED.
SO...I GUESS SOMEONE IS SLEEPING ON THE COUCH TONIGHT.
YOU WANT ME TO GO WITH HER...OR STAY... OR...
I COULD DO EITHER.

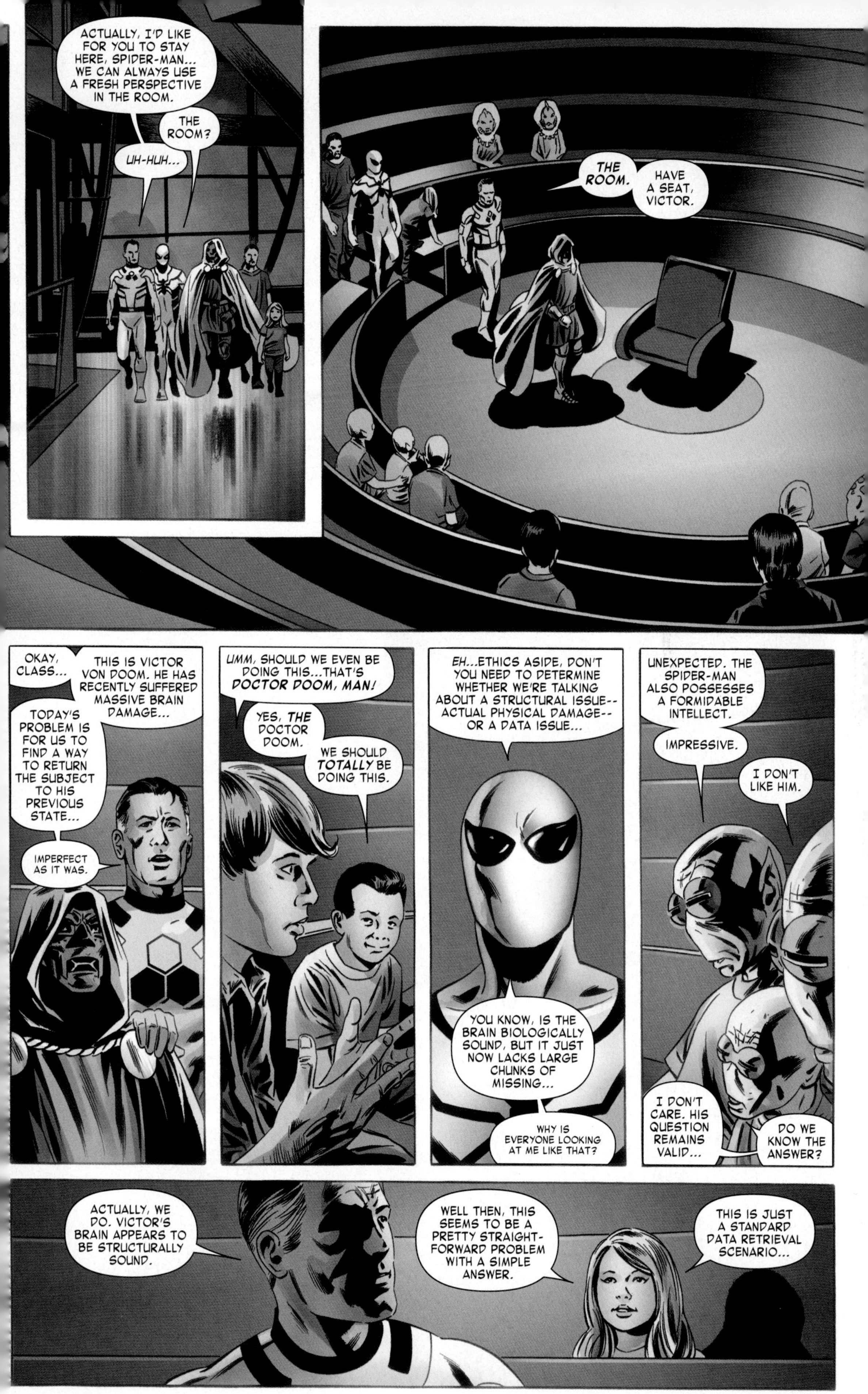
ACTUALLY, I'D LIKE FOR YOU TO STAY HERE, SPIDER-MAN... WE CAN ALWAYS USE A FRESH PERSPECTIVE IN THE ROOM.
THE ROOM?
UH-HUH...
THE ROOM.
HAVE A SEAT, VICTOR.
OKAY, CLASS...
THIS IS VICTOR VON DOOM. HE HAS RECENTLY SUFFERED MASSIVE BRAIN DAMAGE...
TODAY'S PROBLEM IS FOR US TO FIND A WAY TO RETURN THE SUBJECT TO HIS PREVIOUS STATE...
IMPERFECT AS IT WAS.
UMM, SHOULD WE EVEN BE DOING THIS...THAT'S DOCTOR DOOM, MAN!
YES, THE DOCTOR DOOM.
WE SHOULD TOTALLY BE DOING THIS.
EH...ETHICS ASIDE, DON'T YOU NEED TO DETERMINE WHETHER WE'RE TALKING ABOUT A STRUCTURAL ISSUE-- ACTUAL PHYSICAL DAMAGE-- OR A DATA ISSUE...
YOU KNOW, IS THE BRAIN BIOLOGICALLY SOUND, BUT IT JUST NOW LACKS LARGE CHUNKS OF MISSING...
WHY IS EVERYONE LOOKING AT ME LIKE THAT?
UNEXPECTED. THE SPIDER-MAN ALSO POSSESSES A FORMIDABLE INTELLECT.
IMPRESSIVE.
I DON'T LIKE HIM.
I DON'T CARE. HIS QUESTION REMAINS VALID...
DO WE KNOW THE ANSWER?
ACTUALLY, WE DO. VICTOR'S BRAIN APPEARS TO BE STRUCTURALLY SOUND.
WELL THEN, THIS SEEMS TO BE A PRETTY STRAIGHT-FORWARD PROBLEM WITH A SIMPLE ANSWER.
THIS IS JUST A STANDARD DATA RETRIEVAL SCENARIO...

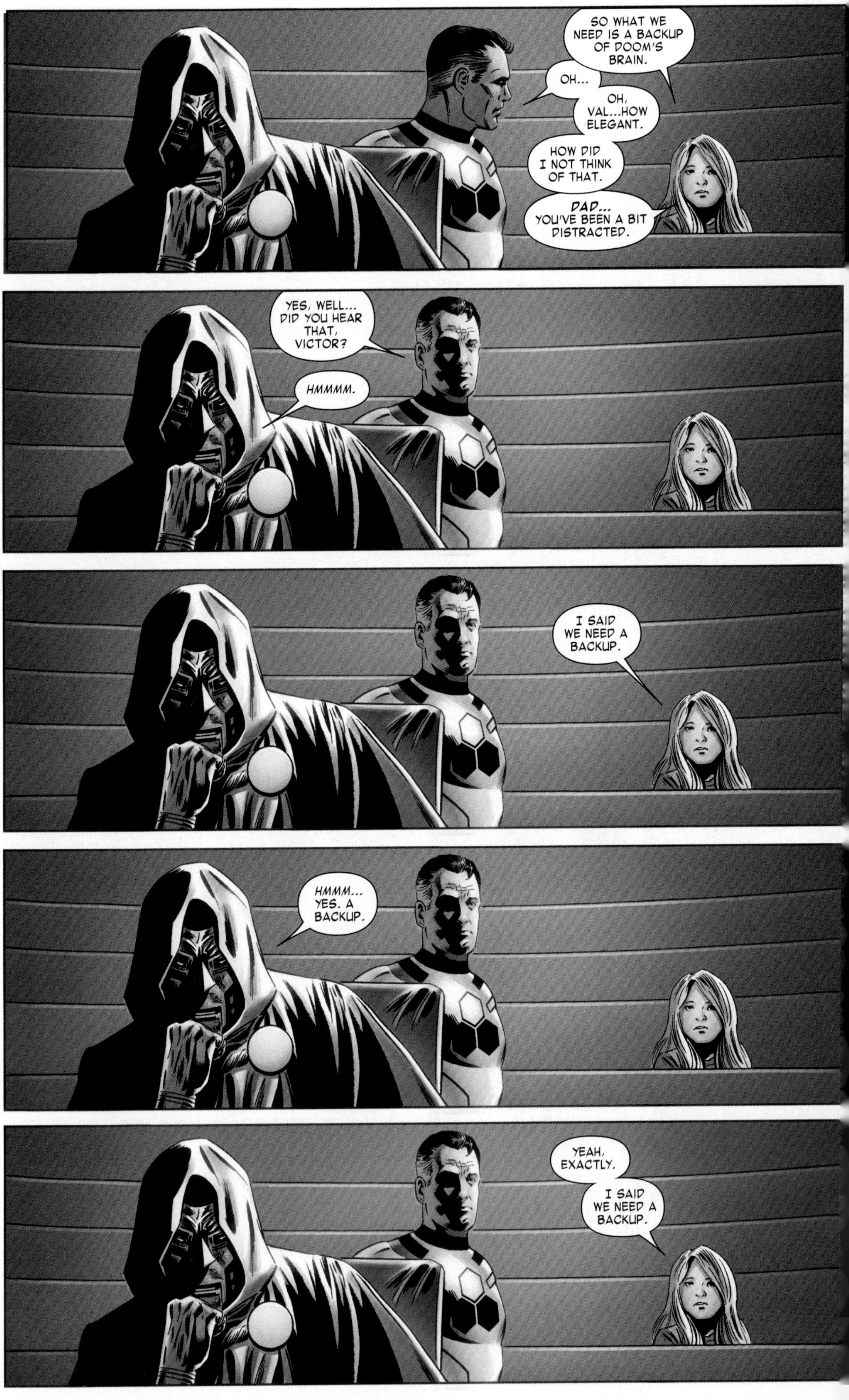
SO WHAT WE NEED IS A BACKUP OF DOOM'S BRAIN.
OH...
OH, VAL...HOW ELEGANT.
HOW DID I NOT THINK OF THAT.
DAD... YOU'VE BEEN A BIT DISTRACTED.
YES, WELL... DID YOU HEAR THAT, VICTOR?
HMMMM.
I SAID WE NEED A BACKUP.
HMMM... YES. A BACKUP.
YEAH, EXACTLY.
I SAID WE NEED A BACKUP.

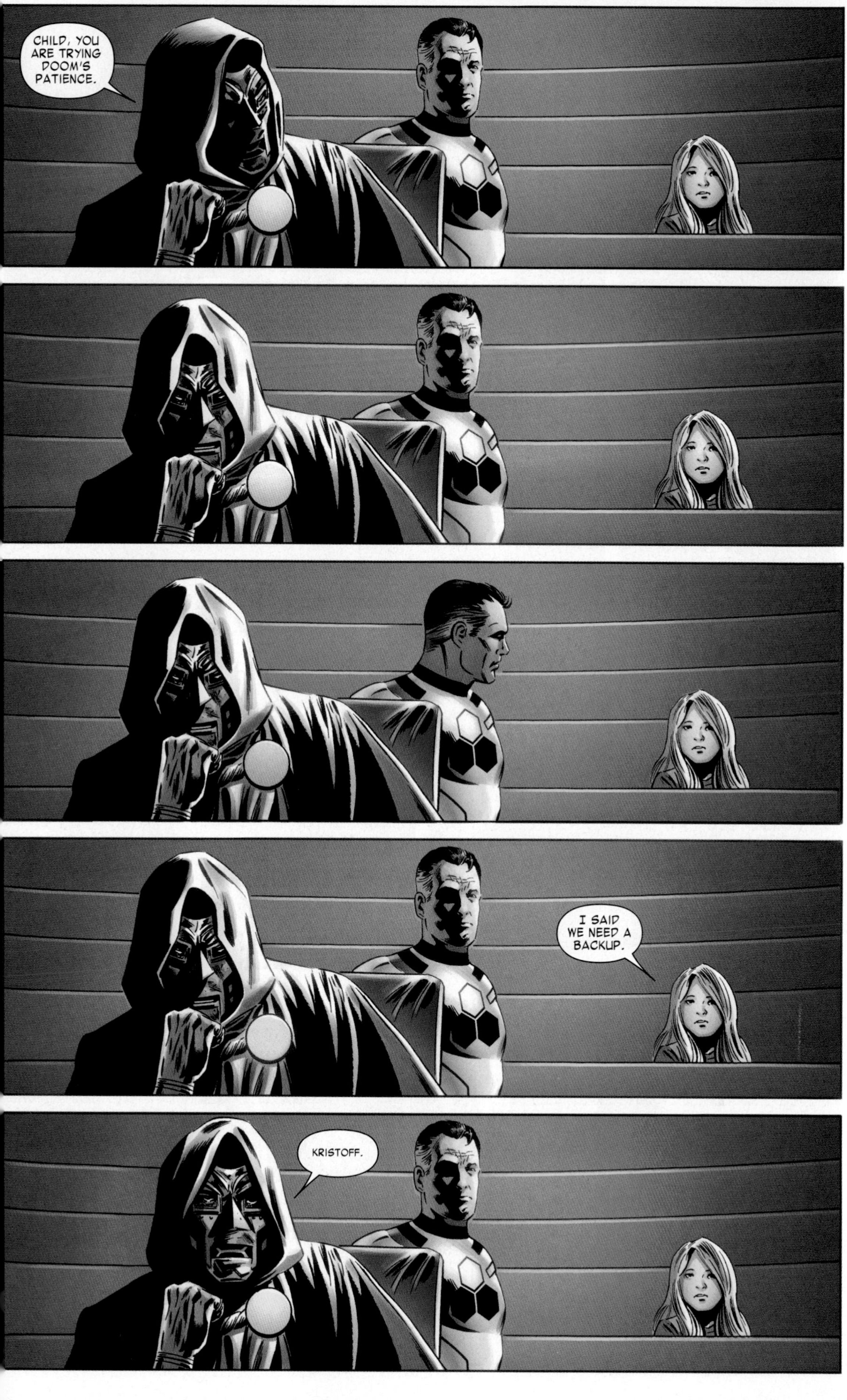
CHILD, YOU ARE TRYING DOOM'S PATIENCE.
I SAID WE NEED A BACKUP.
KRISTOFF.

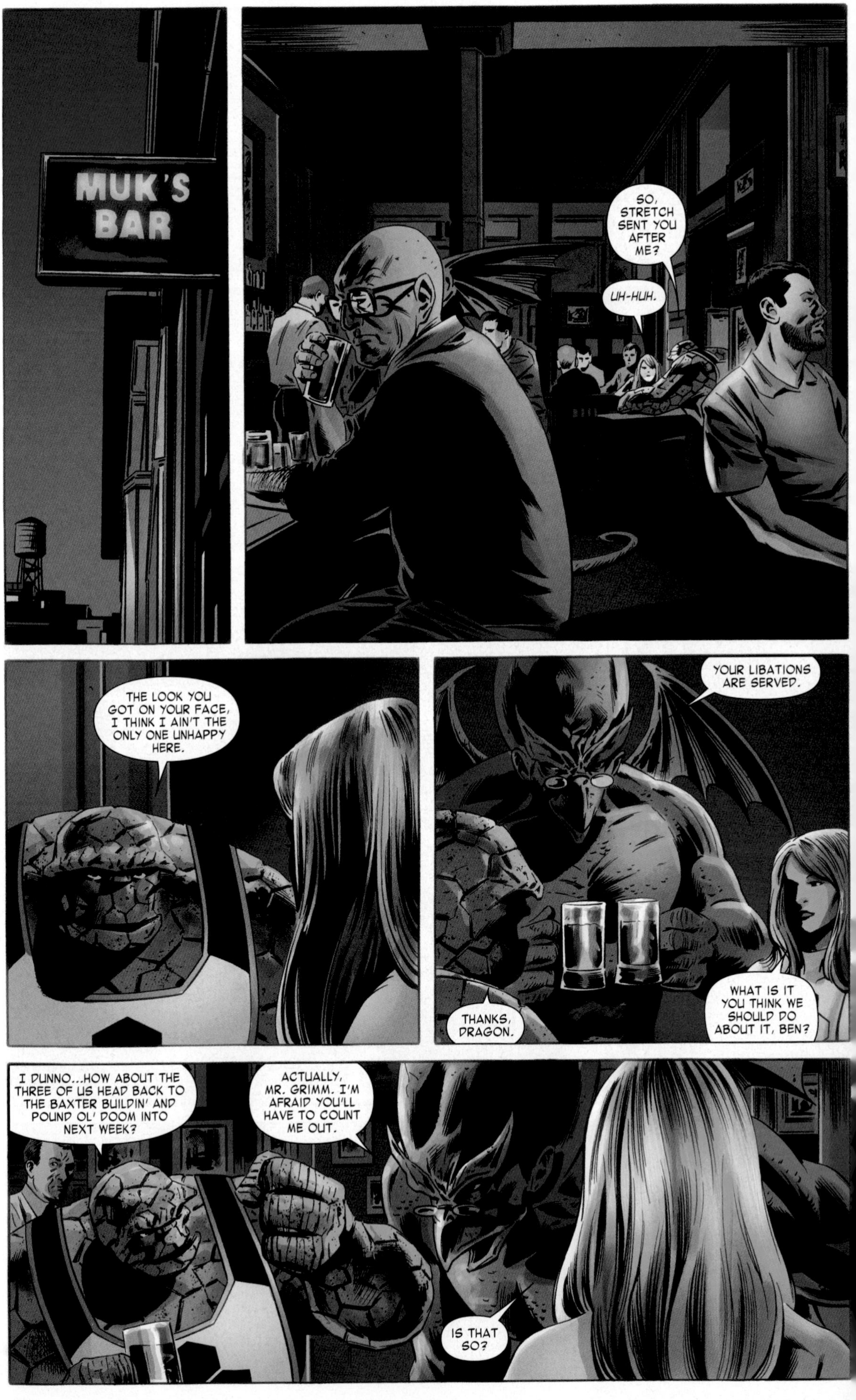
MUK'S BAR
SO, STRETCH SENT YOU AFTER ME?
UH-HUH.
THE LOOK YOU GOT ON YOUR FACE, I THINK I AIN'T THE ONLY ONE UNHAPPY HERE.
YOUR LIBATIONS ARE SERVED.
THANKS, DRAGON.
WHAT IS IT YOU THINK WE SHOULD DO ABOUT IT, BEN?
I DUNNO...HOW ABOUT THE THREE OF US HEAD BACK TO THE BAXTER BUILDIN' AND POUND OL' DOOM INTO NEXT WEEK?
ACTUALLY, MR. GRIMM. I'M AFRAID YOU'LL HAVE TO COUNT ME OUT.
IS THAT SO?

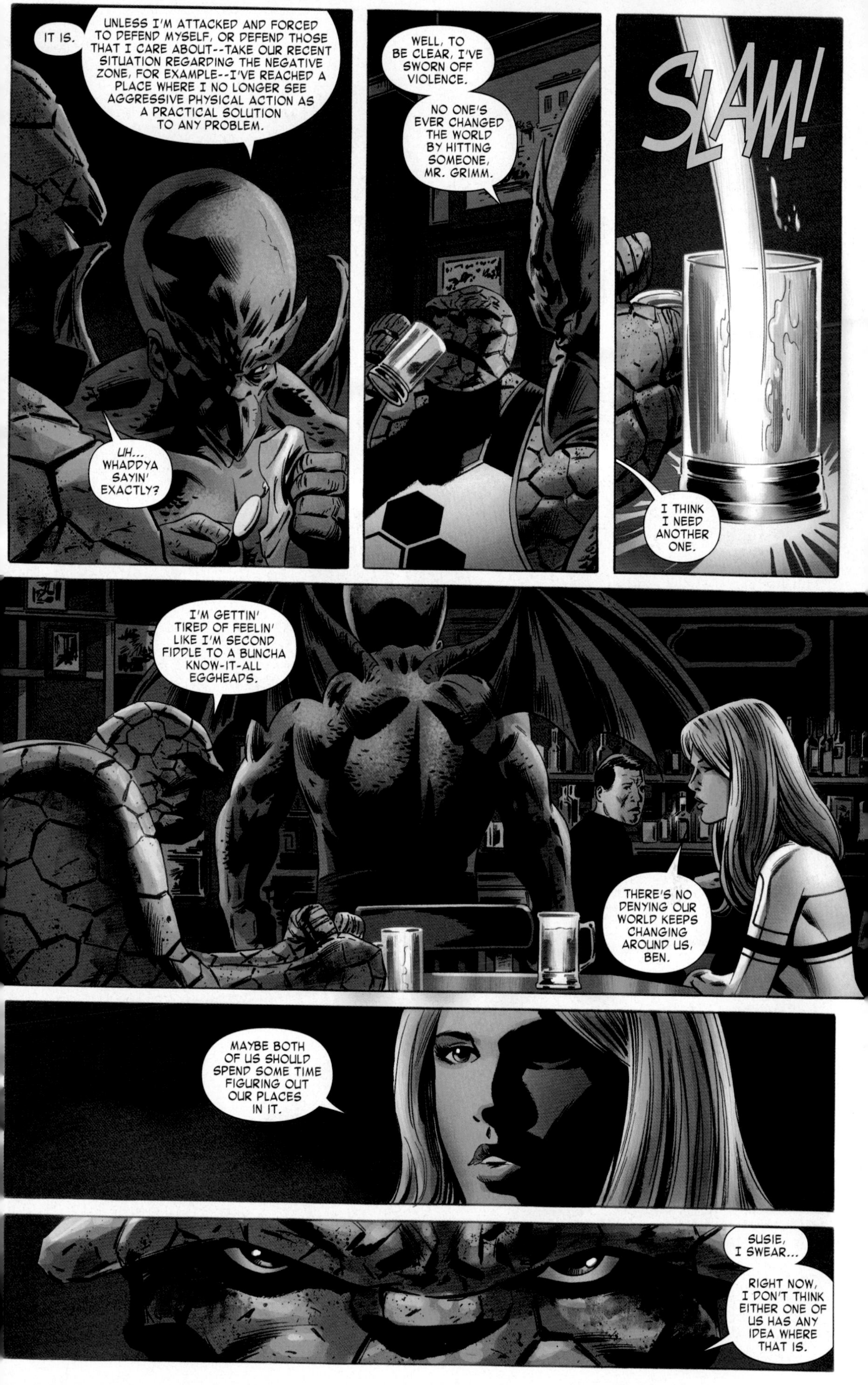
IT IS.
UNLESS I'M ATTACKED AND FORCED TO DEFEND MYSELF, OR DEFEND THOSE THAT I CARE ABOUT--TAKE OUR RECENT SITUATION REGARDING THE NEGATIVE ZONE, FOR EXAMPLE--I'VE REACHED A PLACE WHERE I NO LONGER SEE AGGRESSIVE PHYSICAL ACTION AS A PRACTICAL SOLUTION TO ANY PROBLEM.
UH... WHADDYA SAYIN' EXACTLY?
WELL, TO BE CLEAR, I'VE SWORN OFF VIOLENCE.
NO ONE'S EVER CHANGED THE WORLD BY HITTING SOMEONE, MR. GRIMM.
SLAM!
I THINK I NEED ANOTHER ONE.
I'M GETTIN' TIRED OF FEELIN' LIKE I'M SECOND FIDDLE TO A BUNCHA KNOW-IT-ALL EGGHEADS.
THERE'S NO DENYING OUR WORLD KEEPS CHANGING AROUND US, BEN.
MAYBE BOTH OF US SHOULD SPEND SOME TIME FIGURING OUT OUR PLACES IN IT.
SUSIE, I SWEAR...
RIGHT NOW, I DON'T THINK EITHER ONE OF US HAS ANY IDEA WHERE THAT IS.

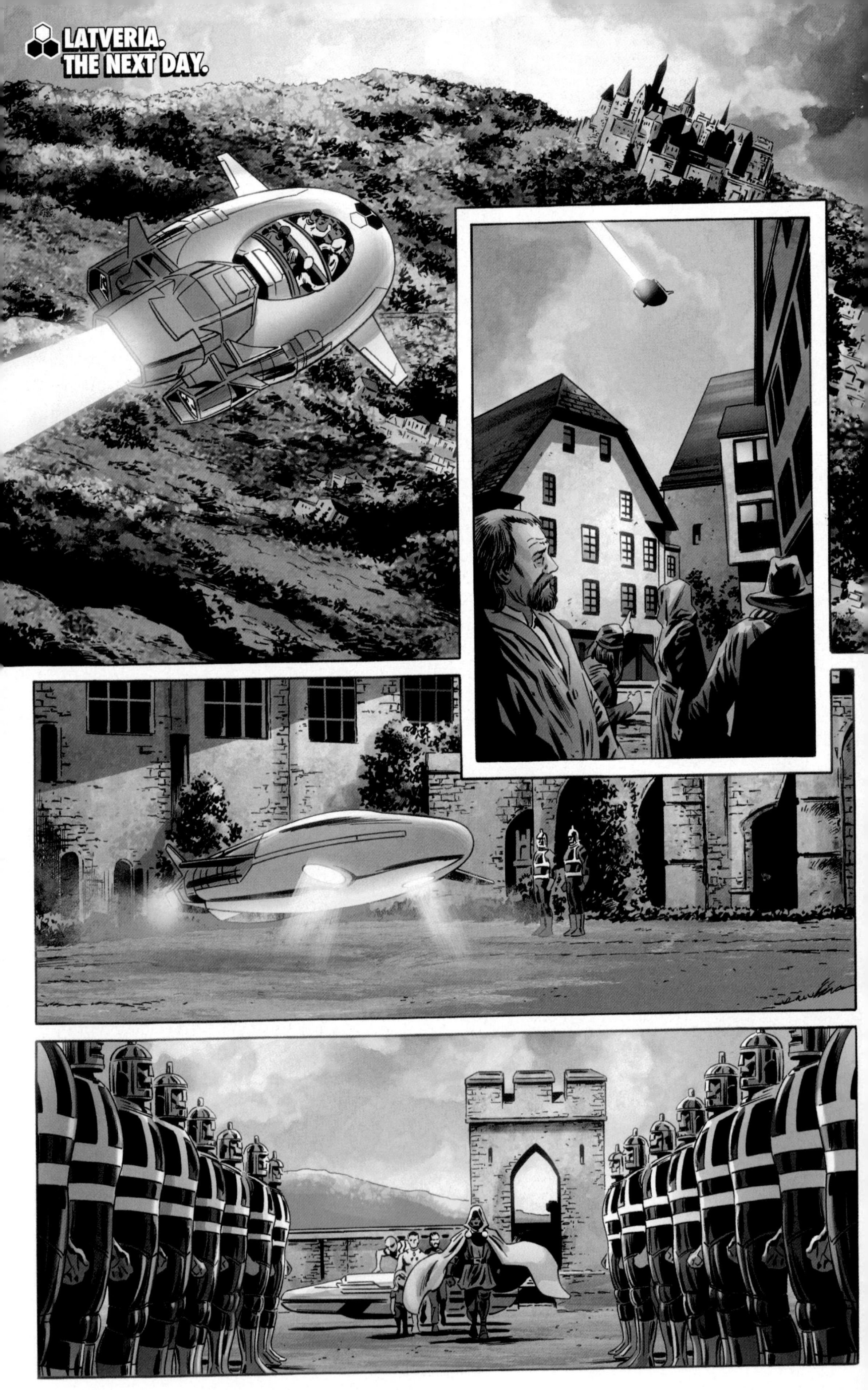
LATVERIA. THE NEXT DAY.

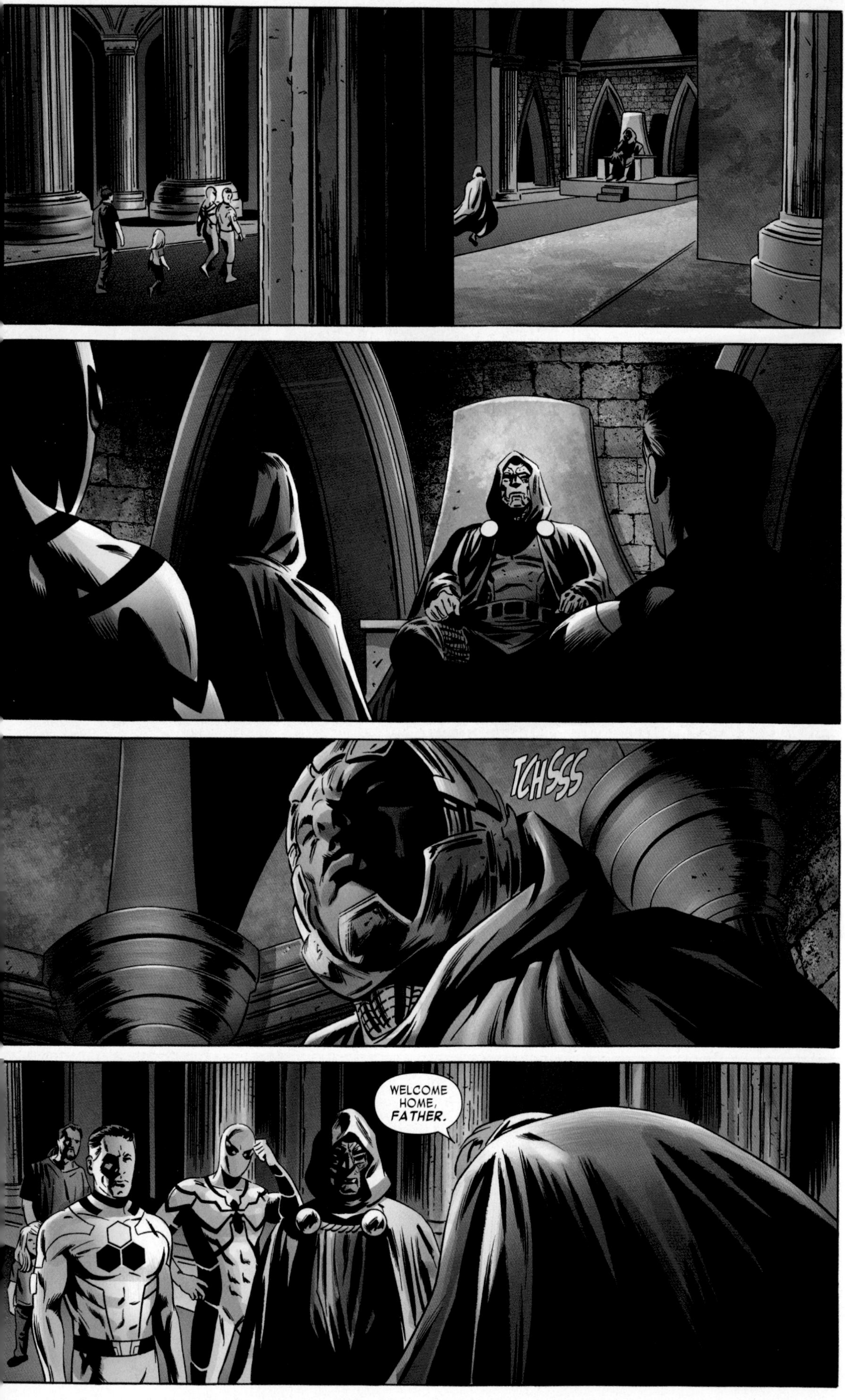
TCHSSS
WELCOME HOME, FATHER.

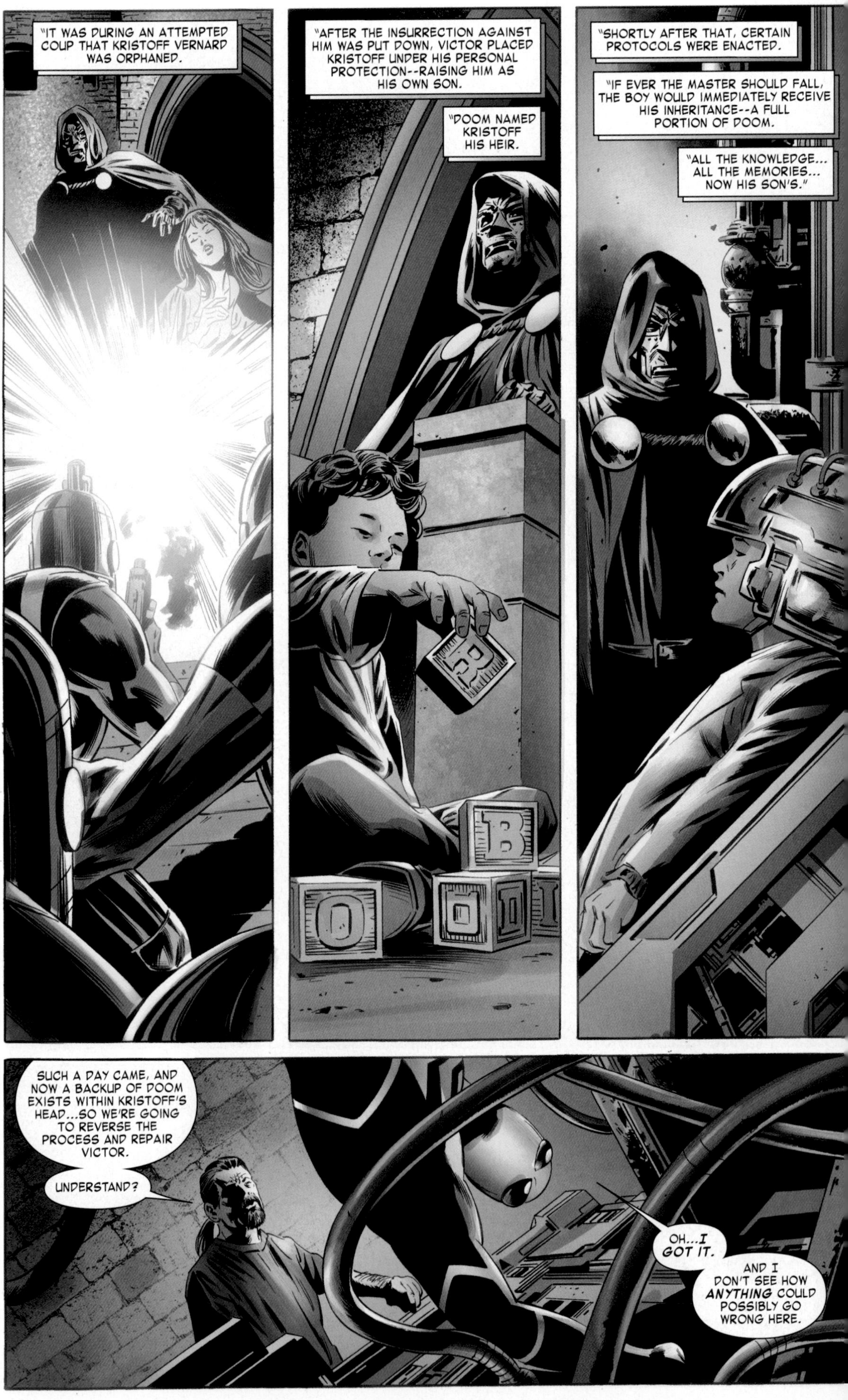
"IT WAS DURING AN ATTEMPTED COUP THAT KRISTOFF VERNARD WAS ORPHANED.
"AFTER THE INSURRECTION AGAINST HIM WAS PUT DOWN, VICTOR PLACED KRISTOFF UNDER HIS PERSONAL PROTECTION--RAISING HIM AS HIS OWN SON.
"DOOM NAMED KRISTOFF HIS HEIR.
"SHORTLY AFTER THAT, CERTAIN PROTOCOLS WERE ENACTED.
"IF EVER THE MASTER SHOULD FALL, THE BOY WOULD IMMEDIATELY RECEIVE HIS INHERITANCE--A FULL PORTION OF DOOM.
"ALL THE KNOWLEDGE... ALL THE MEMORIES... NOW HIS SON'S."
SUCH A DAY CAME, AND NOW A BACKUP OF DOOM EXISTS WITHIN KRISTOFF'S HEAD...SO WE'RE GOING TO REVERSE THE PROCESS AND REPAIR VICTOR.
UNDERSTAND?
OH...*I GOT IT.*
AND I DON'T SEE HOW *ANYTHING* COULD POSSIBLY GO WRONG HERE.

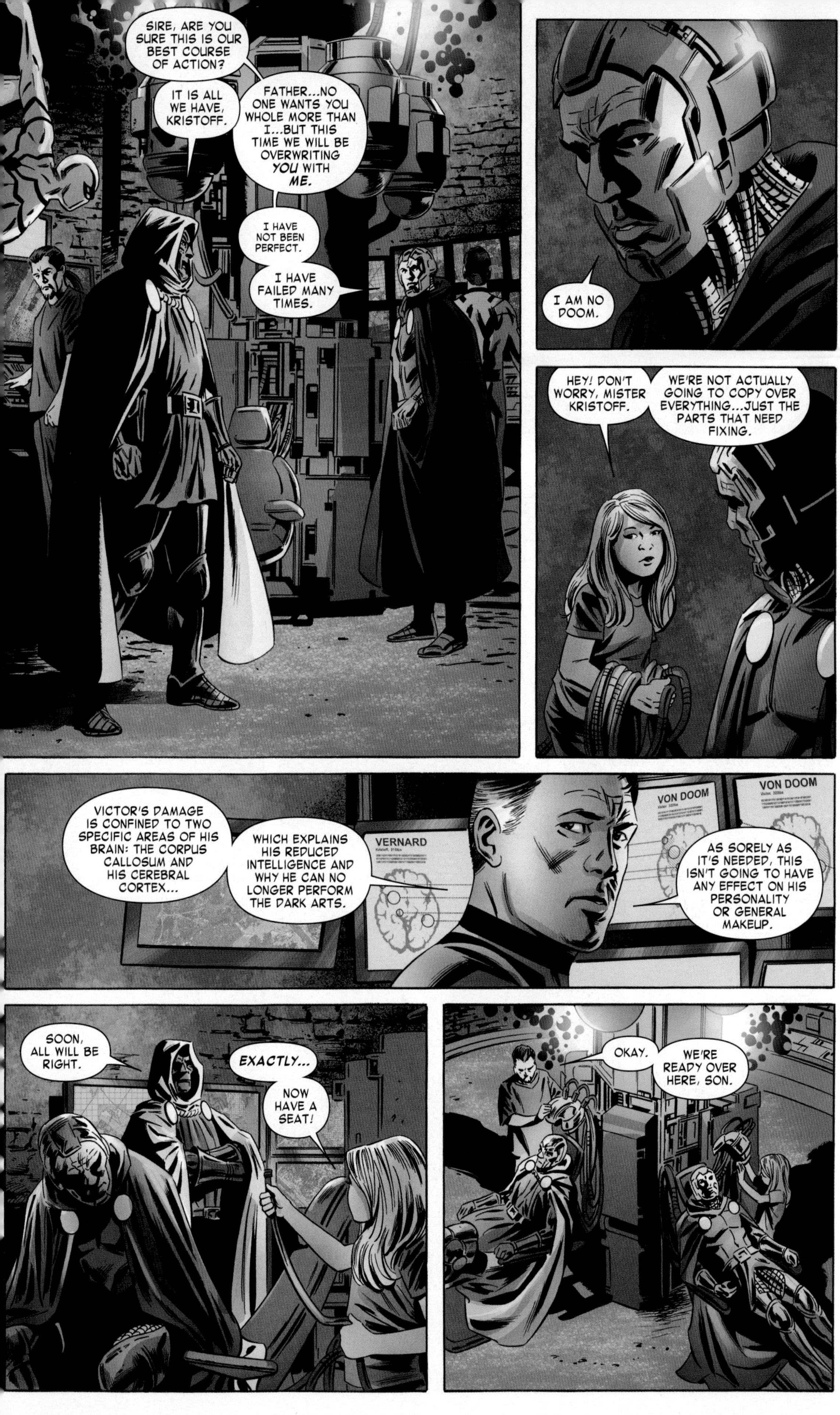
SIRE, ARE YOU SURE THIS IS OUR BEST COURSE OF ACTION?
IT IS ALL WE HAVE, KRISTOFF.
FATHER...NO ONE WANTS YOU WHOLE MORE THAN I...BUT THIS TIME WE WILL BE OVERWRITING *YOU* WITH *ME.*
I HAVE NOT BEEN PERFECT.
I HAVE FAILED MANY TIMES.
I AM NO DOOM.
HEY! DON'T WORRY, MISTER KRISTOFF.
WE'RE NOT ACTUALLY GOING TO COPY OVER EVERYTHING...JUST THE PARTS THAT NEED FIXING.
VICTOR'S DAMAGE IS CONFINED TO TWO SPECIFIC AREAS OF HIS BRAIN: THE CORPUS CALLOSUM AND HIS CEREBRAL CORTEX...
WHICH EXPLAINS HIS REDUCED INTELLIGENCE AND WHY HE CAN NO LONGER PERFORM THE DARK ARTS.
VERNARD
VON DOOM
VON DOOM
AS SORELY AS IT'S NEEDED, THIS ISN'T GOING TO HAVE ANY EFFECT ON HIS PERSONALITY OR GENERAL MAKEUP.
SOON, ALL WILL BE RIGHT.
EXACTLY...
NOW HAVE A SEAT!
OKAY.
WE'RE READY OVER HERE, SON.

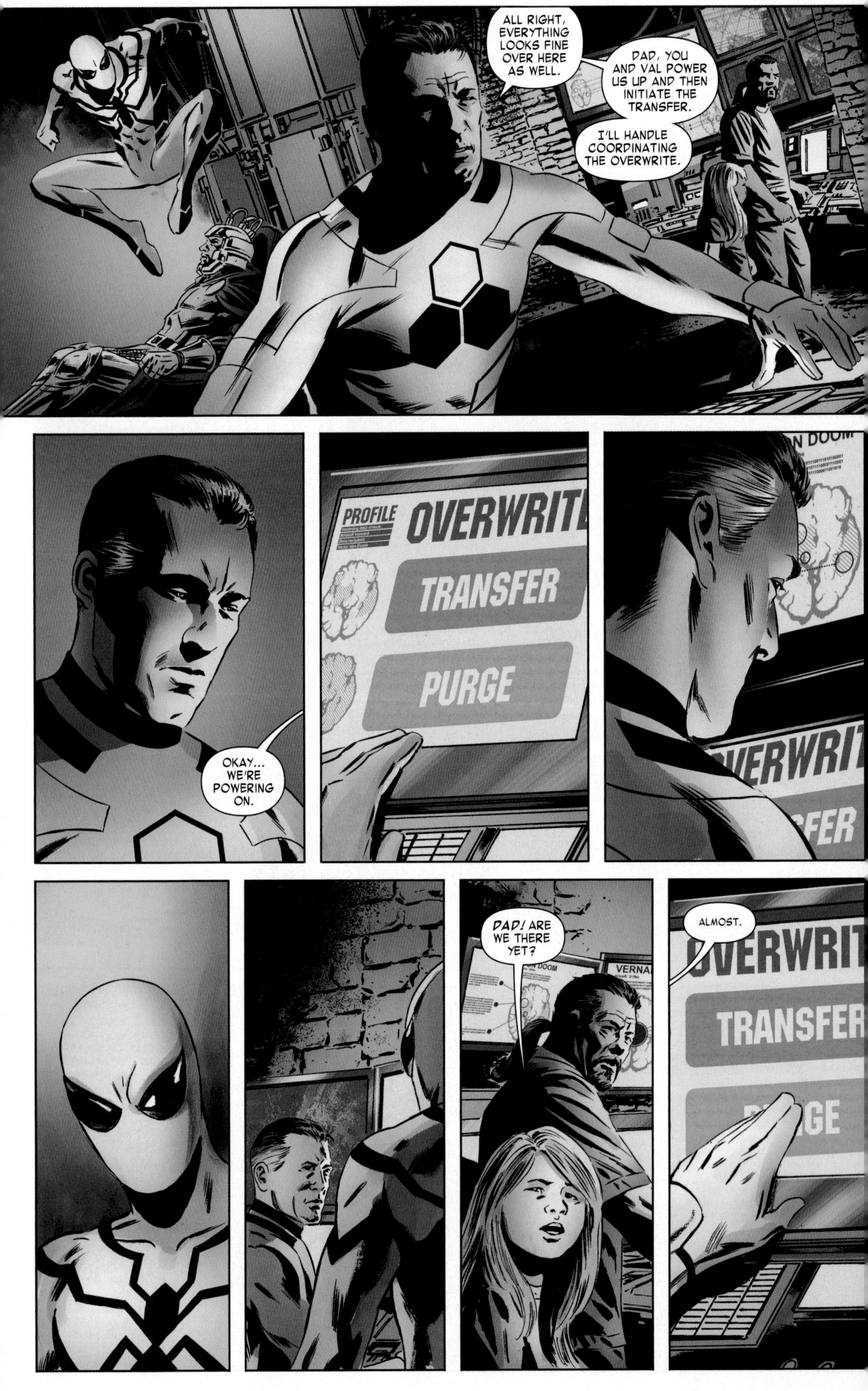
ALL RIGHT, EVERYTHING LOOKS FINE OVER HERE AS WELL.
DAD, YOU AND VAL POWER US UP AND THEN INITIATE THE TRANSFER.
I'LL HANDLE COORDINATING THE OVERWRITE.
OKAY... WE'RE POWERING ON.
PROFILE
OVERWRIT
TRANSFER
PURGE
DAD! ARE WE THERE YET?
ALMOST.
OVERWRIT
TRANSFER

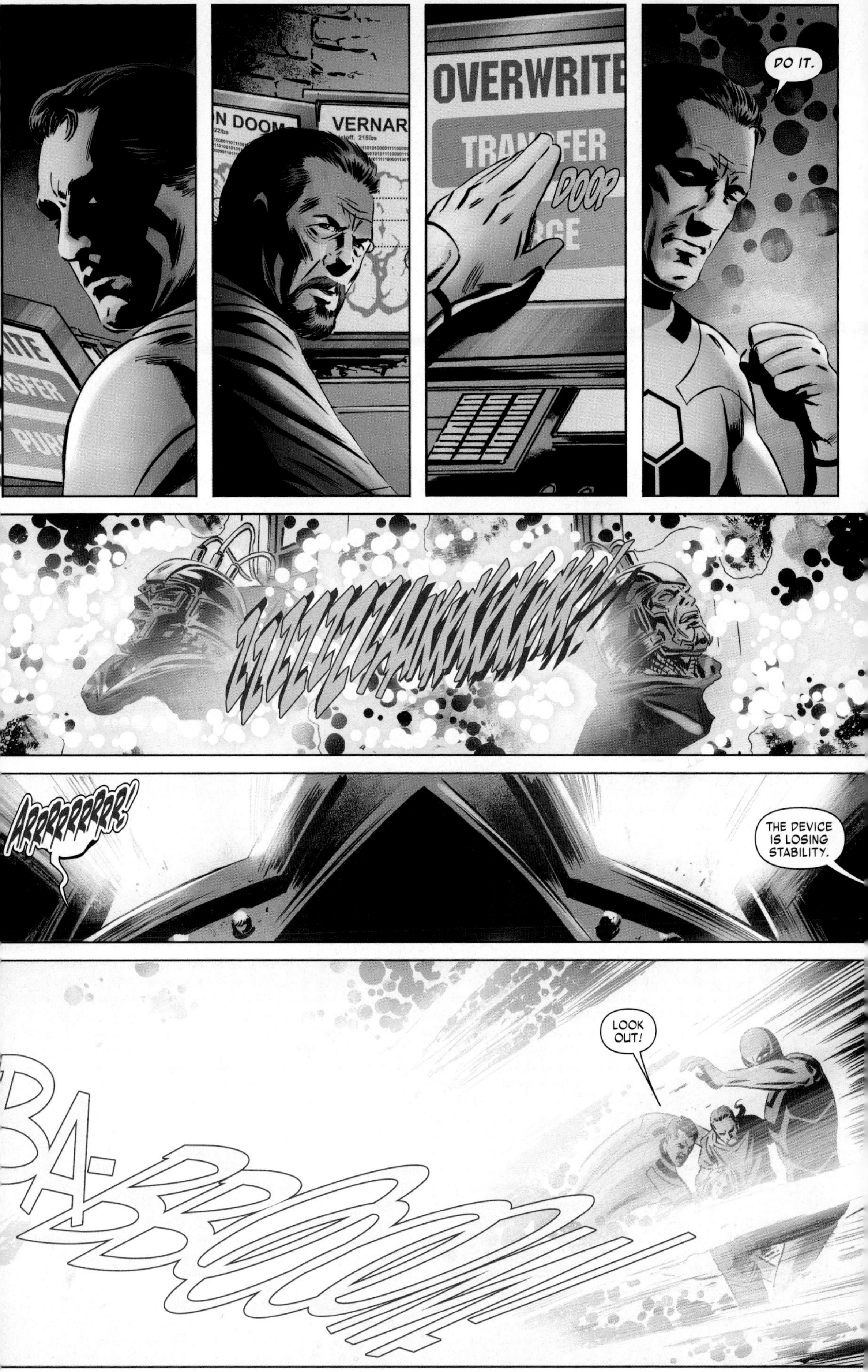
OVERWRITE
DOOP
DO IT.
THE DEVICE IS LOSING STABILITY.
LOOK OUT!

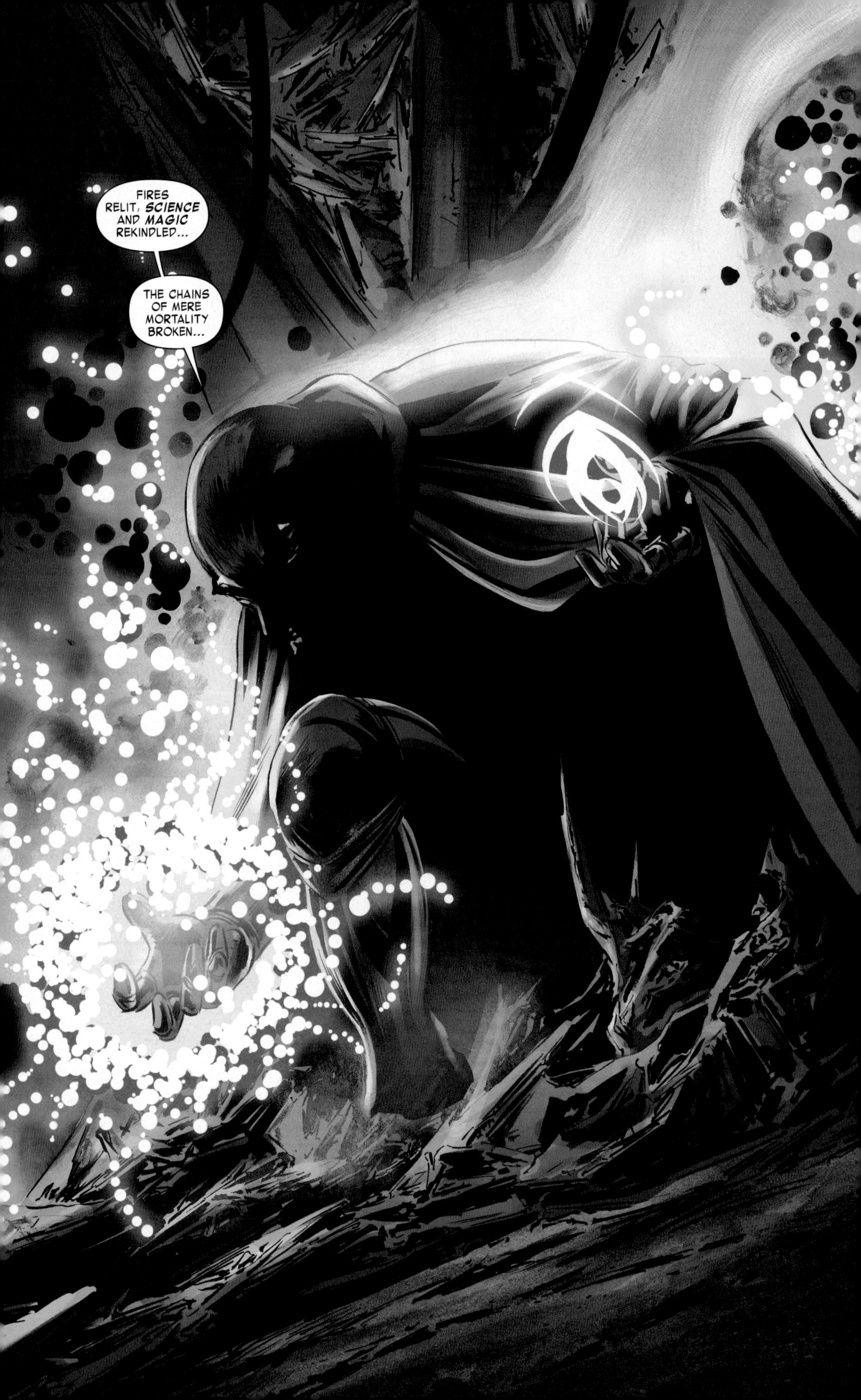
FIRES RELIT, SCIENCE AND MAGIC REKINDLED...
THE CHAINS OF MERE MORTALITY BROKEN...

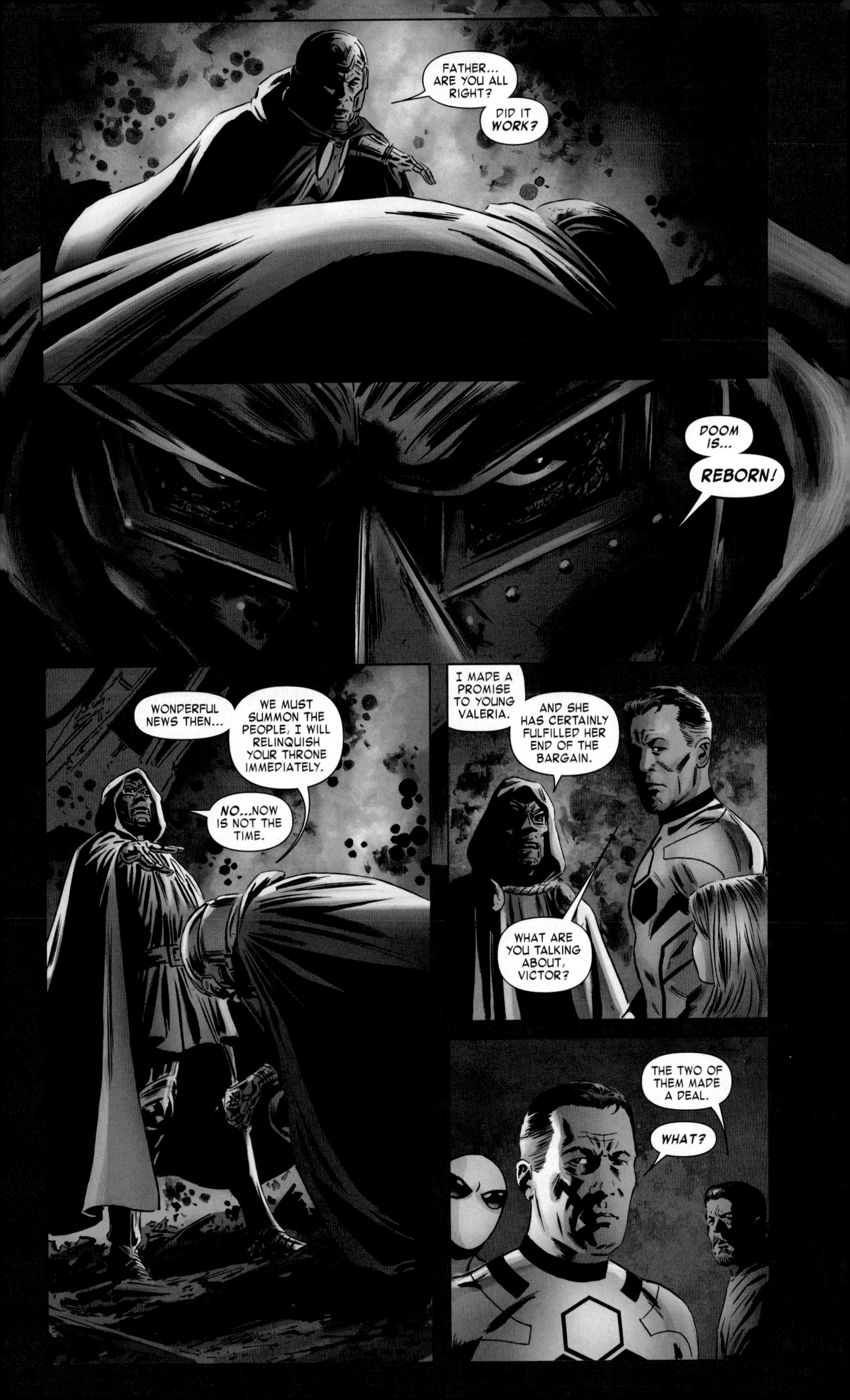
FATHER... ARE YOU ALL RIGHT?
DID IT WORK?
DOOM IS... REBORN!
WONDERFUL NEWS THEN...
WE MUST SUMMON THE PEOPLE, I WILL RELINQUISH YOUR THRONE IMMEDIATELY.
NO...NOW IS NOT THE TIME.
I MADE A PROMISE TO YOUNG VALERIA.
AND SHE HAS CERTAINLY FULFILLED HER END OF THE BARGAIN.
WHAT ARE YOU TALKING ABOUT, VICTOR?
THE TWO OF THEM MADE A DEAL.
WHAT?

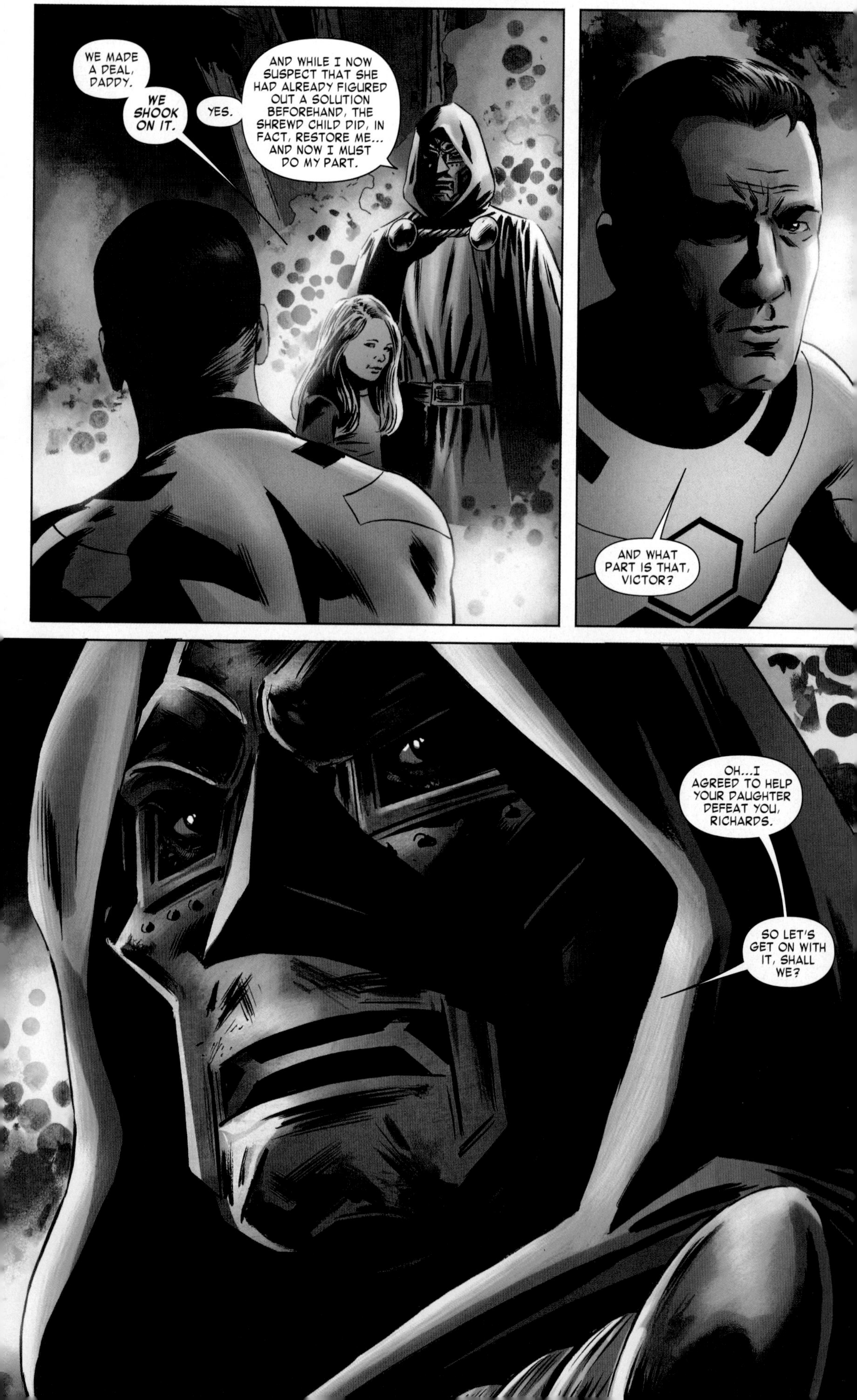
WE MADE A DEAL, DADDY.
WE SHOOK ON IT.
YES.
AND WHILE I NOW SUSPECT THAT SHE HAD ALREADY FIGURED OUT A SOLUTION BEFOREHAND, THE SHREWD CHILD DID, IN FACT, RESTORE ME... AND NOW I MUST DO MY PART.
AND WHAT PART IS THAT, VICTOR?
OH...I AGREED TO HELP YOUR DAUGHTER DEFEAT YOU, RICHARDS.
SO LET'S GET ON WITH IT, SHALL WE?

FIND ME SOMETHING I CAN USE

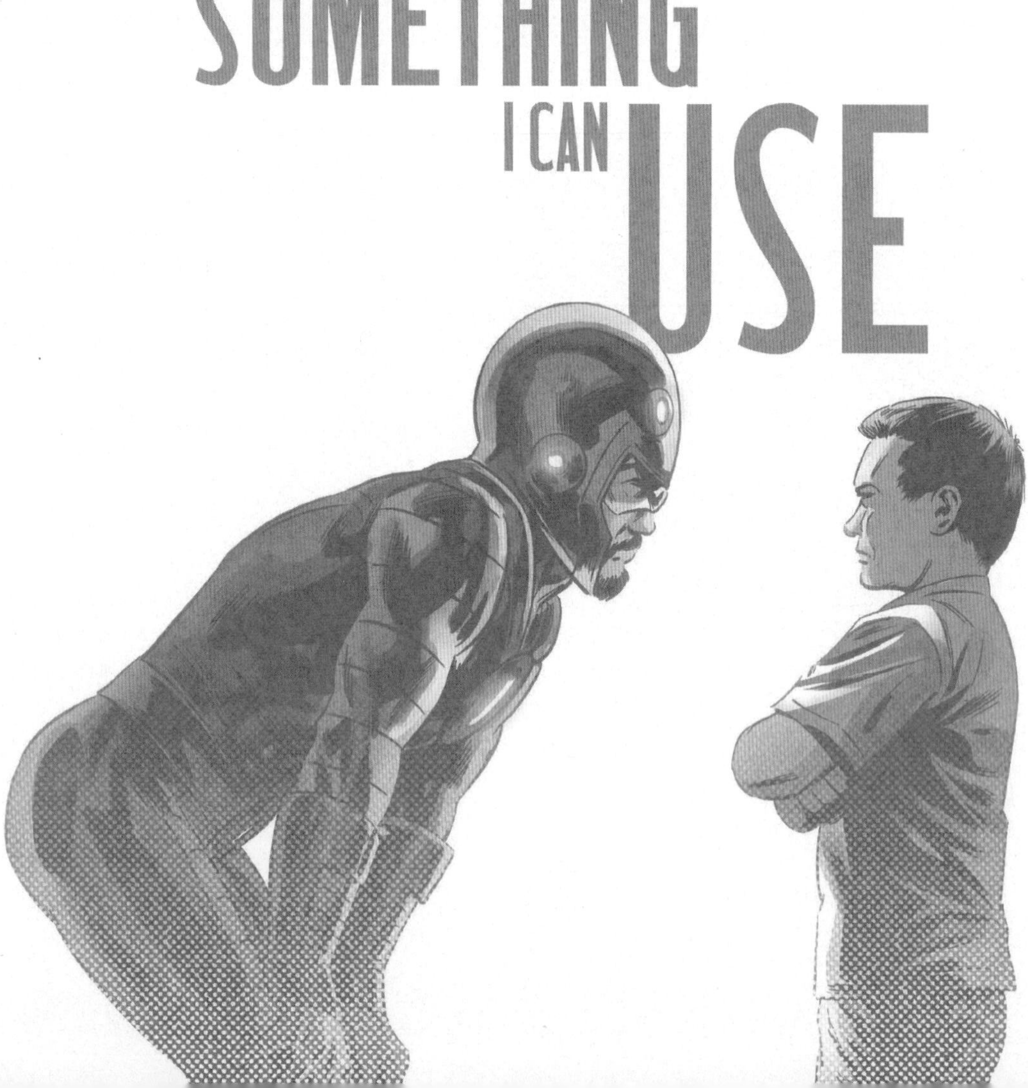

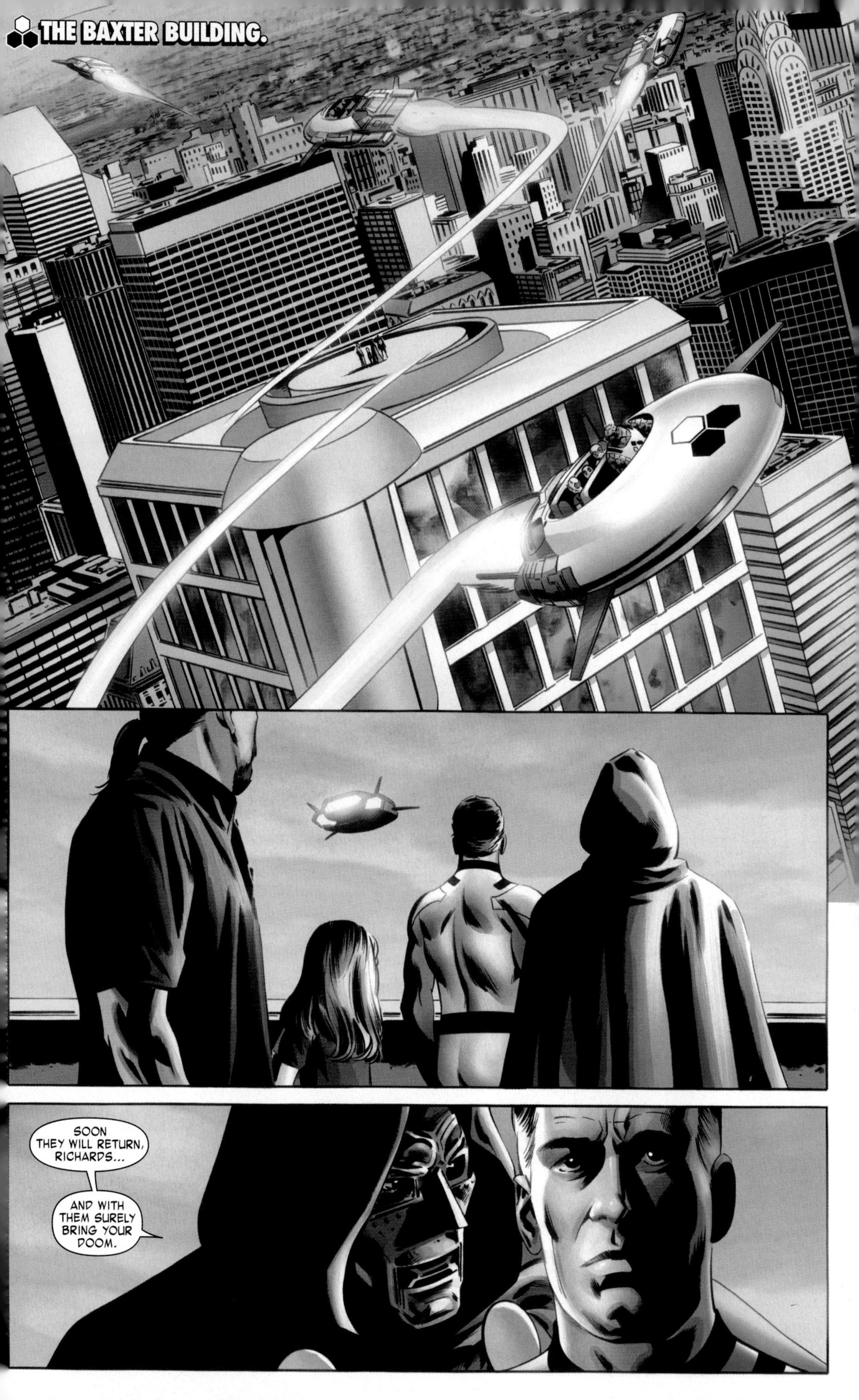
THE BAXTER BUILDING.
SOON THEY WILL RETURN, RICHARDS...
AND WITH THEM SURELY BRING YOUR DOOM.

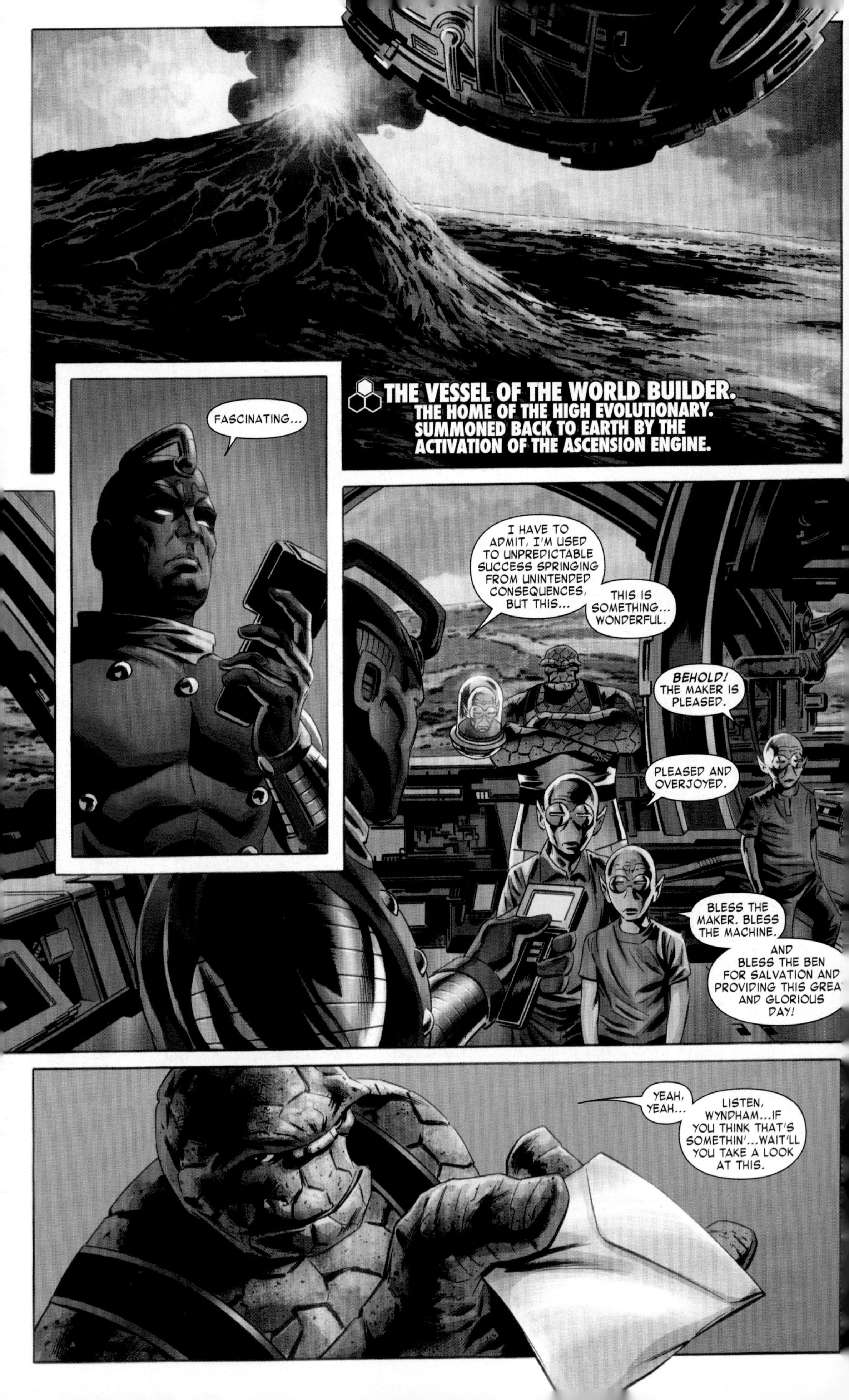
THE VESSEL OF THE WORLD BUILDER.
THE HOME OF THE HIGH EVOLUTIONARY. SUMMONED BACK TO EARTH BY THE ACTIVATION OF THE ASCENSION ENGINE.
FASCINATING...
I HAVE TO ADMIT, I'M USED TO UNPREDICTABLE SUCCESS SPRINGING FROM UNINTENDED CONSEQUENCES, BUT THIS...
THIS IS SOMETHING... WONDERFUL.
BEHOLD! THE MAKER IS PLEASED.
PLEASED AND OVERJOYED.
BLESS THE MAKER. BLESS THE MACHINE.
AND BLESS THE BEN FOR SALVATION AND PROVIDING THIS GREAT AND GLORIOUS DAY!
YEAH, YEAH...
LISTEN, WYNDHAM...IF YOU THINK THAT'S SOMETHIN'...WAIT'LL YOU TAKE A LOOK AT THIS.

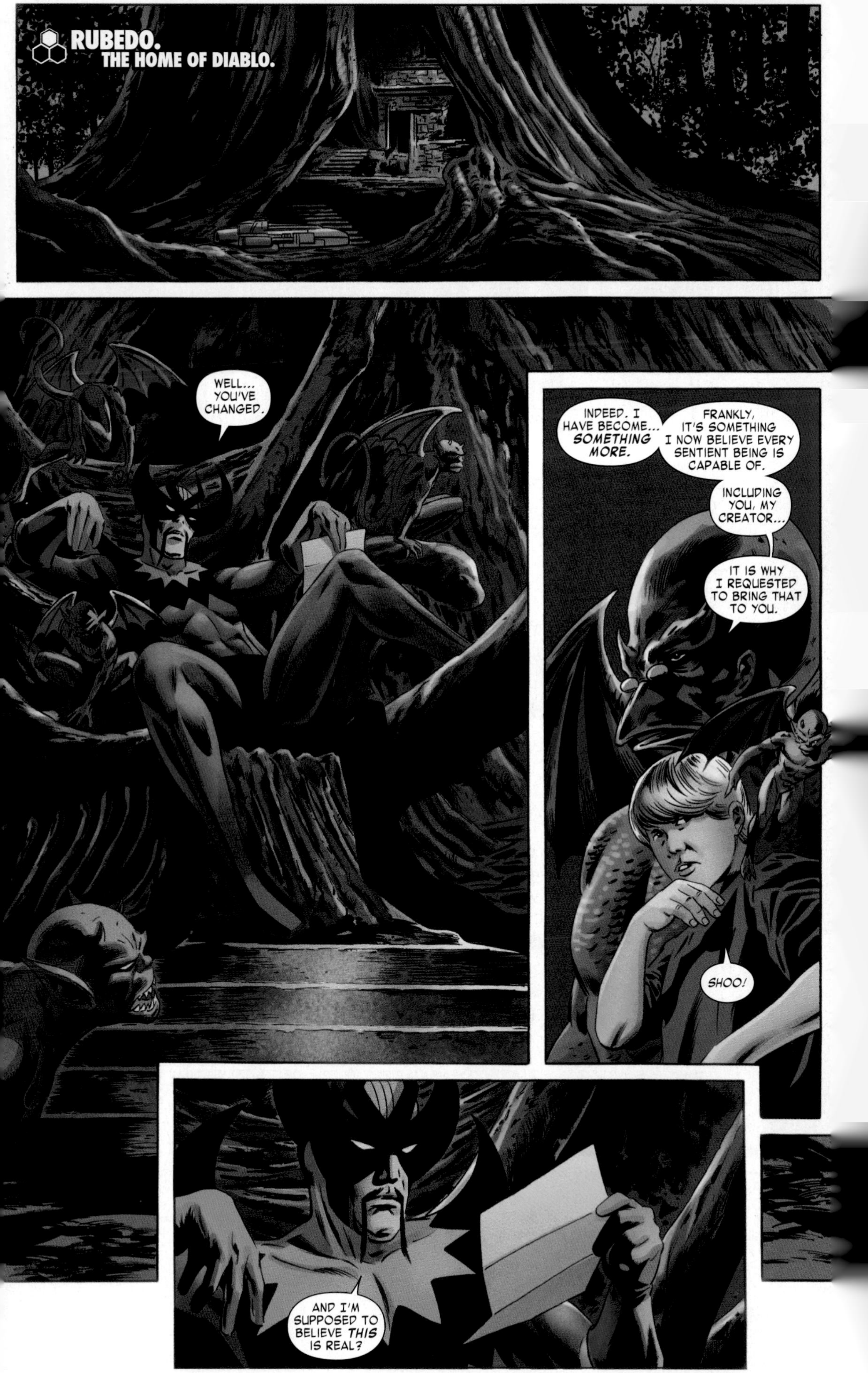
RUBEDO.
THE HOME OF DIABLO.
WELL... YOU'VE CHANGED.
INDEED. I HAVE BECOME... SOMETHING MORE.
FRANKLY, IT'S SOMETHING I NOW BELIEVE EVERY SENTIENT BEING IS CAPABLE OF.
INCLUDING YOU, MY CREATOR...
IT IS WHY I REQUESTED TO BRING THAT TO YOU.
SHOO!
AND I'M SUPPOSED TO BELIEVE THIS IS REAL?

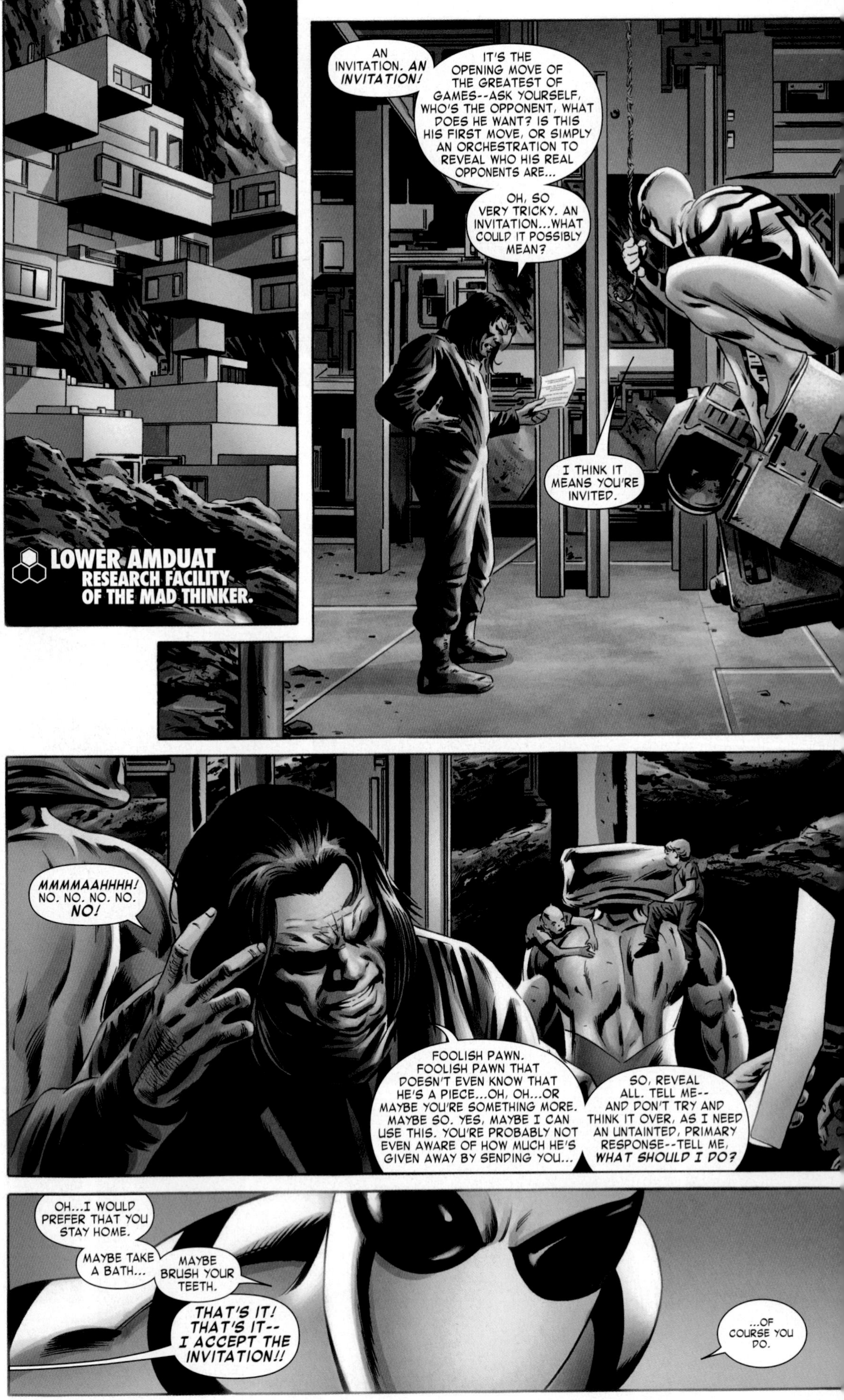
LOWER AMDUAT RESEARCH FACILITY OF THE MAD THINKER.
AN INVITATION. *AN INVITATION!*
IT'S THE OPENING MOVE OF THE GREATEST OF GAMES--ASK YOURSELF, WHO'S THE OPPONENT, WHAT DOES HE WANT? IS THIS HIS FIRST MOVE, OR SIMPLY AN ORCHESTRATION TO REVEAL WHO HIS REAL OPPONENTS ARE...
OH, SO VERY TRICKY. AN INVITATION...WHAT COULD IT POSSIBLY MEAN?
I THINK IT MEANS YOU'RE INVITED.
MMMMAAHHHH! NO. NO. NO. NO. *NO!*
FOOLISH PAWN. FOOLISH PAWN THAT DOESN'T EVEN KNOW THAT HE'S A PIECE...OH, OH...OR MAYBE YOU'RE SOMETHING MORE. MAYBE SO. YES, MAYBE I CAN USE THIS. YOU'RE PROBABLY NOT EVEN AWARE OF HOW MUCH HE'S GIVEN AWAY BY SENDING YOU...
SO, REVEAL ALL. TELL ME-- AND DON'T TRY AND THINK IT OVER, AS I NEED AN UNTAINTED, PRIMARY RESPONSE--TELL ME, *WHAT SHOULD I DO?*
OH...I WOULD PREFER THAT YOU STAY HOME.
MAYBE TAKE A BATH...
MAYBE BRUSH YOUR TEETH.
THAT'S IT! THAT'S IT-- I ACCEPT THE INVITATION!!
...OF COURSE YOU DO.

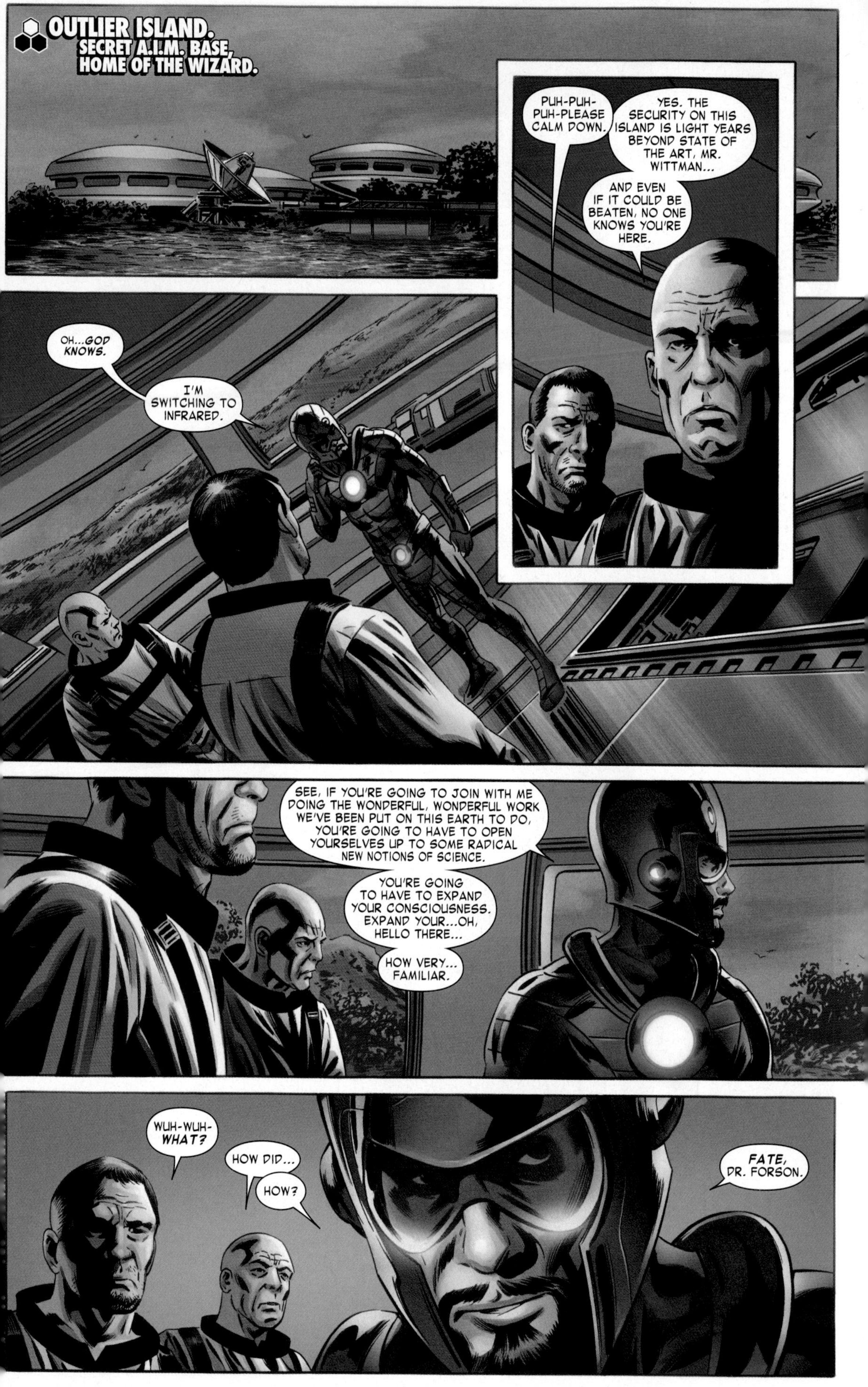
OUTLIER ISLAND.
SECRET A.I.M. BASE, HOME OF THE WIZARD.
PUH-PUH-PUH-PLEASE CALM DOWN.
YES. THE SECURITY ON THIS ISLAND IS LIGHT YEARS BEYOND STATE OF THE ART, MR. WITTMAN...
AND EVEN IF IT COULD BE BEATEN, NO ONE KNOWS YOU'RE HERE.
OH...GOD KNOWS.
I'M SWITCHING TO INFRARED.
SEE, IF YOU'RE GOING TO JOIN WITH ME DOING THE WONDERFUL, WONDERFUL WORK WE'VE BEEN PUT ON THIS EARTH TO DO, YOU'RE GOING TO HAVE TO OPEN YOURSELVES UP TO SOME RADICAL NEW NOTIONS OF SCIENCE.
YOU'RE GOING TO HAVE TO EXPAND YOUR CONSCIOUSNESS. EXPAND YOUR...OH, HELLO THERE...
HOW VERY... FAMILIAR.
WUH-WUH-WHAT?
HOW DID...
HOW?
FATE, DR. FORSON.

NO. THEY SHOULD NOT HAVE BEEN ABLE TO FIND US.

∻TT∻ THE WIZARD'S HELMET ONLY SHIELDS HIS BRAINWAVES WHEN HE WEARS IT. IF SOMEONE HAS AN EXACT COPY--AND WE DO--MR. WITTMAN WOULD BE BEST ADVISED TO WEAR IT ALL THE TIME.

I CAN ONLY BEAR SO MUCH OF A BURDEN...IT ITCHES WHEN I SLEEP.

HELLO, LITTLE TWENTY-THREE.

MY NAME IS BENTLEY NOW.

I'VE EARNED IT.

BE THAT AS IT MAY...HAVE YOU DECIDED TO COME HOME, LITTLE PRODIGAL?

NO. THAT'S NOT WHY WE'RE HERE.

THIS IS.

WE NEED TO KNOW IF YOU'RE COMING.

HMMMMM....

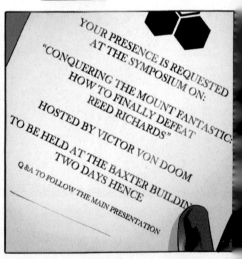

YOUR PRESENCE IS REQUESTED AT THE SYMPOSIUM ON:

"CONQUERING THE MOUNT FANTASTIC: HOW TO FINALLY DEFEAT REED RICHARDS"

HOSTED BY VICTOR VON DOOM

TO BE HELD AT THE BAXTER BUILDIN

TWO DAYS HENCE

Q&A TO FOLLOW THE MAIN PRESENTATION

HOW COULD WE REFUSE?

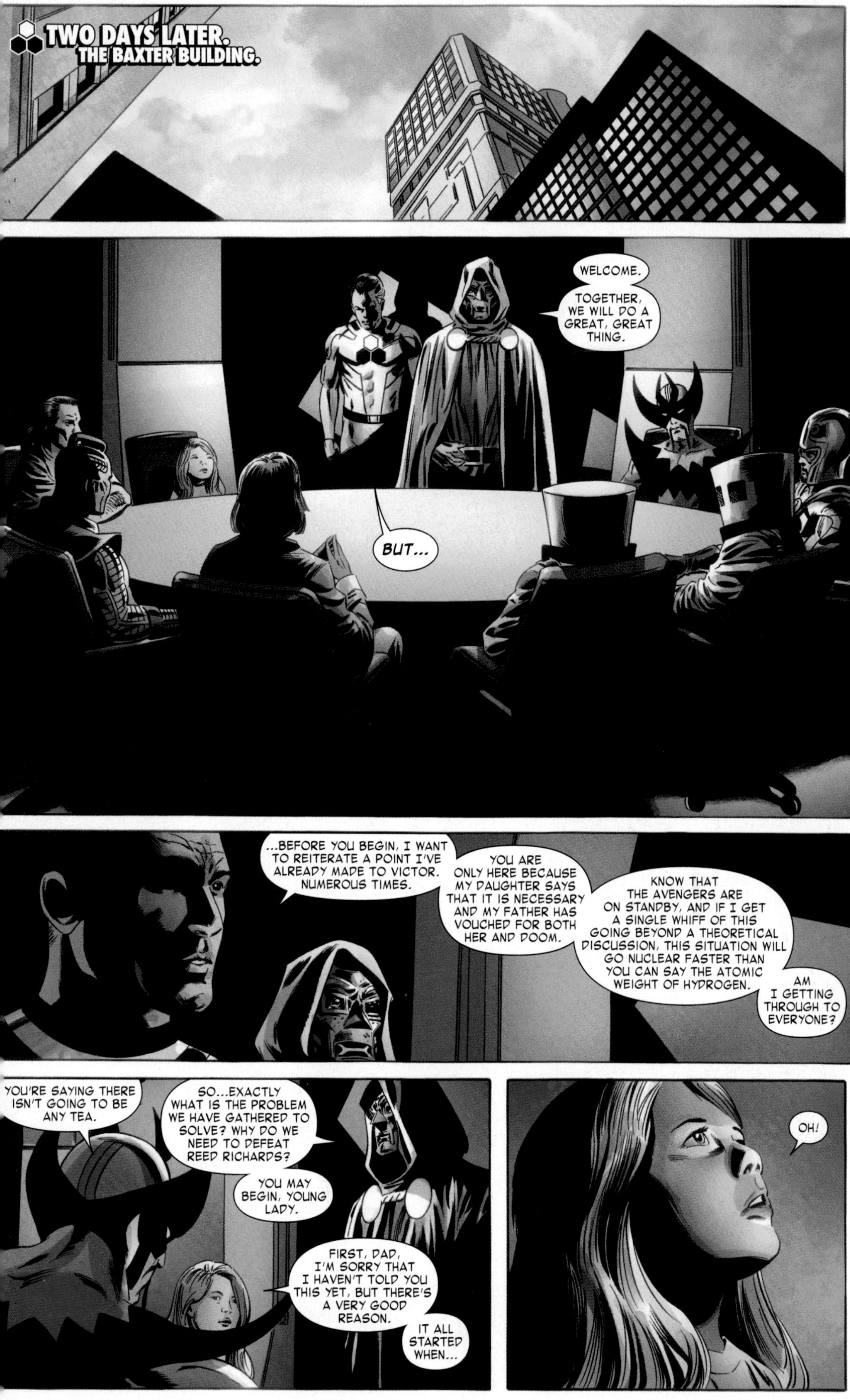
TWO DAYS LATER. THE BAXTER BUILDING.
WELCOME.
TOGETHER, WE WILL DO A GREAT, GREAT THING.
BUT...
...BEFORE YOU BEGIN, I WANT TO REITERATE A POINT I'VE ALREADY MADE TO VICTOR. NUMEROUS TIMES.
YOU ARE ONLY HERE BECAUSE MY DAUGHTER SAYS THAT IT IS NECESSARY AND MY FATHER HAS VOUCHED FOR BOTH HER AND DOOM.
KNOW THAT THE AVENGERS ARE ON STANDBY, AND IF I GET A SINGLE WHIFF OF THIS GOING BEYOND A THEORETICAL DISCUSSION, THIS SITUATION WILL GO NUCLEAR FASTER THAN YOU CAN SAY THE ATOMIC WEIGHT OF HYDROGEN.
AM I GETTING THROUGH TO EVERYONE?
YOU'RE SAYING THERE ISN'T GOING TO BE ANY TEA.
SO...EXACTLY WHAT IS THE PROBLEM WE HAVE GATHERED TO SOLVE? WHY DO WE NEED TO DEFEAT REED RICHARDS?
YOU MAY BEGIN, YOUNG LADY.
FIRST, DAD, I'M SORRY THAT I HAVEN'T TOLD YOU THIS YET, BUT THERE'S A VERY GOOD REASON.
IT ALL STARTED WHEN...
OH!

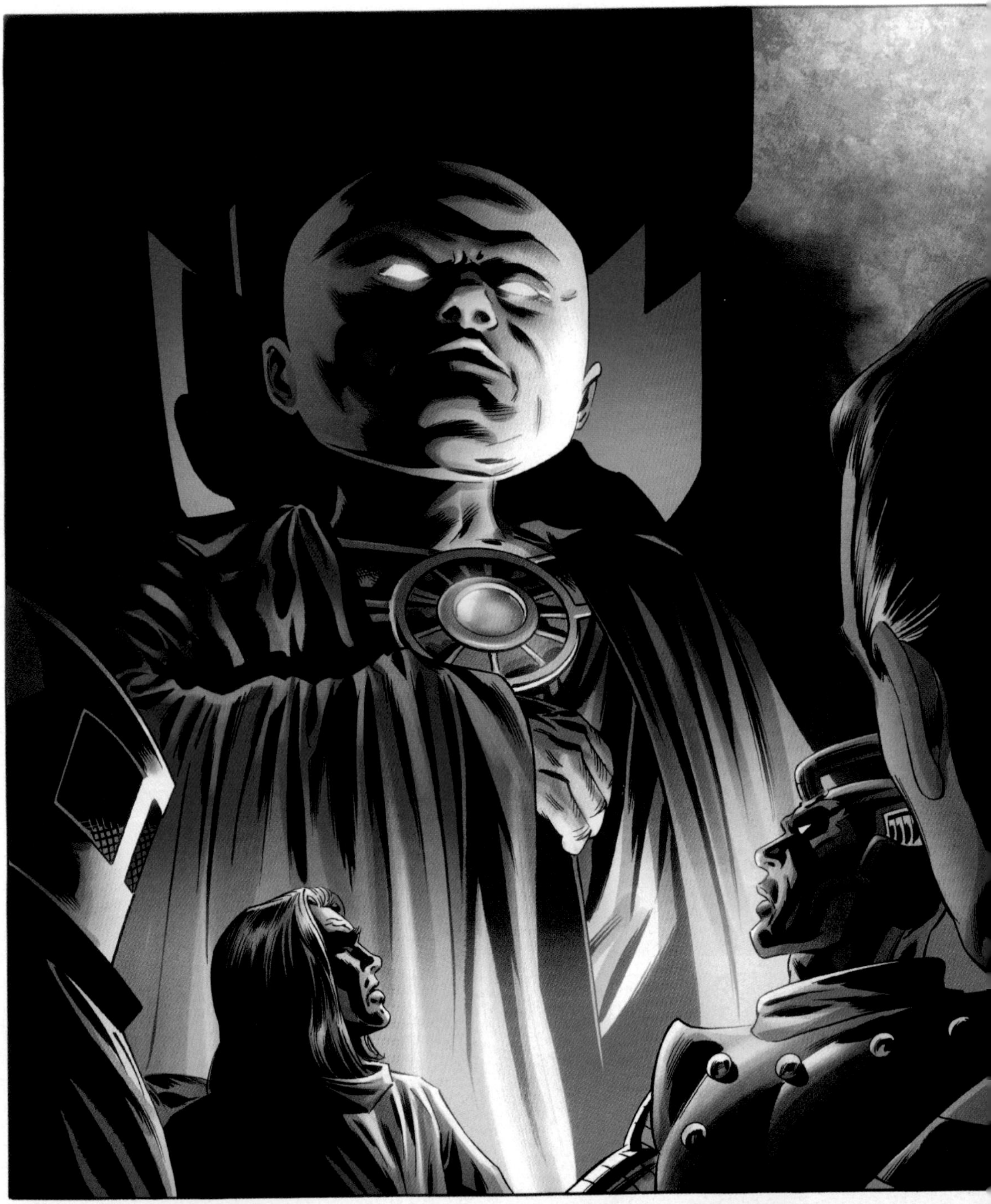

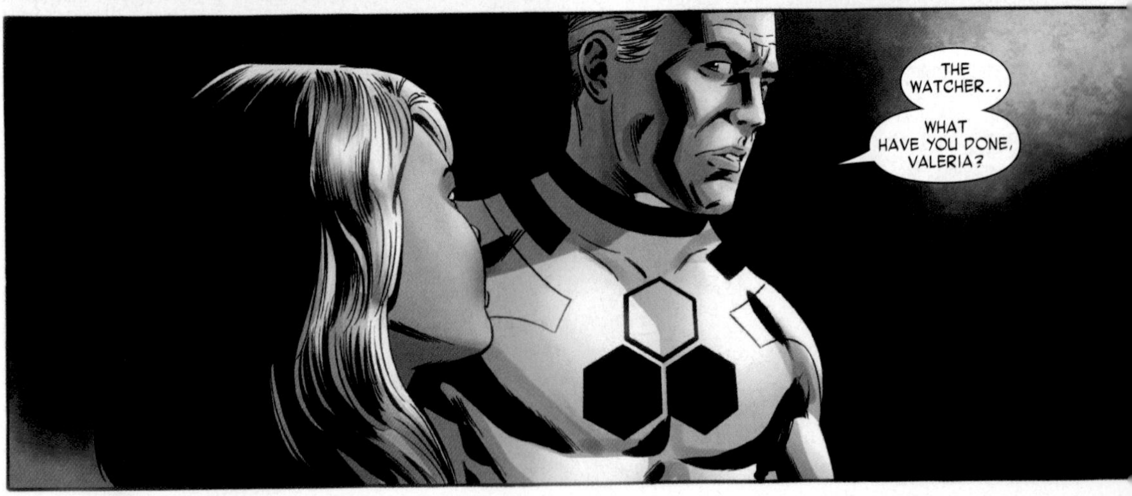
THE WATCHER...
WHAT HAVE YOU DONE, VALERIA?

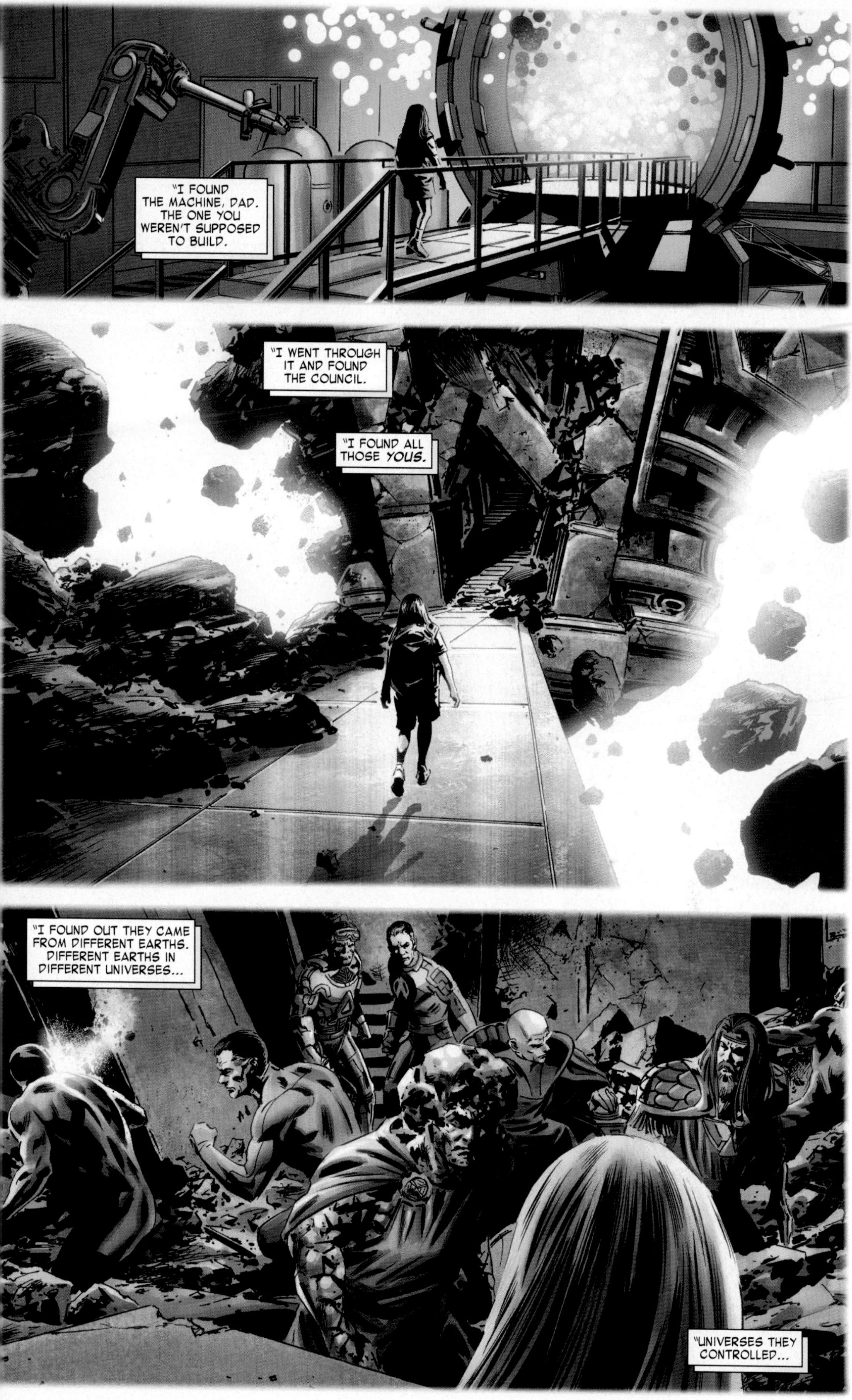
"I FOUND THE MACHINE, DAD. THE ONE YOU WEREN'T SUPPOSED TO BUILD.
"I WENT THROUGH IT AND FOUND THE COUNCIL.
"I FOUND ALL THOSE *YOUS.*
"I FOUND OUT THEY CAME FROM DIFFERENT EARTHS. DIFFERENT EARTHS IN DIFFERENT UNIVERSES...
"UNIVERSES THEY CONTROLLED...

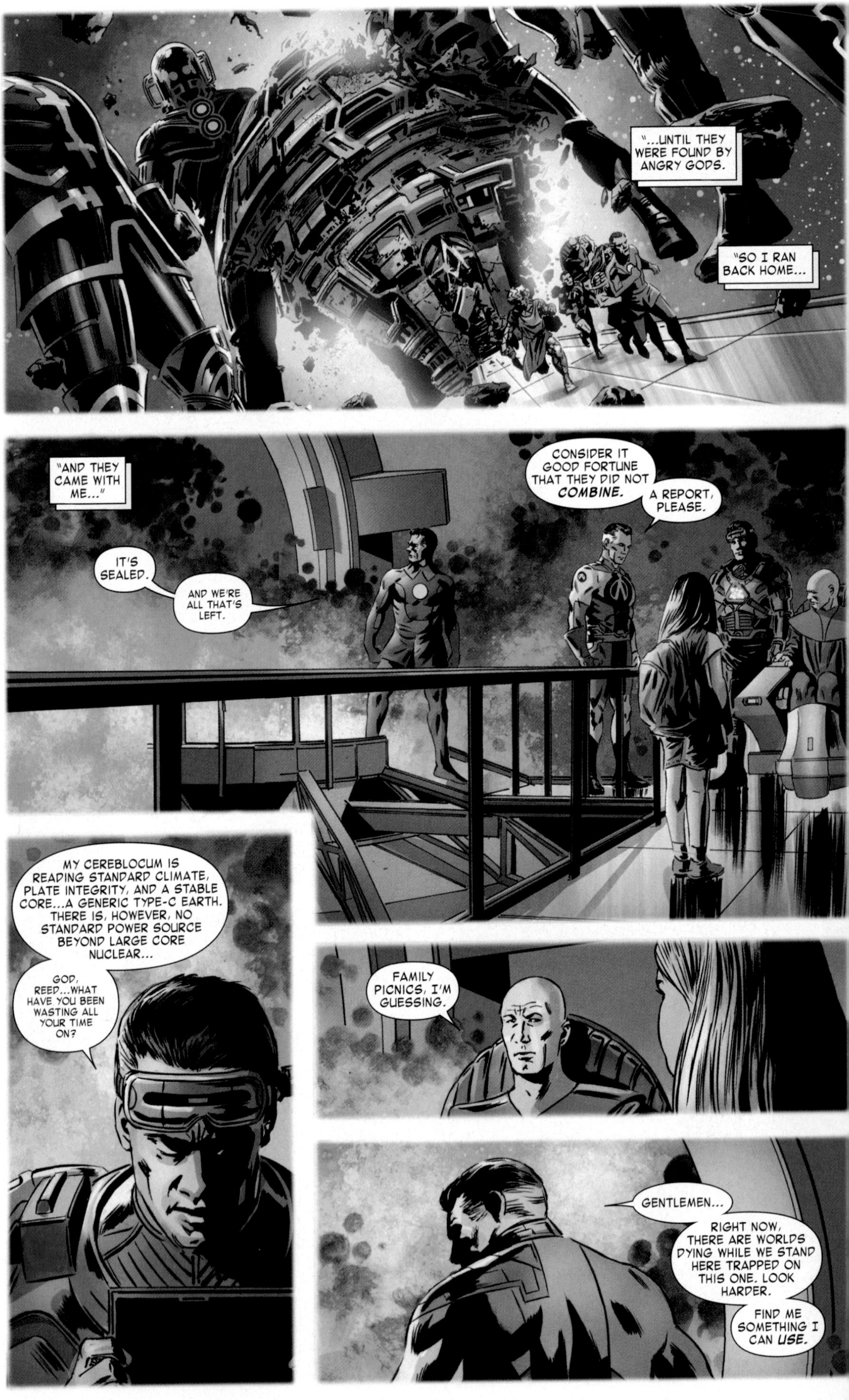
"...UNTIL THEY WERE FOUND BY ANGRY GODS.
"SO I RAN BACK HOME...
"AND THEY CAME WITH ME..."
CONSIDER IT GOOD FORTUNE THAT THEY DID NOT COMBINE.
A REPORT, PLEASE.
IT'S SEALED.
AND WE'RE ALL THAT'S LEFT.
MY CEREBLOCUM IS READING STANDARD CLIMATE, PLATE INTEGRITY, AND A STABLE CORE...A GENERIC TYPE-C EARTH. THERE IS, HOWEVER, NO STANDARD POWER SOURCE BEYOND LARGE CORE NUCLEAR...
GOD, REED...WHAT HAVE YOU BEEN WASTING ALL YOUR TIME ON?
FAMILY PICNICS, I'M GUESSING.
GENTLEMEN...
RIGHT NOW, THERE ARE WORLDS DYING WHILE WE STAND HERE TRAPPED ON THIS ONE. LOOK HARDER.
FIND ME SOMETHING I CAN USE.

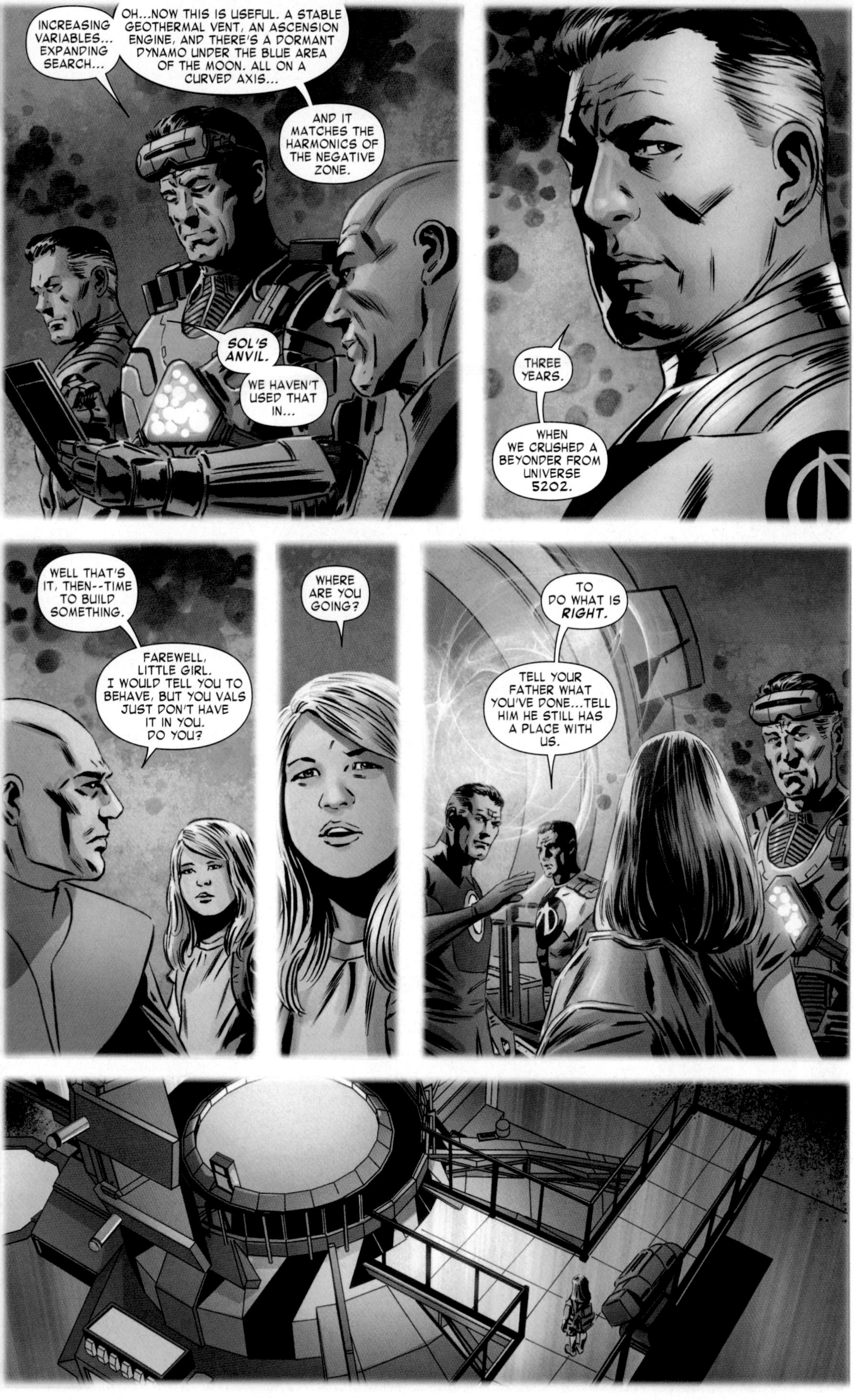
INCREASING VARIABLES... EXPANDING SEARCH...
OH...NOW THIS IS USEFUL. A STABLE GEOTHERMAL VENT, AN ASCENSION ENGINE, AND THERE'S A DORMANT DYNAMO UNDER THE BLUE AREA OF THE MOON. ALL ON A CURVED AXIS...
AND IT MATCHES THE HARMONICS OF THE NEGATIVE ZONE.
SOL'S ANVIL.
WE HAVEN'T USED THAT IN...
THREE YEARS.
WHEN WE CRUSHED A BEYONDER FROM UNIVERSE 5202.
WELL THAT'S IT, THEN--TIME TO BUILD SOMETHING.
FAREWELL, LITTLE GIRL. I WOULD TELL YOU TO BEHAVE, BUT YOU VALS JUST DON'T HAVE IT IN YOU. DO YOU?
WHERE ARE YOU GOING?
TO DO WHAT IS RIGHT.
TELL YOUR FATHER WHAT YOU'VE DONE...TELL HIM HE STILL HAS A PLACE WITH US.

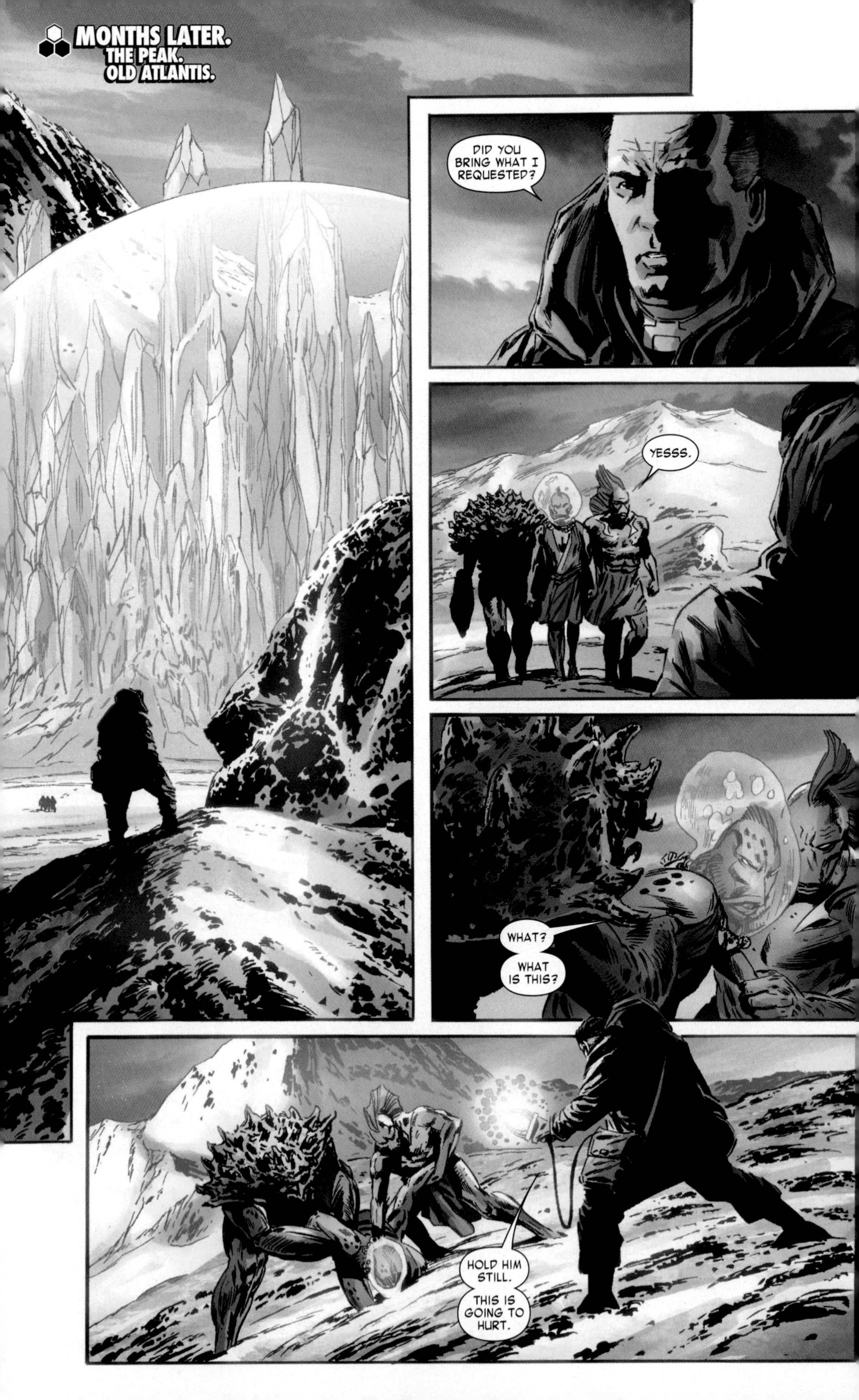
MONTHS LATER.
THE PEAK.
OLD ATLANTIS.
DID YOU BRING WHAT I REQUESTED?
YESSS.
WHAT?
WHAT IS THIS?
HOLD HIM STILL.
THIS IS GOING TO HURT.

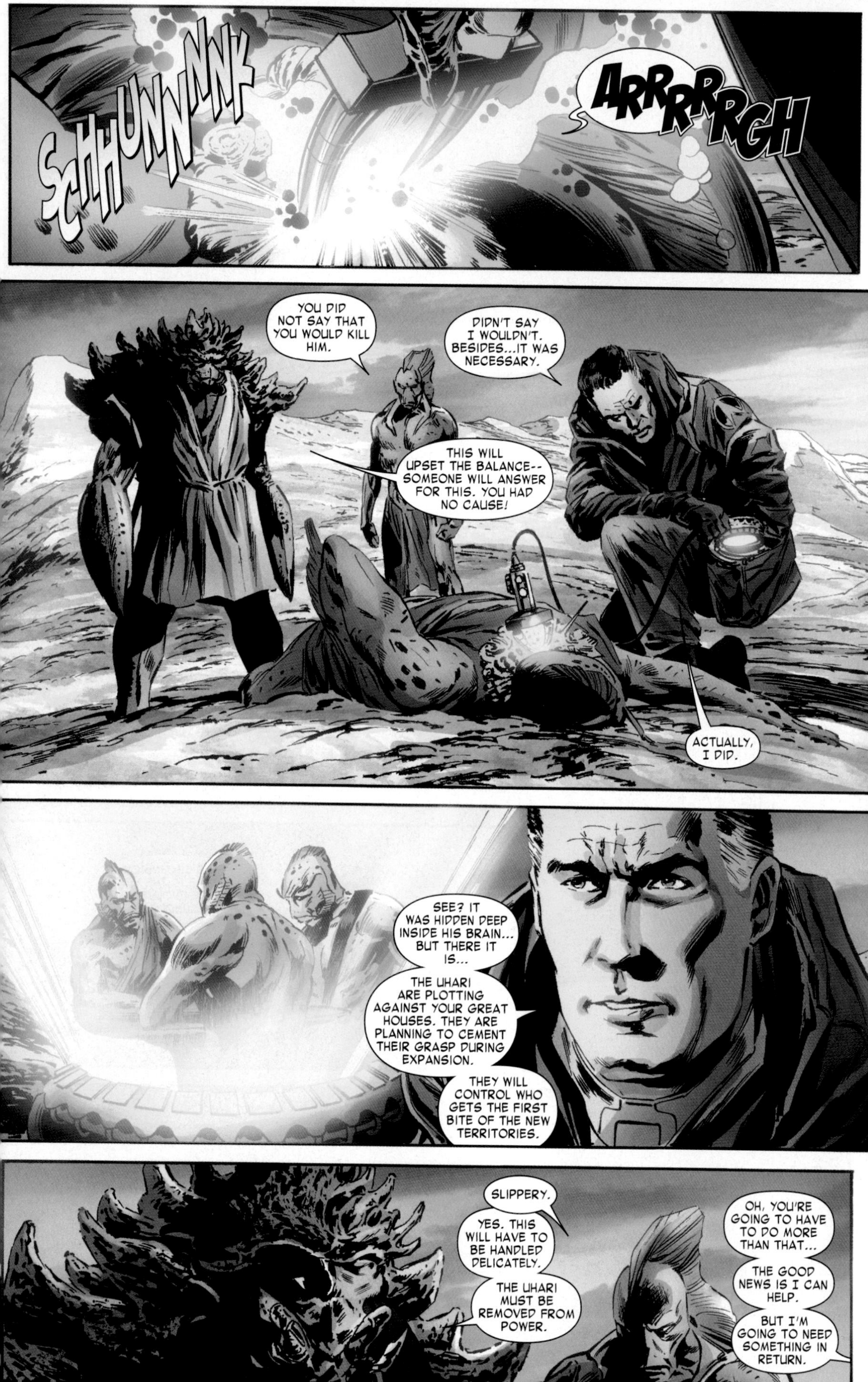

SCHHUNNNNK
ARRRRRGH
YOU DID NOT SAY THAT YOU WOULD KILL HIM.
DIDN'T SAY I WOULDN'T. BESIDES...IT WAS NECESSARY.
THIS WILL UPSET THE BALANCE--SOMEONE WILL ANSWER FOR THIS. YOU HAD NO CAUSE!
ACTUALLY, I DID.
SEE? IT WAS HIDDEN DEEP INSIDE HIS BRAIN... BUT THERE IT IS...
THE UHARI ARE PLOTTING AGAINST YOUR GREAT HOUSES. THEY ARE PLANNING TO CEMENT THEIR GRASP DURING EXPANSION.
THEY WILL CONTROL WHO GETS THE FIRST BITE OF THE NEW TERRITORIES.
SLIPPERY.
YES. THIS WILL HAVE TO BE HANDLED DELICATELY.
THE UHARI MUST BE REMOVED FROM POWER.
OH, YOU'RE GOING TO HAVE TO DO MORE THAN THAT...
THE GOOD NEWS IS I CAN HELP.
BUT I'M GOING TO NEED SOMETHING IN RETURN.

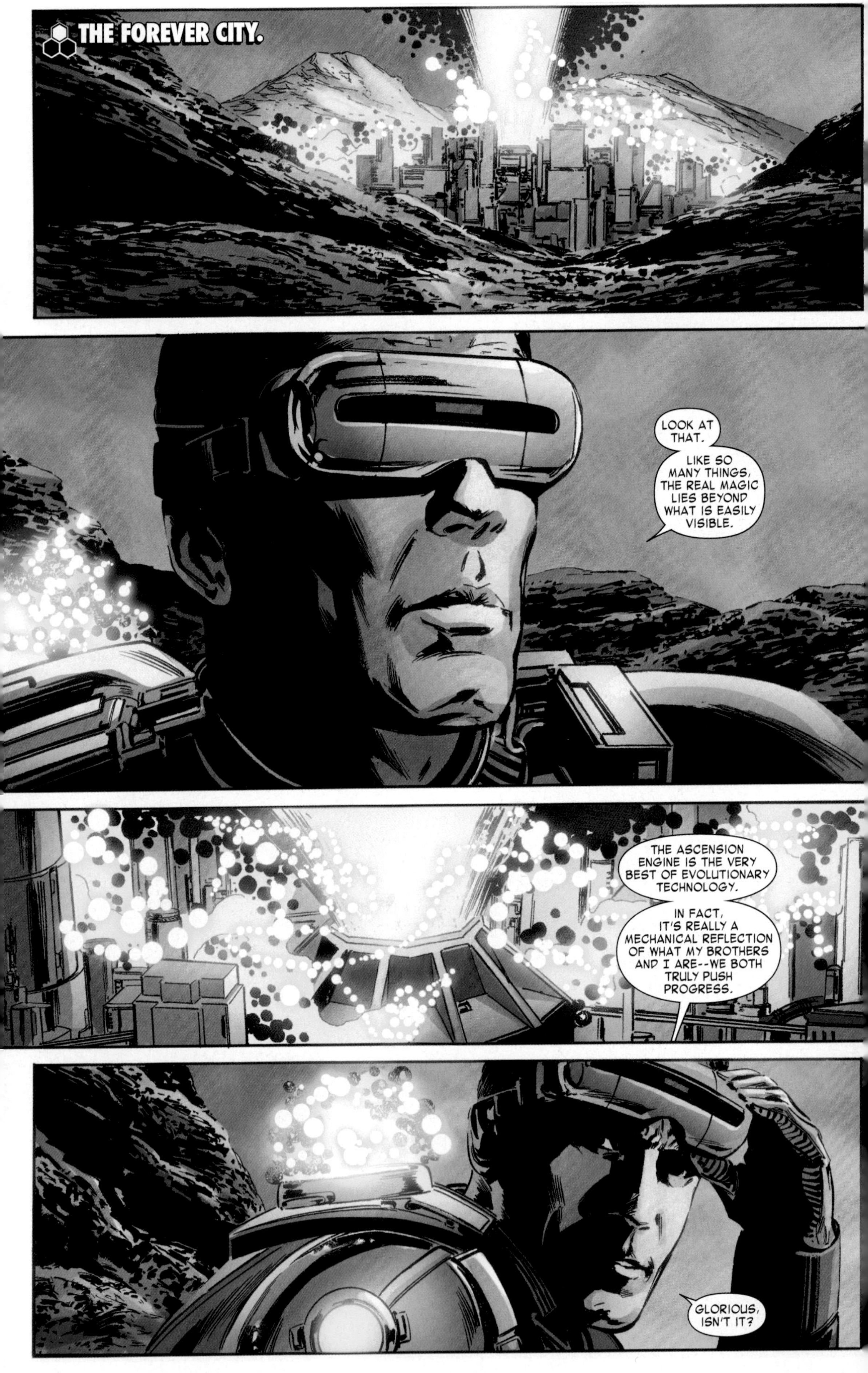
THE FOREVER CITY.
LOOK AT THAT.
LIKE SO MANY THINGS, THE REAL MAGIC LIES BEYOND WHAT IS EASILY VISIBLE.
THE ASCENSION ENGINE IS THE VERY BEST OF EVOLUTIONARY TECHNOLOGY.
IN FACT, IT'S REALLY A MECHANICAL REFLECTION OF WHAT MY BROTHERS AND I ARE--WE BOTH TRULY PUSH PROGRESS.
GLORIOUS, ISN'T IT?

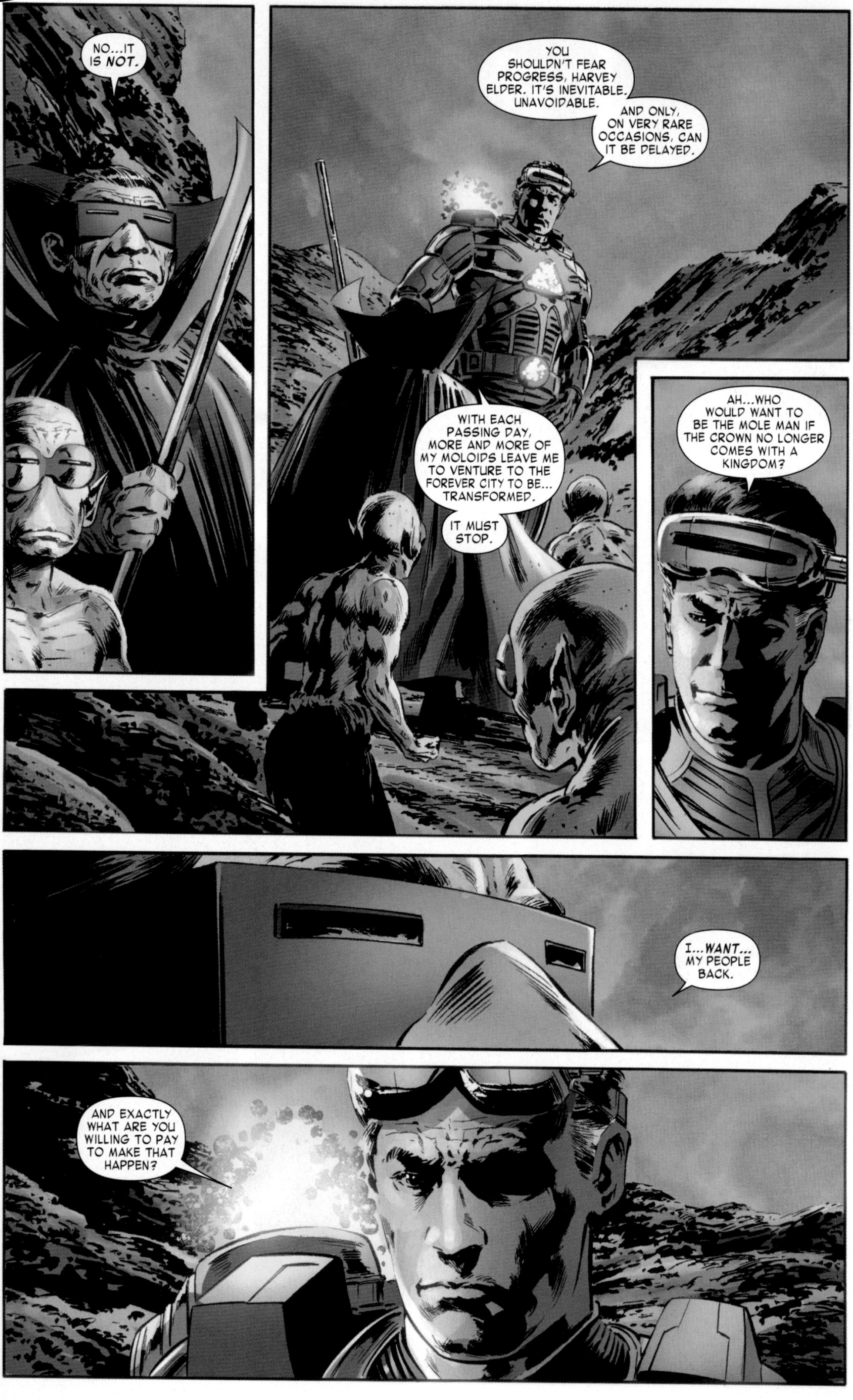
NO...IT IS NOT.
YOU SHOULDN'T FEAR PROGRESS, HARVEY ELDER. IT'S INEVITABLE. UNAVOIDABLE.
AND ONLY, ON VERY RARE OCCASIONS, CAN IT BE DELAYED.
WITH EACH PASSING DAY, MORE AND MORE OF MY MOLOIDS LEAVE ME TO VENTURE TO THE FOREVER CITY TO BE... TRANSFORMED.
IT MUST STOP.
AH...WHO WOULD WANT TO BE THE MOLE MAN IF THE CROWN NO LONGER COMES WITH A KINGDOM?
I...WANT... MY PEOPLE BACK.
AND EXACTLY WHAT ARE YOU WILLING TO PAY TO MAKE THAT HAPPEN?

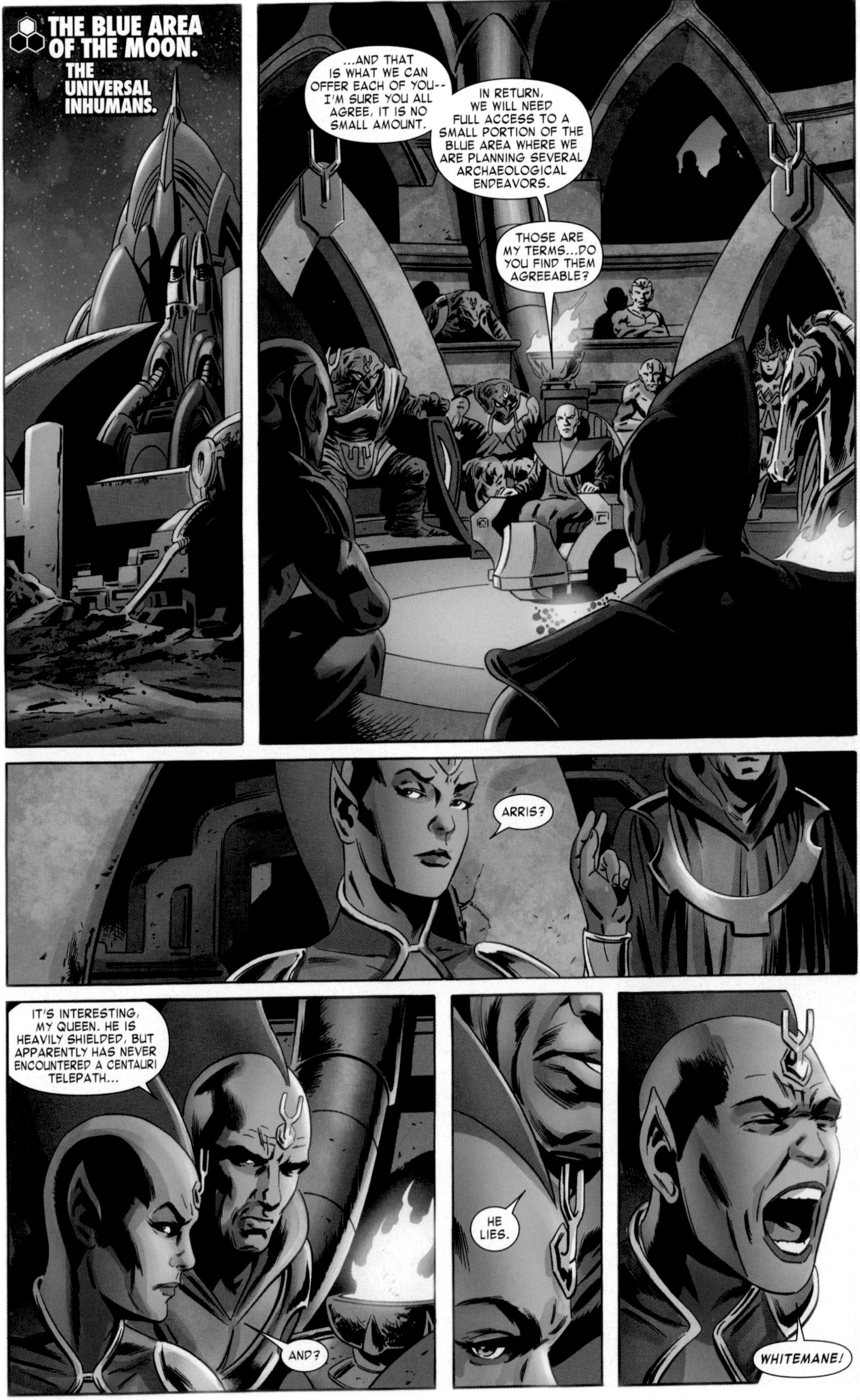
THE BLUE AREA OF THE MOON.
THE UNIVERSAL INHUMANS.
...AND THAT IS WHAT WE CAN OFFER EACH OF YOU-- I'M SURE YOU ALL AGREE, IT IS NO SMALL AMOUNT.
IN RETURN, WE WILL NEED FULL ACCESS TO A SMALL PORTION OF THE BLUE AREA WHERE WE ARE PLANNING SEVERAL ARCHAEOLOGICAL ENDEAVORS.
THOSE ARE MY TERMS...DO YOU FIND THEM AGREEABLE?
ARRIS?
IT'S INTERESTING, MY QUEEN. HE IS HEAVILY SHIELDED, BUT APPARENTLY HAS NEVER ENCOUNTERED A CENTAURI TELEPATH...
AND?
HE LIES.
WHITEMANE!

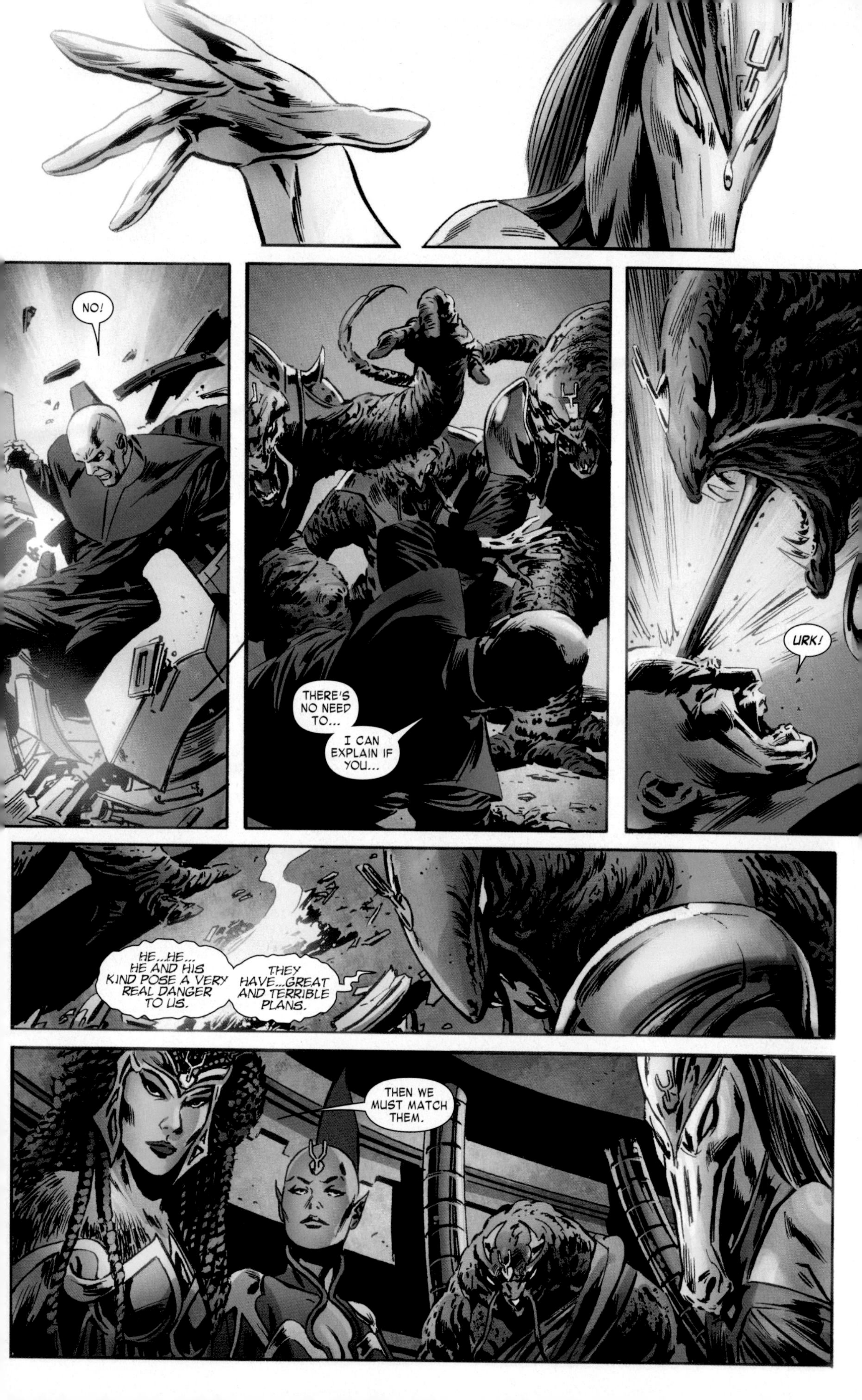

NO!
THERE'S NO NEED TO...
I CAN EXPLAIN IF YOU...
URK!
HE...HE... HE AND HIS KIND POSE A VERY REAL DANGER TO US.
THEY HAVE...GREAT AND TERRIBLE PLANS.
THEN WE MUST MATCH THEM.

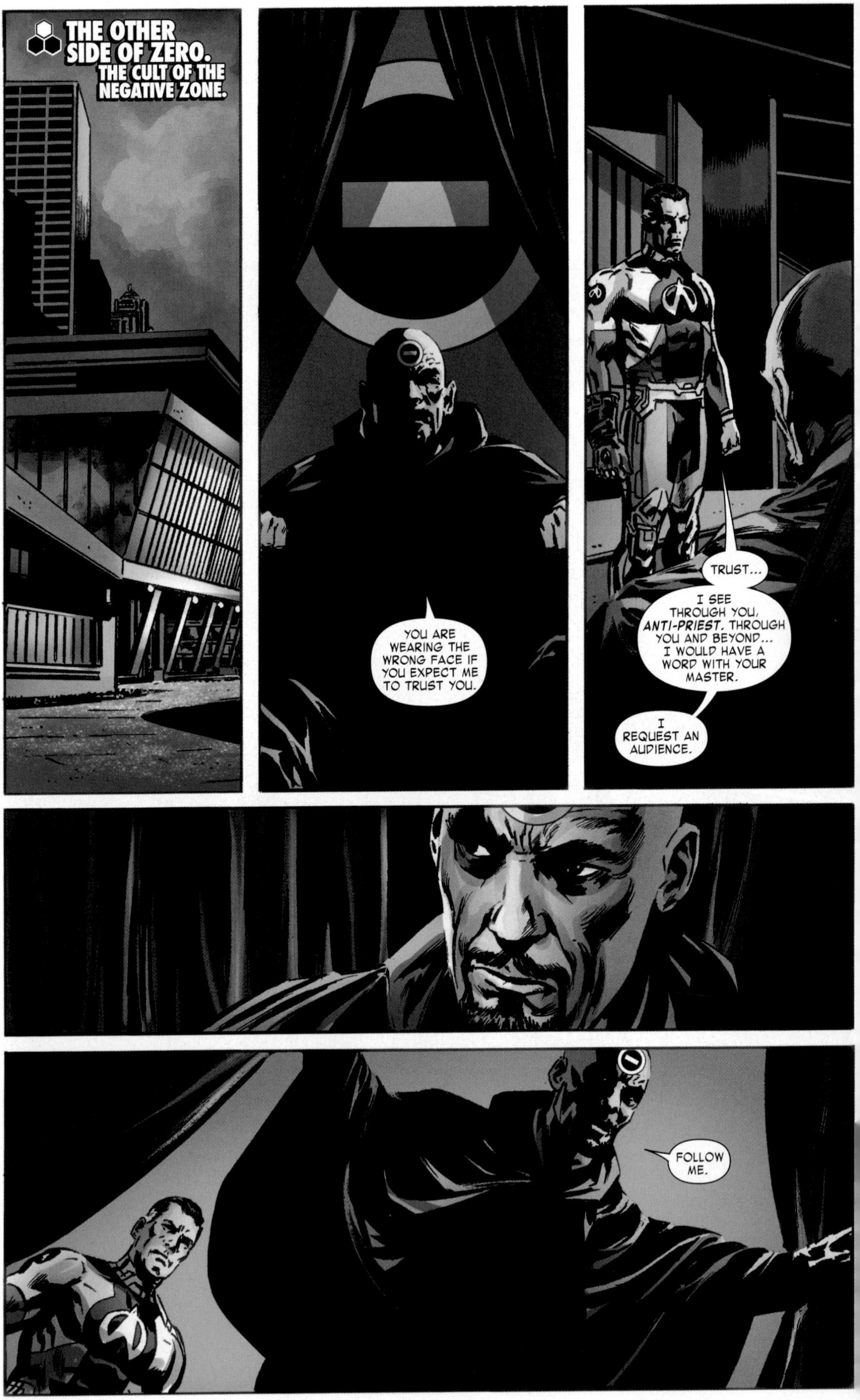
THE OTHER SIDE OF ZERO.
THE CULT OF THE NEGATIVE ZONE.
YOU ARE WEARING THE WRONG FACE IF YOU EXPECT ME TO TRUST YOU.
TRUST...
I SEE THROUGH YOU, ANTI-PRIEST. THROUGH YOU AND BEYOND... I WOULD HAVE A WORD WITH YOUR MASTER.
I REQUEST AN AUDIENCE.
FOLLOW ME.

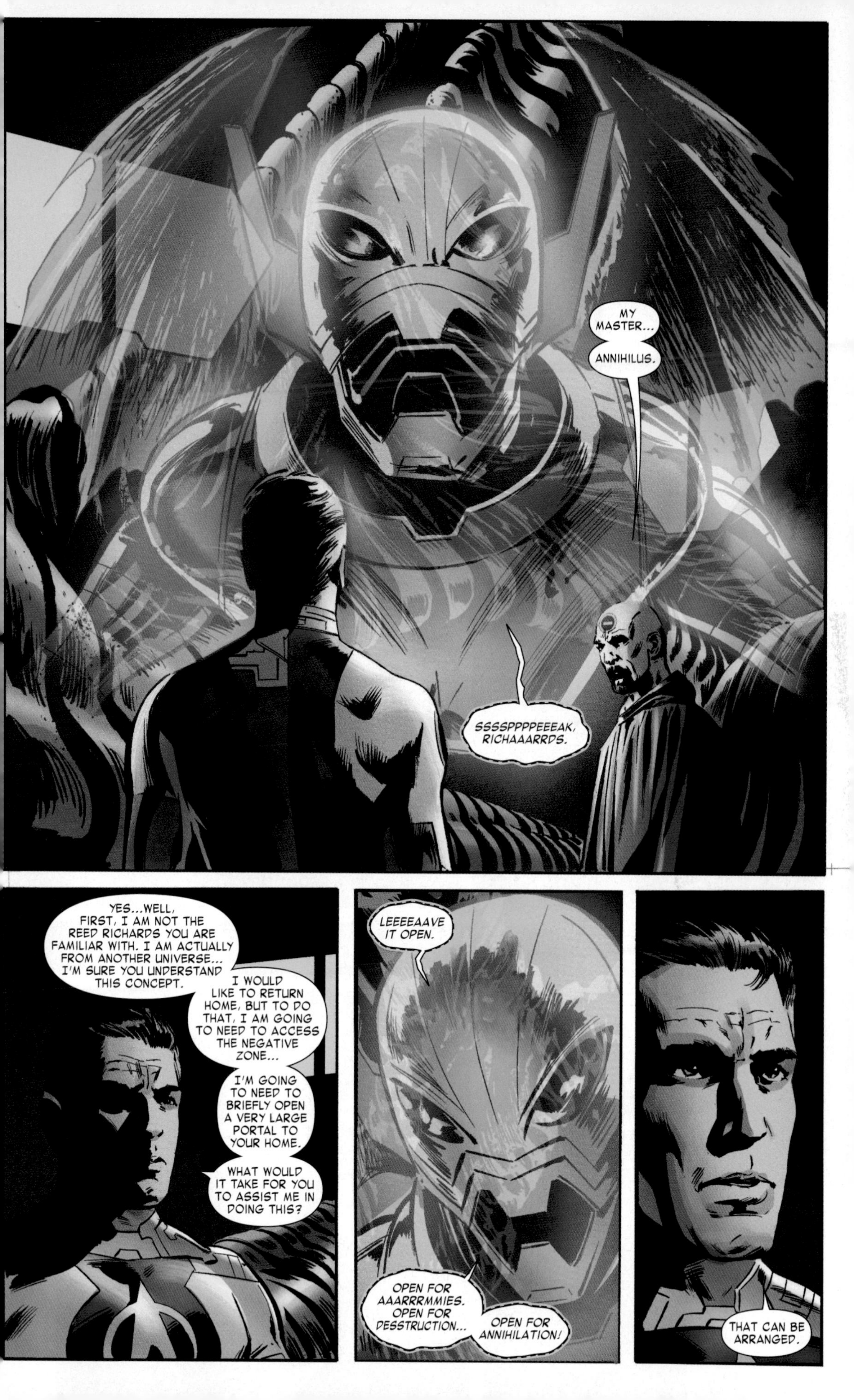

MY MASTER...
ANNIHILUS.
SSSSPPPPEEEAK, RICHAAARRDS.
YES...WELL, FIRST, I AM NOT THE REED RICHARDS YOU ARE FAMILIAR WITH. I AM ACTUALLY FROM ANOTHER UNIVERSE... I'M SURE YOU UNDERSTAND THIS CONCEPT.
I WOULD LIKE TO RETURN HOME, BUT TO DO THAT, I AM GOING TO NEED TO ACCESS THE NEGATIVE ZONE...
I'M GOING TO NEED TO BRIEFLY OPEN A VERY LARGE PORTAL TO YOUR HOME.
WHAT WOULD IT TAKE FOR YOU TO ASSIST ME IN DOING THIS?
LEEEEAAVE IT OPEN.
OPEN FOR AAARRRMMIES. OPEN FOR DESSTRUCTION...
OPEN FOR ANNIHILATION!
THAT CAN BE ARRANGED.

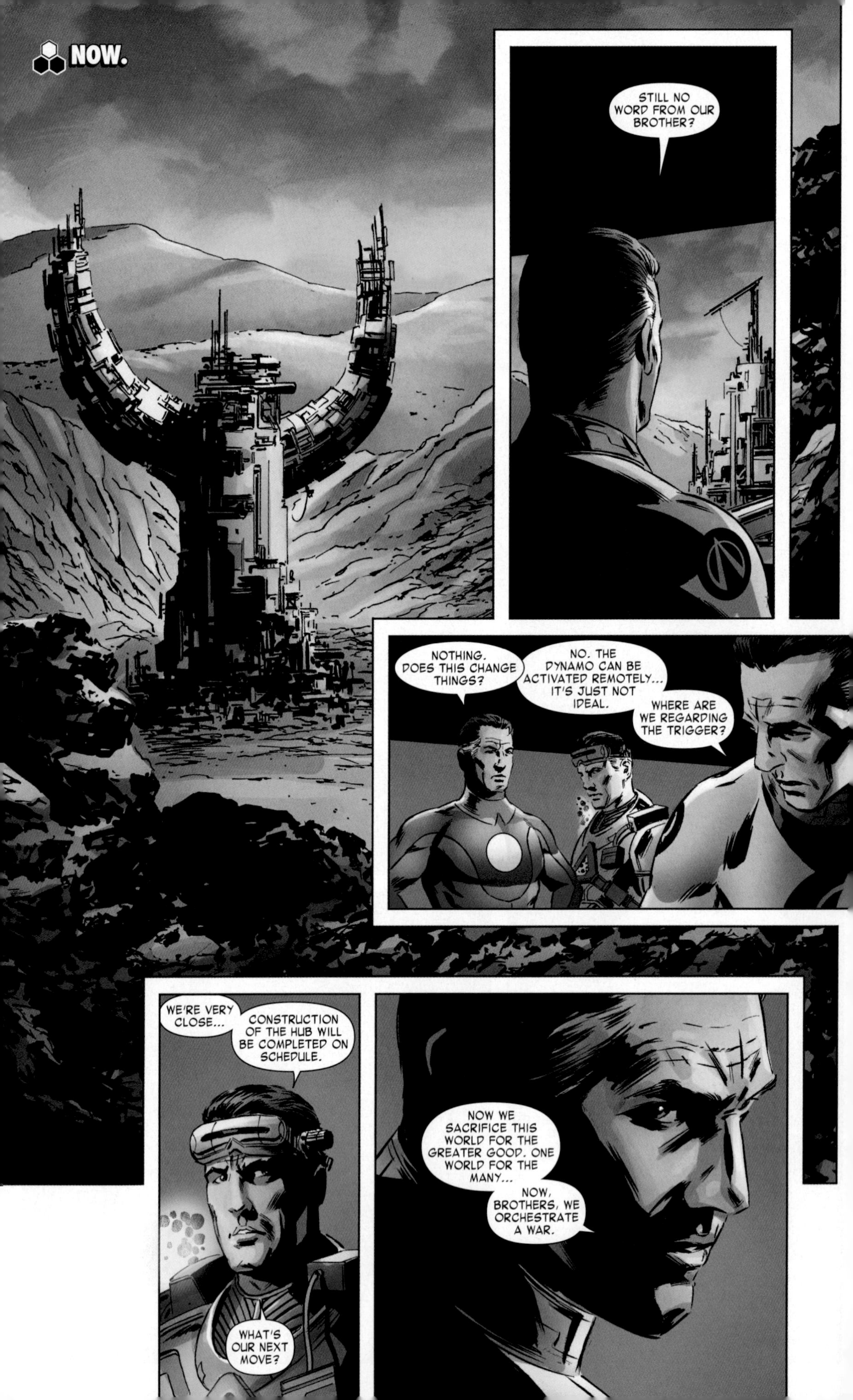
NOW.
STILL NO WORD FROM OUR BROTHER?
NOTHING. DOES THIS CHANGE THINGS?
NO. THE DYNAMO CAN BE ACTIVATED REMOTELY... IT'S JUST NOT IDEAL.
WHERE ARE WE REGARDING THE TRIGGER?
WE'RE VERY CLOSE...
CONSTRUCTION OF THE HUB WILL BE COMPLETED ON SCHEDULE.
WHAT'S OUR NEXT MOVE?
NOW WE SACRIFICE THIS WORLD FOR THE GREATER GOOD. ONE WORLD FOR THE MANY...
NOW, BROTHERS, WE ORCHESTRATE A WAR.

THE BEATING OF DRUMS

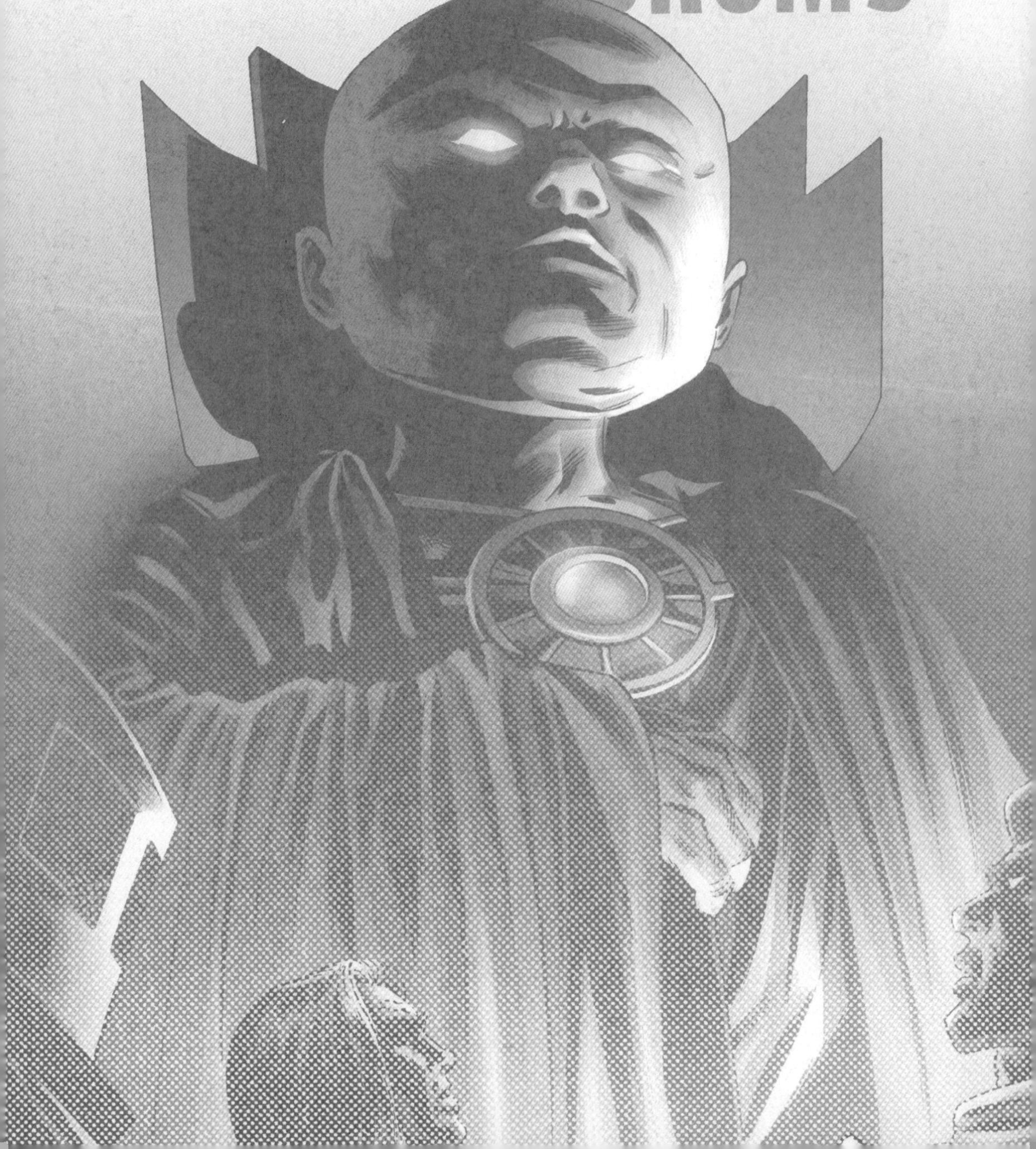

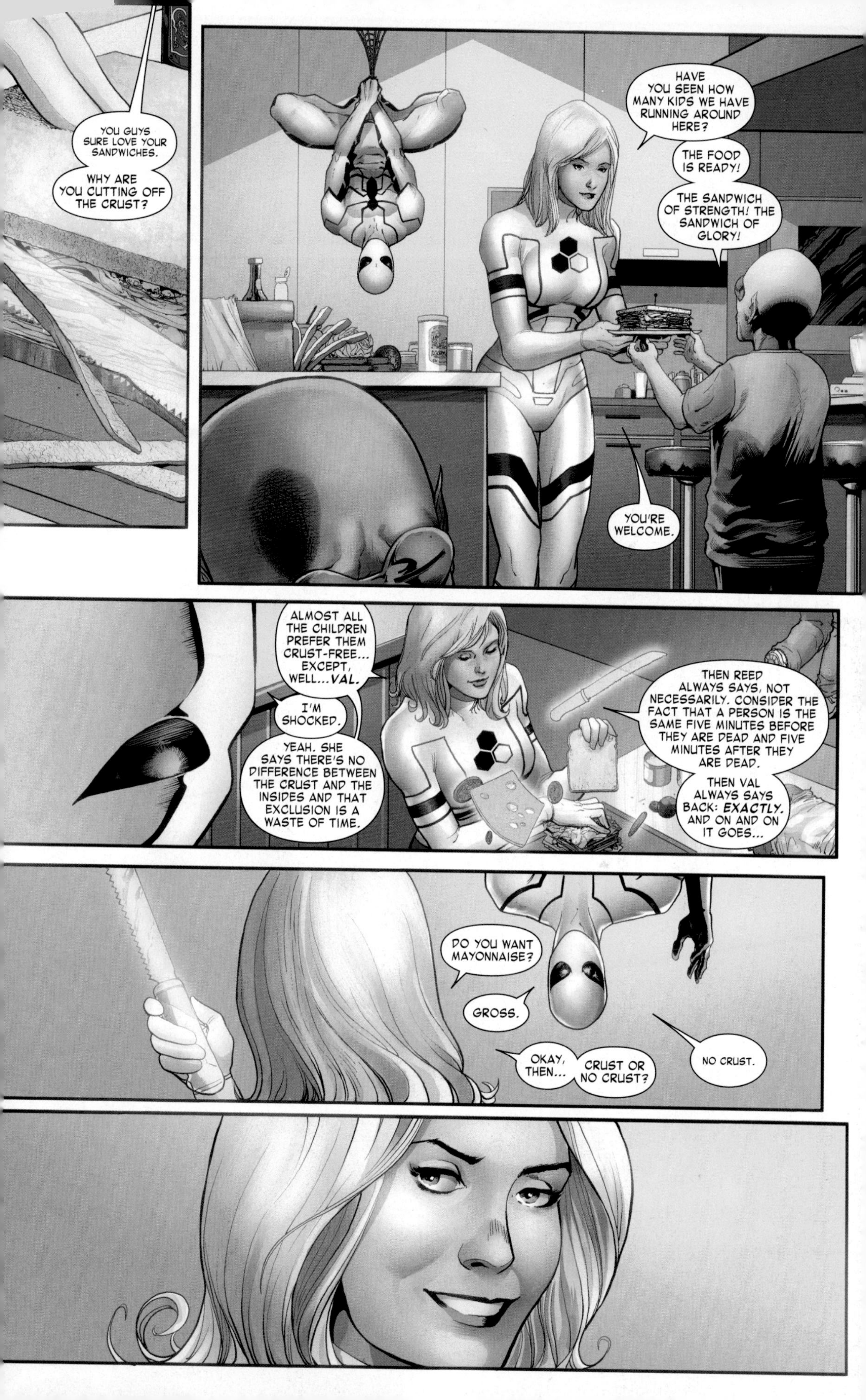
YOU GUYS SURE LOVE YOUR SANDWICHES.
WHY ARE YOU CUTTING OFF THE CRUST?
HAVE YOU SEEN HOW MANY KIDS WE HAVE RUNNING AROUND HERE?
THE FOOD IS READY!
THE SANDWICH OF STRENGTH! THE SANDWICH OF GLORY!
YOU'RE WELCOME.
ALMOST ALL THE CHILDREN PREFER THEM CRUST-FREE... EXCEPT, WELL...VAL.
I'M SHOCKED.
YEAH. SHE SAYS THERE'S NO DIFFERENCE BETWEEN THE CRUST AND THE INSIDES AND THAT EXCLUSION IS A WASTE OF TIME.
THEN REED ALWAYS SAYS, NOT NECESSARILY. CONSIDER THE FACT THAT A PERSON IS THE SAME FIVE MINUTES BEFORE THEY ARE DEAD AND FIVE MINUTES AFTER THEY ARE DEAD.
THEN VAL ALWAYS SAYS BACK: EXACTLY. AND ON AND ON IT GOES...
DO YOU WANT MAYONNAISE?
GROSS.
OKAY, THEN...
CRUST OR NO CRUST?
NO CRUST.

HERE YOU GO.
THANKS, SUSAN.
SO, I'VE GOT TO ASK...HOW IS IT YOU'RE SO COOL WITH EVERYTHING THAT'S GOING ON?
I MEAN, HAVE YOU SEEN WHO ALL WENT IN THAT ROOM WITH REED, HIS OLD MAN, AND VAL?
LET'S SEE... I SAW YOU SHOW UP WITH THE MAD THINKER. I BROUGHT THE WIZARD AND HIS A.I.M. LIEUTENANTS.
I ALSO SAW DIABLO AND THE HIGH EVOLUTIONARY... OH, AND WHO COULD FORGET ONE VICTOR VON DOOM.
DO YOU KNOW WHAT THEY ALL HAVE IN COMMON?
Butter
KETCHUP
<MUNCH> WHAT'S THAT?
THROUGH THE YEARS, I'VE BEATEN EVERY ONE OF THEM.
OVER AND OVER.
BADLY.
SO YOU TELL ME...
DO YOU THINK I SHOULD BE AFRAID OF THEM...
OR SHOULD THEY BE AFRAID OF ME?
FAIR POINT.
EEEEEEEEEEEEEEEEEEEEEEE
HEY... DO YOU HEAR THAT?

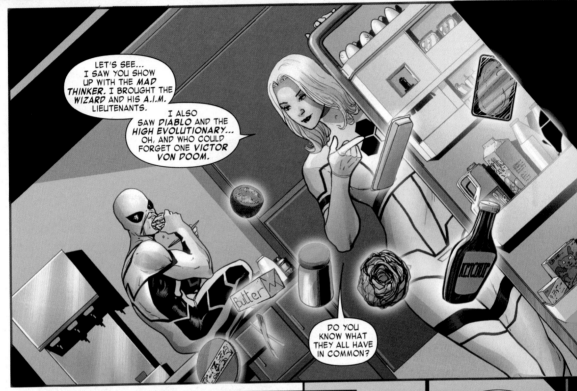

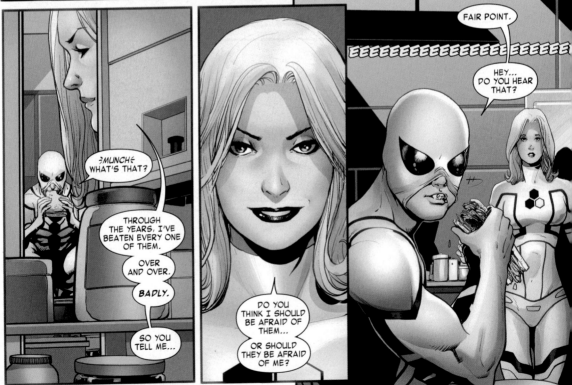

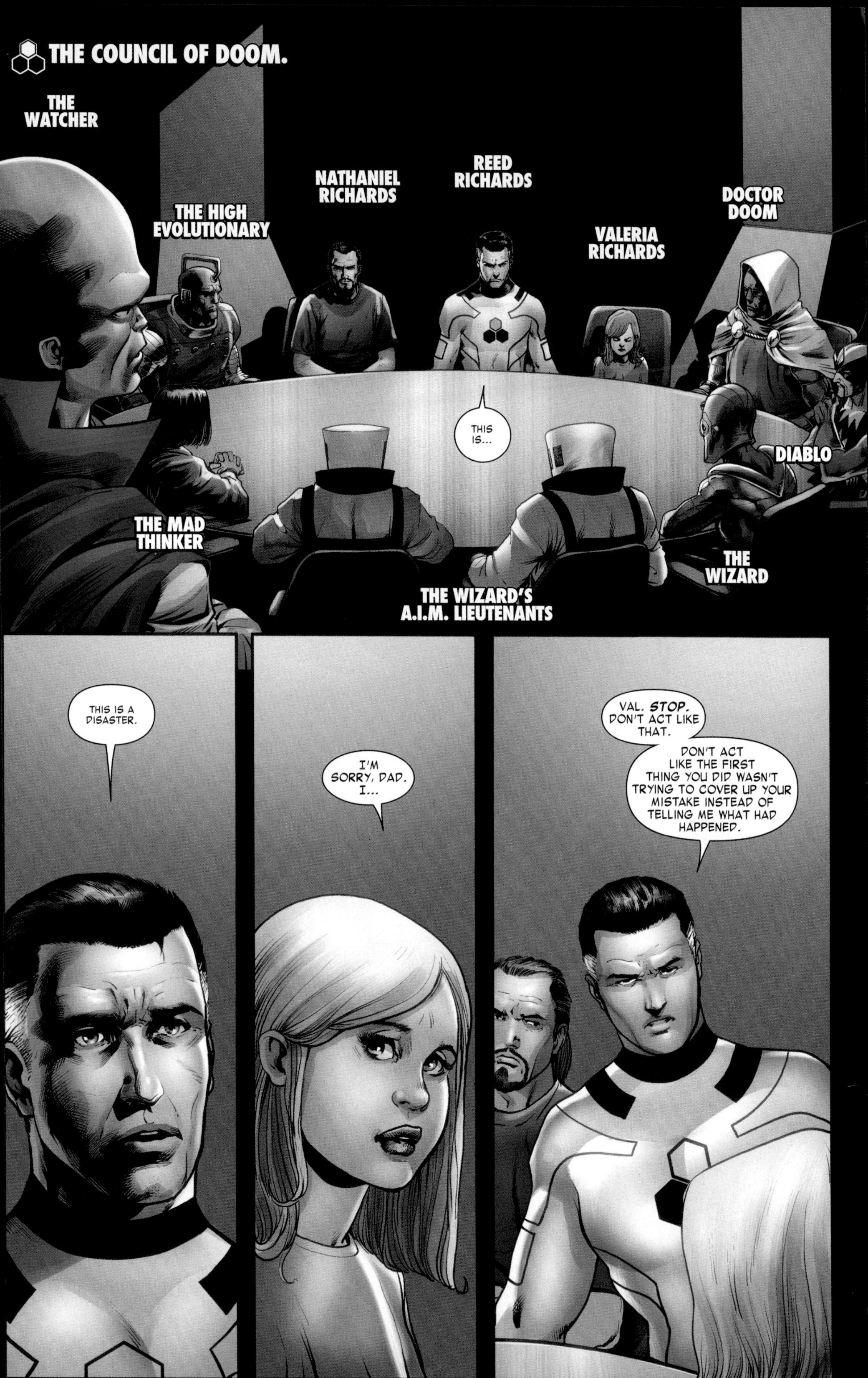
THE COUNCIL OF DOOM.
THE WATCHER
THE HIGH EVOLUTIONARY
NATHANIEL RICHARDS
REED RICHARDS
VALERIA RICHARDS
DOCTOR DOOM
THIS IS...
DIABLO
THE MAD THINKER
THE WIZARD
THE WIZARD'S A.I.M. LIEUTENANTS
THIS IS A DISASTER.
I'M SORRY, DAD. I...
VAL. STOP. DON'T ACT LIKE THAT.
DON'T ACT LIKE THE FIRST THING YOU DID WASN'T TRYING TO COVER UP YOUR MISTAKE INSTEAD OF TELLING ME WHAT HAD HAPPENED.

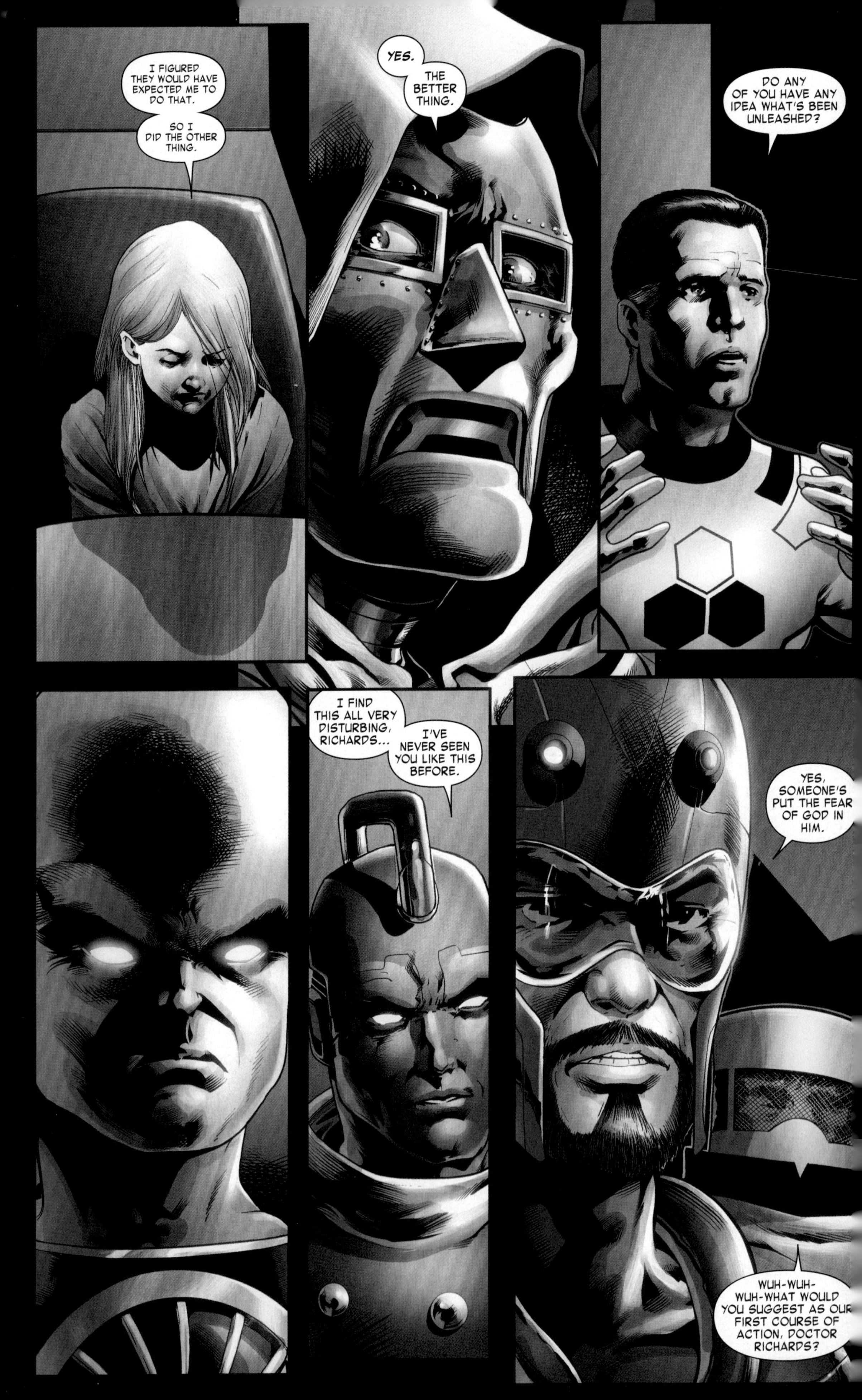
I FIGURED THEY WOULD HAVE EXPECTED ME TO DO THAT.
SO I DID THE OTHER THING.
YES.
THE BETTER THING.
DO ANY OF YOU HAVE ANY IDEA WHAT'S BEEN UNLEASHED?
I FIND THIS ALL VERY DISTURBING, RICHARDS...
I'VE NEVER SEEN YOU LIKE THIS BEFORE.
YES, SOMEONE'S PUT THE FEAR OF GOD IN HIM.
WUH-WUH-WUH-WHAT WOULD YOU SUGGEST AS OUR FIRST COURSE OF ACTION, DOCTOR RICHARDS?

WHY ARE YOU ASKING HIM, MAN OF SCIENCE?

IS THAT NOT WHY WE HAVE CONVENED HERE?

YOU HAVE A SUGGESTION?

OF COURSE... WE CONCENTRATE ON HIS WEAKNESSES.

MAYBE WE FIND OUT WHO THEIR SUSANS ARE, MAYBE WE FIND OUT WHAT THEY LOVE AND TAKE IT FROM THEM--USE IT TO BARGAIN WITH THEM, MAKE THEM OUR POSSESSIONS.

MAYBE WE TAKE THEIR CHILDREN.

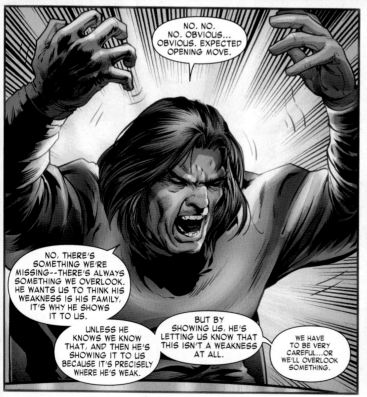

NO. NO. NO. OBVIOUS... OBVIOUS. EXPECTED OPENING MOVE.

NO, THERE'S SOMETHING WE'RE MISSING--THERE'S ALWAYS SOMETHING WE OVERLOOK. HE WANTS US TO THINK HIS WEAKNESS IS HIS FAMILY, IT'S WHY HE SHOWS IT TO US.

UNLESS HE KNOWS WE KNOW THAT, AND THEN HE'S SHOWING IT TO US BECAUSE IT'S PRECISELY WHERE HE'S WEAK.

BUT BY SHOWING US, HE'S LETTING US KNOW THAT THIS ISN'T A WEAKNESS AT ALL.

WE HAVE TO BE VERY CAREFUL...OR WE'LL OVERLOOK SOMETHING.

HMMMMM. IT SEEMS THERE ARE TWO OPTIONS...TWO CHOICES.

TWO WOMEN CAME BEFORE KING SOLOMON AND CLAIMED A CHILD AS THEIR OWN. HE PROPOSED TO CUT THE BABY IN HALF, GIVING ONE PART TO EACH MOTHER.

SO, LET'S DO THAT! LET'S CUT ALL THE BABIES IN HALF!

STOP!

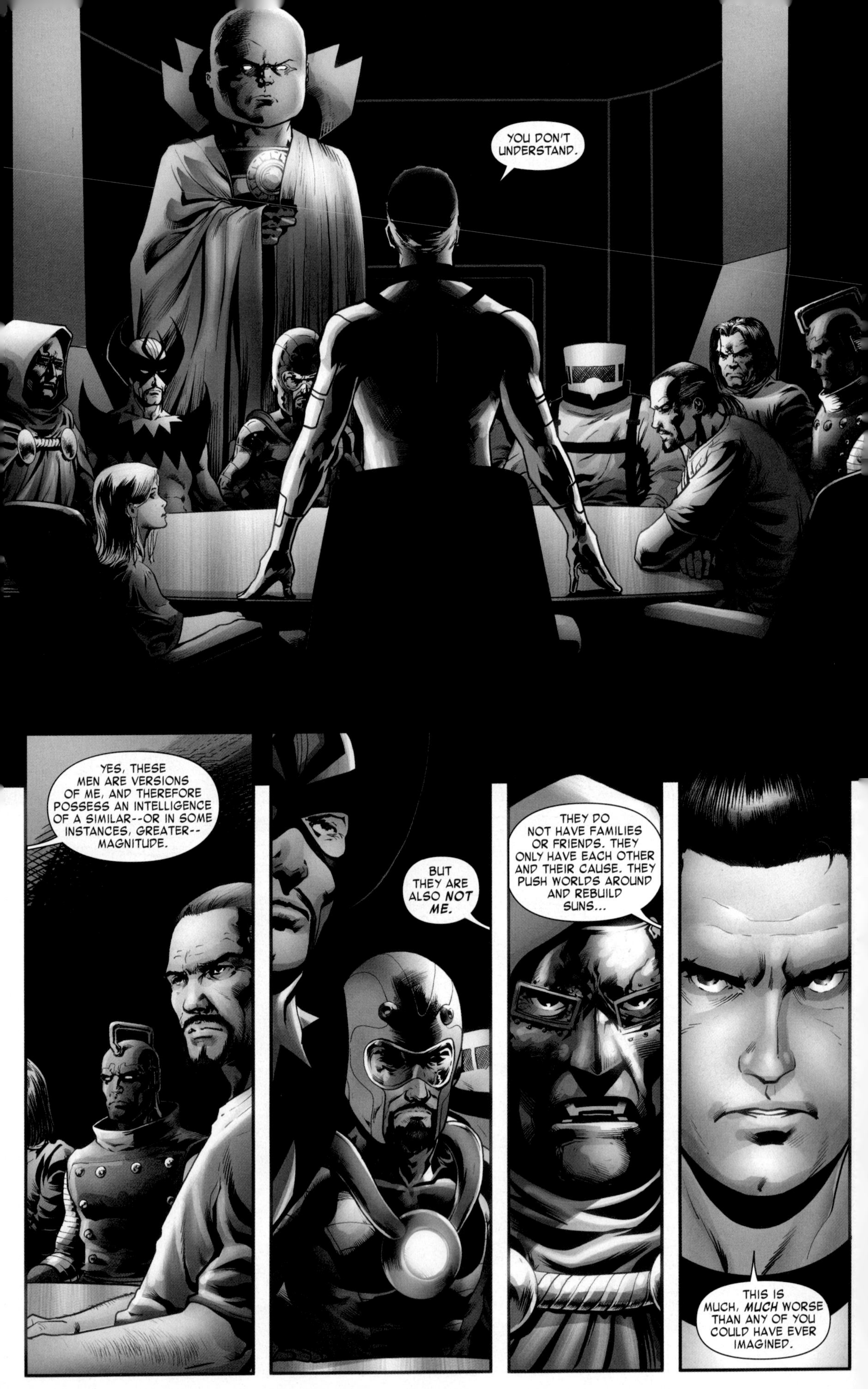
YOU DON'T UNDERSTAND.
YES, THESE MEN ARE VERSIONS OF ME, AND THEREFORE POSSESS AN INTELLIGENCE OF A SIMILAR--OR IN SOME INSTANCES, GREATER--MAGNITUDE.
BUT THEY ARE ALSO *NOT ME.*
THEY DO NOT HAVE FAMILIES OR FRIENDS. THEY ONLY HAVE EACH OTHER AND THEIR CAUSE. THEY PUSH WORLDS AROUND AND REBUILD SUNS...
THIS IS MUCH, *MUCH* WORSE THAN ANY OF YOU COULD HAVE EVER IMAGINED.

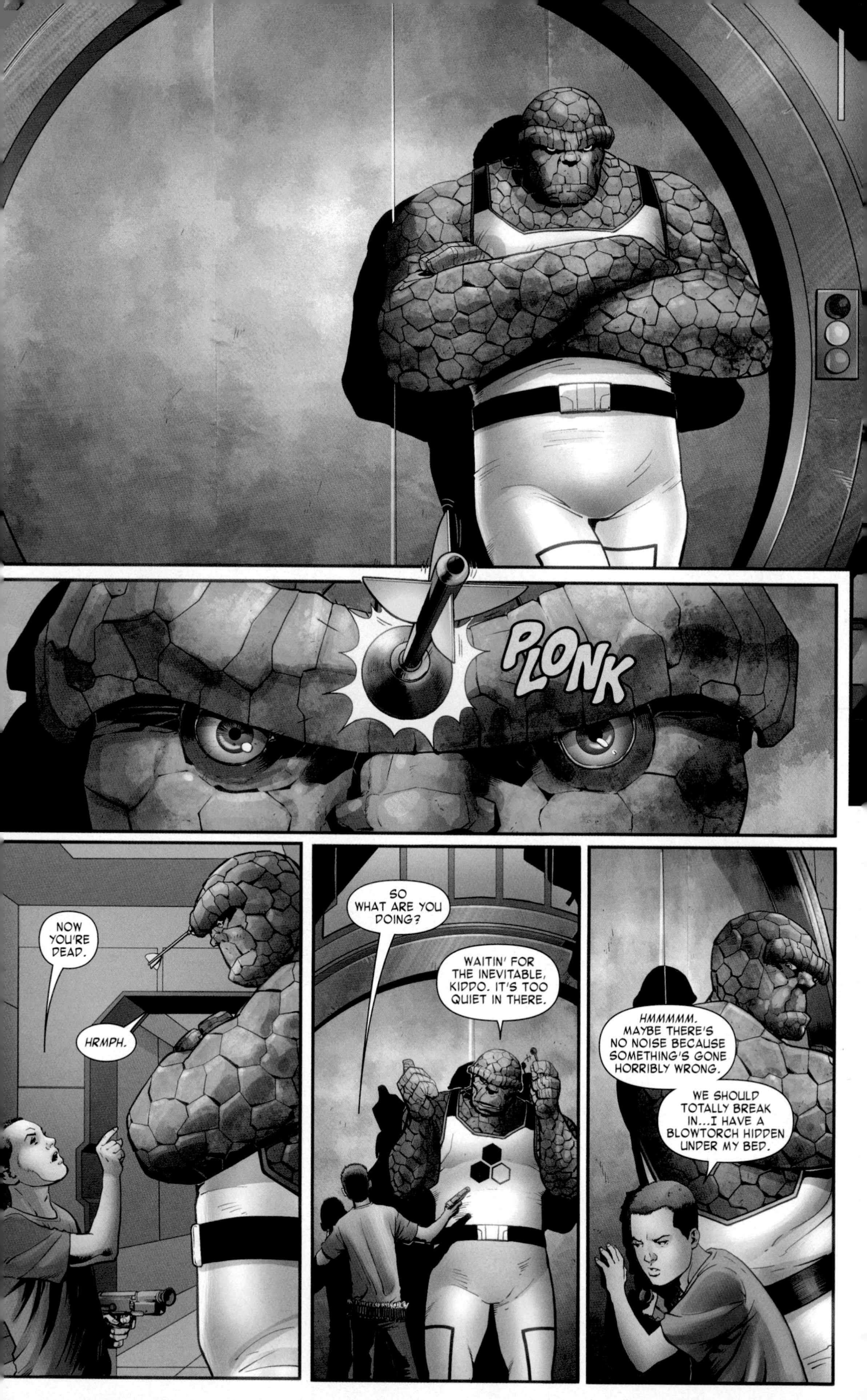
PLONK
NOW YOU'RE DEAD.
HRMPH.
SO WHAT ARE YOU DOING?
WAITIN' FOR THE INEVITABLE, KIDDO. IT'S TOO QUIET IN THERE.
HMMMMM. MAYBE THERE'S NO NOISE BECAUSE SOMETHING'S GONE HORRIBLY WRONG.
WE SHOULD TOTALLY BREAK IN...I HAVE A BLOWTORCH HIDDEN UNDER MY BED.

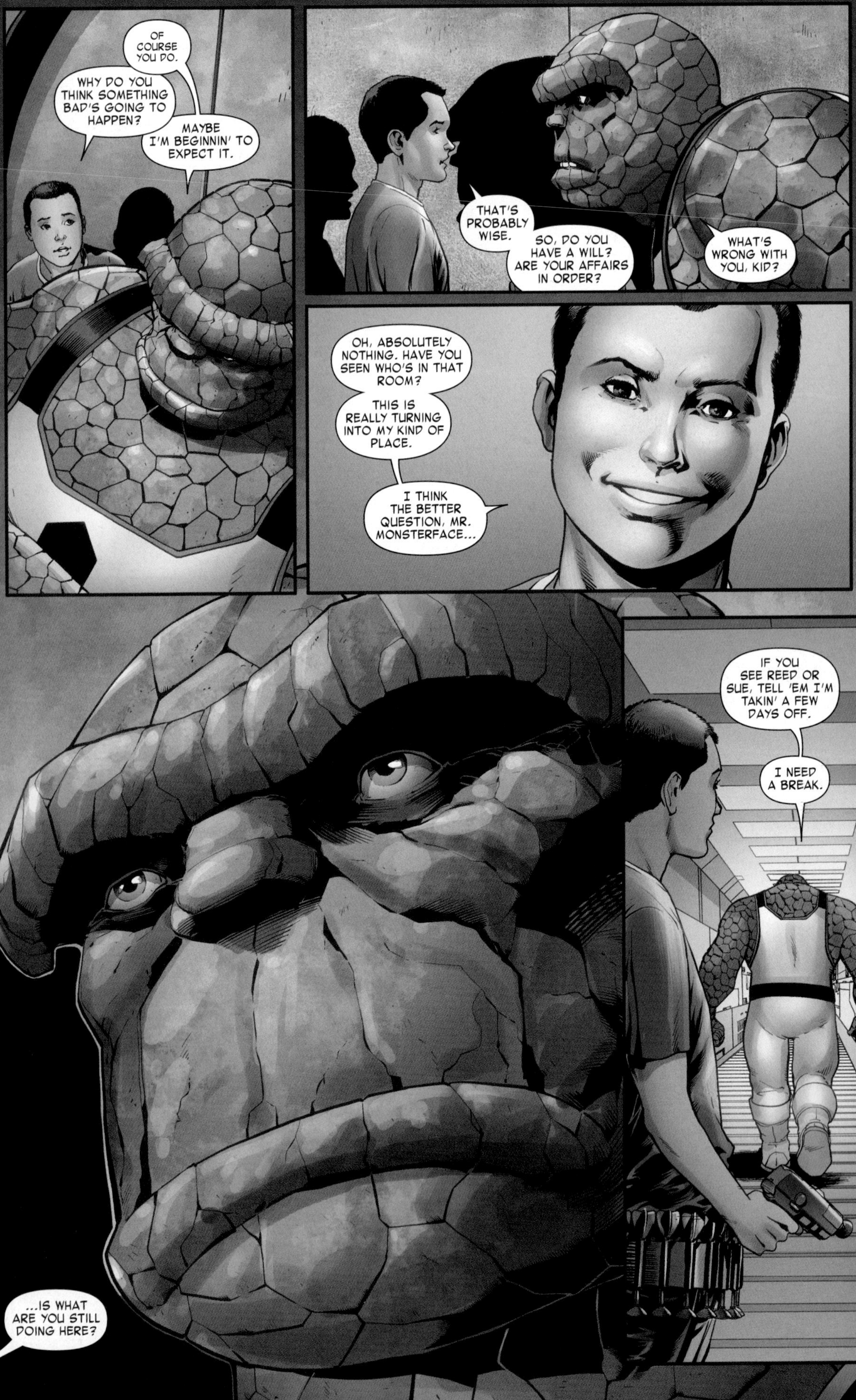
WHY DO YOU THINK SOMETHING BAD'S GOING TO HAPPEN?
OF COURSE YOU DO.
MAYBE I'M BEGINNIN' TO EXPECT IT.
THAT'S PROBABLY WISE.
SO, DO YOU HAVE A WILL? ARE YOUR AFFAIRS IN ORDER?
WHAT'S WRONG WITH YOU, KID?
OH, ABSOLUTELY NOTHING. HAVE YOU SEEN WHO'S IN THAT ROOM?
THIS IS REALLY TURNING INTO MY KIND OF PLACE.
I THINK THE BETTER QUESTION, MR. MONSTERFACE...
...IS WHAT ARE YOU STILL DOING HERE?
IF YOU SEE REED OR SUE, TELL 'EM I'M TAKIN' A FEW DAYS OFF.
I NEED A BREAK.

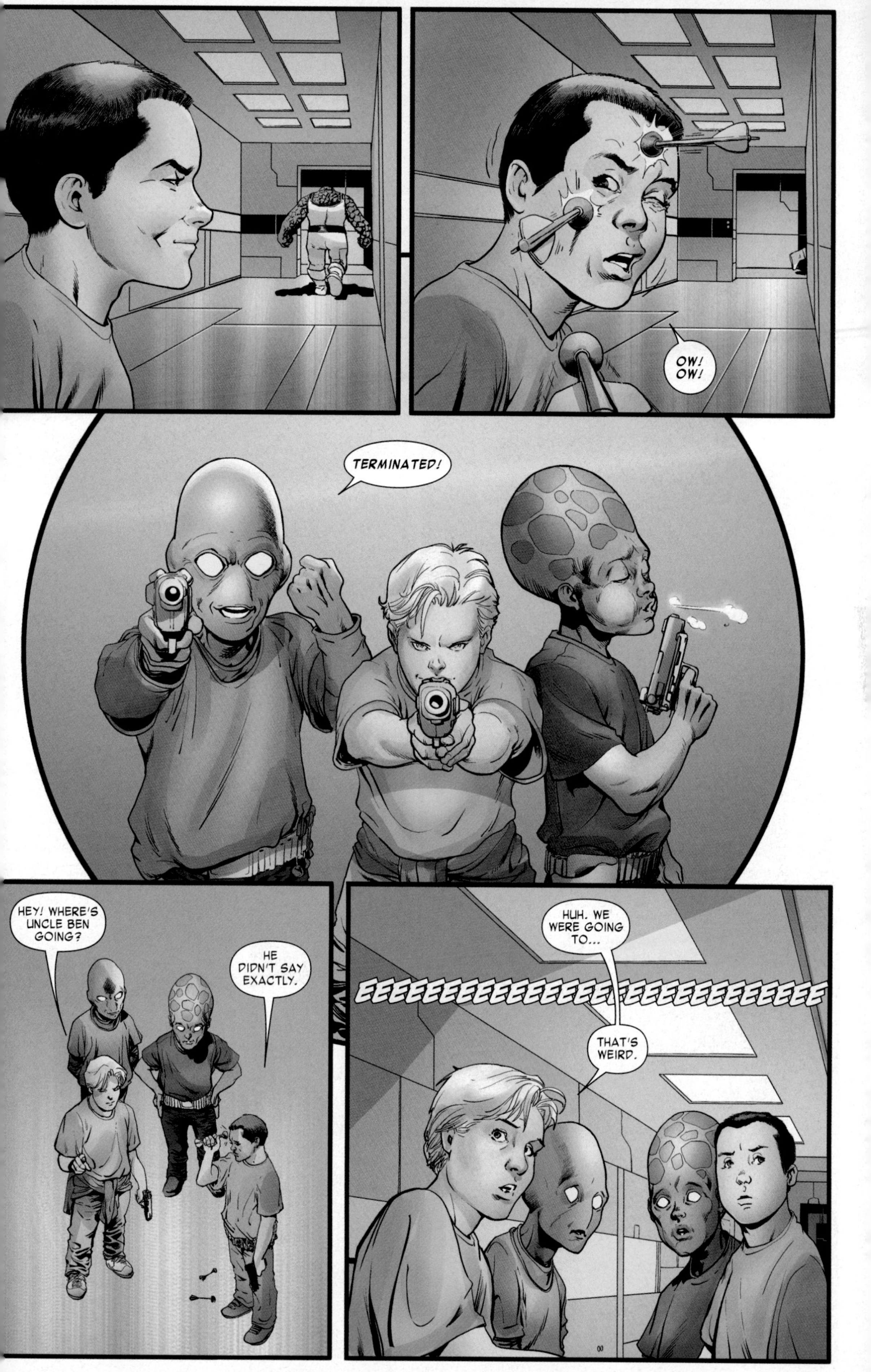
OW! OW!
TERMINATED!
HEY! WHERE'S UNCLE BEN GOING?
HE DIDN'T SAY EXACTLY.
HUH. WE WERE GOING TO...
EEEEEEEEEEEEEEEEEEEEEEEEEEEE
THAT'S WEIRD.

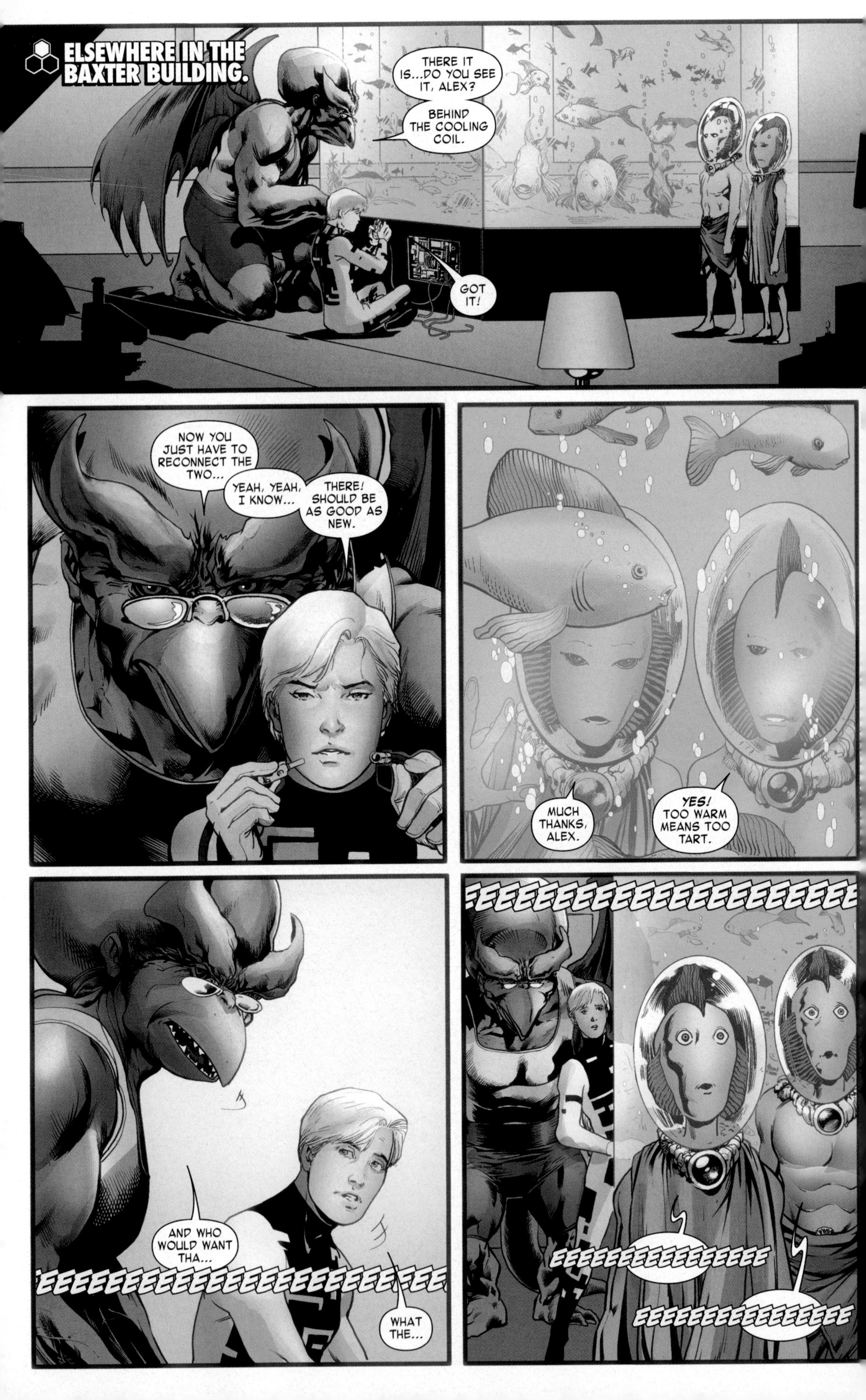

ELSEWHERE IN THE BAXTER BUILDING.
THERE IT IS...DO YOU SEE IT, ALEX?
BEHIND THE COOLING COIL.
GOT IT!
NOW YOU JUST HAVE TO RECONNECT THE TWO...
YEAH, YEAH, I KNOW...
THERE! SHOULD BE AS GOOD AS NEW.
MUCH THANKS, ALEX.
YES! TOO WARM MEANS TOO TART.
AND WHO WOULD WANT THA...
EEEEEEEEEEEEEEEEEEEEEEEEE
WHAT THE...
EEEEEEEEEEEEEEEEEEEEEEEE
EEEEEEEEEEEEEEEE
EEEEEEEEEEEEEEEE

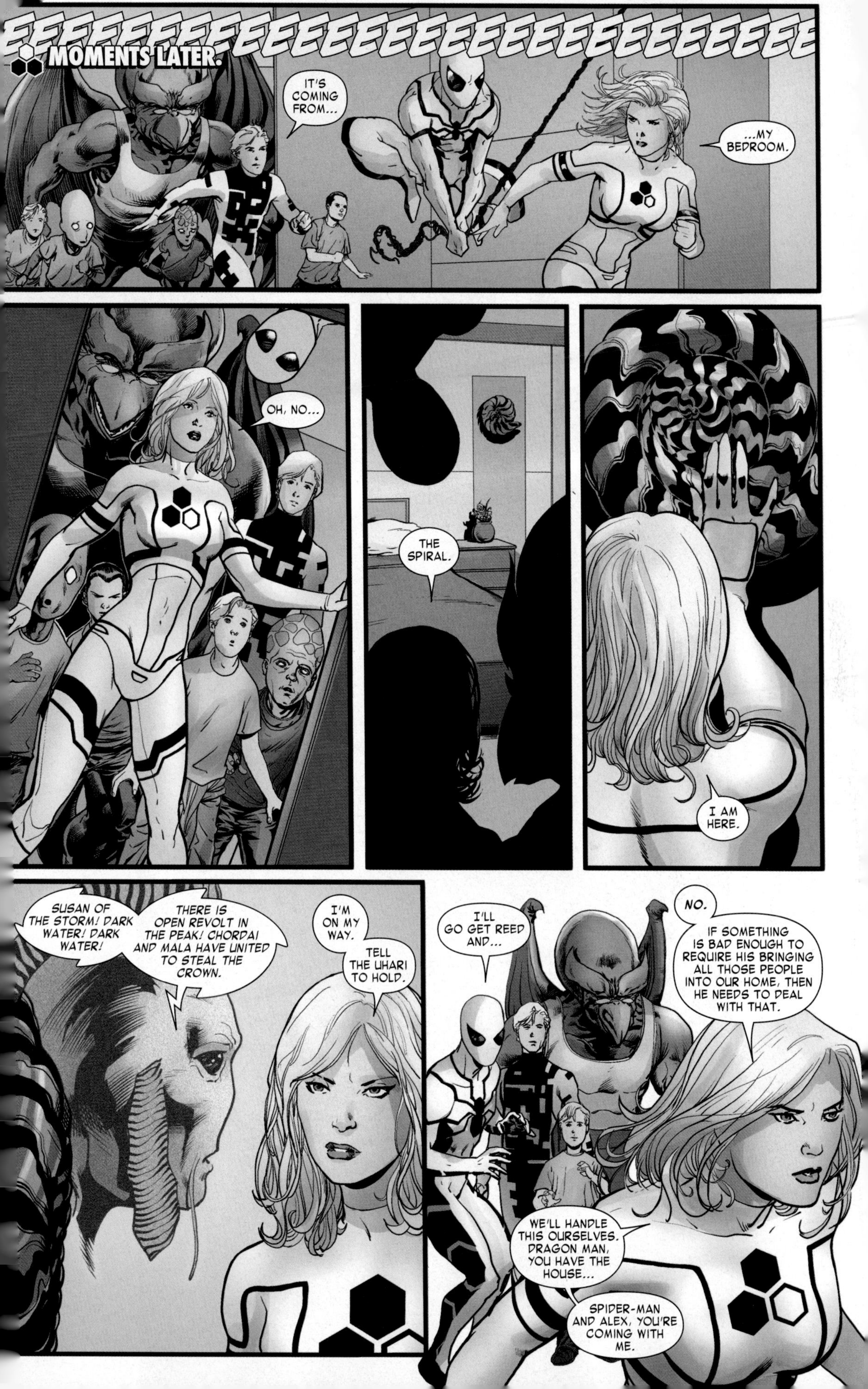
EEEEEEEEEEEEEEEEEEEEEEEEEEEEEEE
MOMENTS LATER.
IT'S COMING FROM...
...MY BEDROOM.
OH, NO...
THE SPIRAL.
I AM HERE.
SUSAN OF THE STORM! DARK WATER! DARK WATER!
THERE IS OPEN REVOLT IN THE PEAK! CHORDAI AND MALA HAVE UNITED TO STEAL THE CROWN.
I'M ON MY WAY.
TELL THE UHARI TO HOLD.
I'LL GO GET REED AND...
NO.
IF SOMETHING IS BAD ENOUGH TO REQUIRE HIS BRINGING ALL THOSE PEOPLE INTO OUR HOME, THEN HE NEEDS TO DEAL WITH THAT.
WE'LL HANDLE THIS OURSELVES. DRAGON MAN, YOU HAVE THE HOUSE...
SPIDER-MAN AND ALEX, YOU'RE COMING WITH ME.

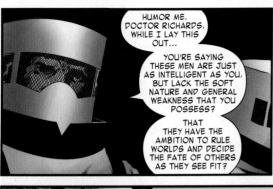

HUMOR ME, DOCTOR RICHARDS, WHILE I LAY THIS OUT...

YOU'RE SAYING THESE MEN ARE JUST AS INTELLIGENT AS YOU, BUT LACK THE SOFT NATURE AND GENERAL WEAKNESS THAT YOU POSSESS?

THAT THEY HAVE THE AMBITION TO RULE WORLDS AND DECIDE THE FATE OF OTHERS AS THEY SEE FIT?

I DO BELIEVE I LIKE THESE REEDS.

YOU WOULDN'T...

ONE OF THE THINGS THEY DO IS TURN ANY VICTOR VON DOOMS THEY ENCOUNTER ON ANY WORLD INTO VEGETABLES.

THEY CONSIDER YOU TOO DANGEROUS TO JUST LET WANDER AROUND.

WELL THEN... I DO BELIEVE I LIKE THESE REEDS.

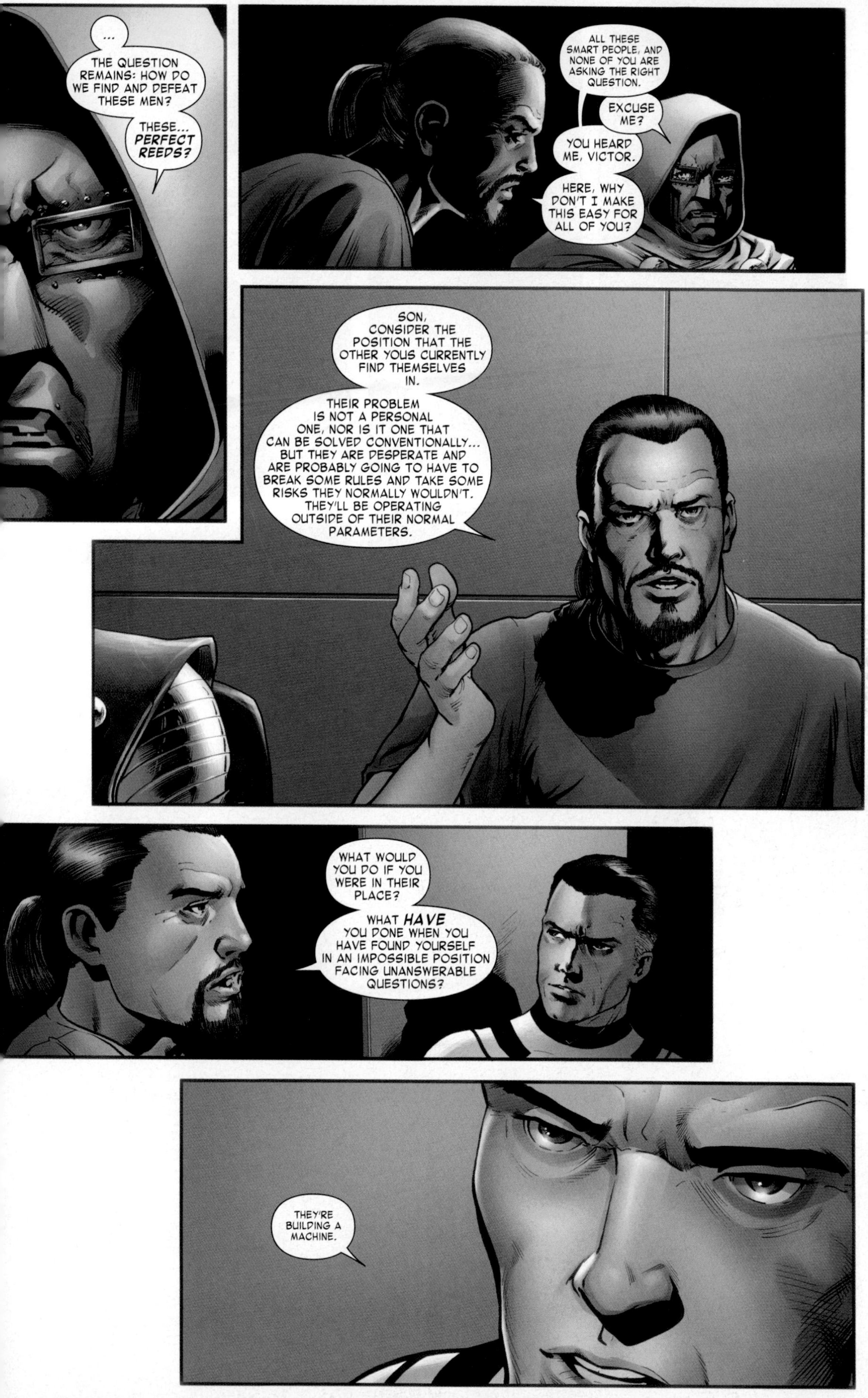
...
THE QUESTION REMAINS: HOW DO WE FIND AND DEFEAT THESE MEN?
THESE... PERFECT REEDS?
ALL THESE SMART PEOPLE, AND NONE OF YOU ARE ASKING THE RIGHT QUESTION.
EXCUSE ME?
YOU HEARD ME, VICTOR.
HERE, WHY DON'T I MAKE THIS EASY FOR ALL OF YOU?
SON, CONSIDER THE POSITION THAT THE OTHER YOUS CURRENTLY FIND THEMSELVES IN.
THEIR PROBLEM IS NOT A PERSONAL ONE, NOR IS IT ONE THAT CAN BE SOLVED CONVENTIONALLY... BUT THEY ARE DESPERATE AND ARE PROBABLY GOING TO HAVE TO BREAK SOME RULES AND TAKE SOME RISKS THEY NORMALLY WOULDN'T. THEY'LL BE OPERATING OUTSIDE OF THEIR NORMAL PARAMETERS.
WHAT WOULD YOU DO IF YOU WERE IN THEIR PLACE?
WHAT HAVE YOU DONE WHEN YOU HAVE FOUND YOURSELF IN AN IMPOSSIBLE POSITION FACING UNANSWERABLE QUESTIONS?
THEY'RE BUILDING A MACHINE.

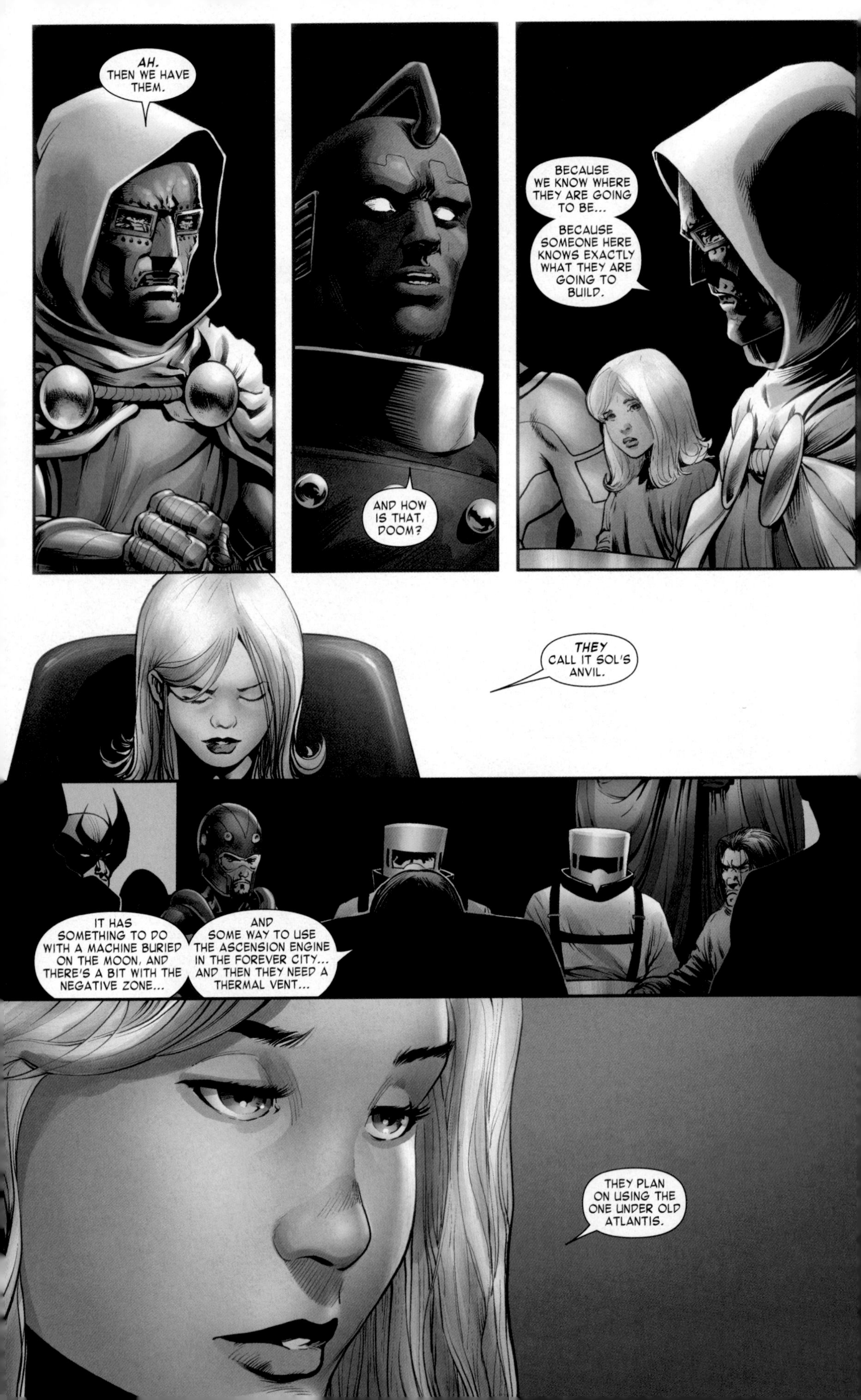
AH. THEN WE HAVE THEM.
AND HOW IS THAT, DOOM?
BECAUSE WE KNOW WHERE THEY ARE GOING TO BE...
BECAUSE SOMEONE HERE KNOWS EXACTLY WHAT THEY ARE GOING TO BUILD.
THEY CALL IT SOL'S ANVIL.
IT HAS SOMETHING TO DO WITH A MACHINE BURIED ON THE MOON, AND THERE'S A BIT WITH THE NEGATIVE ZONE...
AND SOME WAY TO USE THE ASCENSION ENGINE IN THE FOREVER CITY... AND THEN THEY NEED A THERMAL VENT...
THEY PLAN ON USING THE ONE UNDER OLD ATLANTIS.

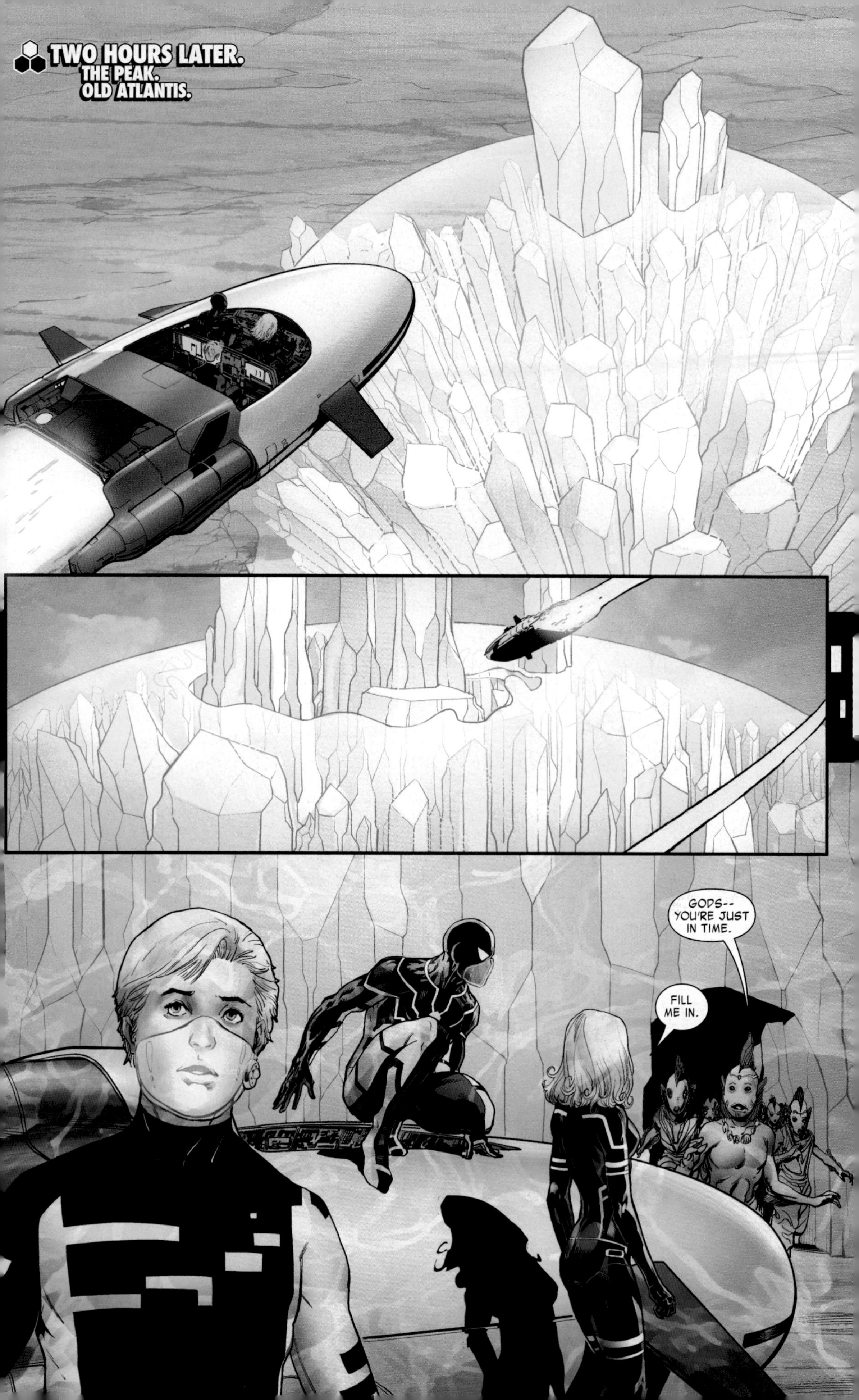
TWO HOURS LATER.
THE PEAK.
OLD ATLANTIS.
GODS-- YOU'RE JUST IN TIME.
FILL ME IN.

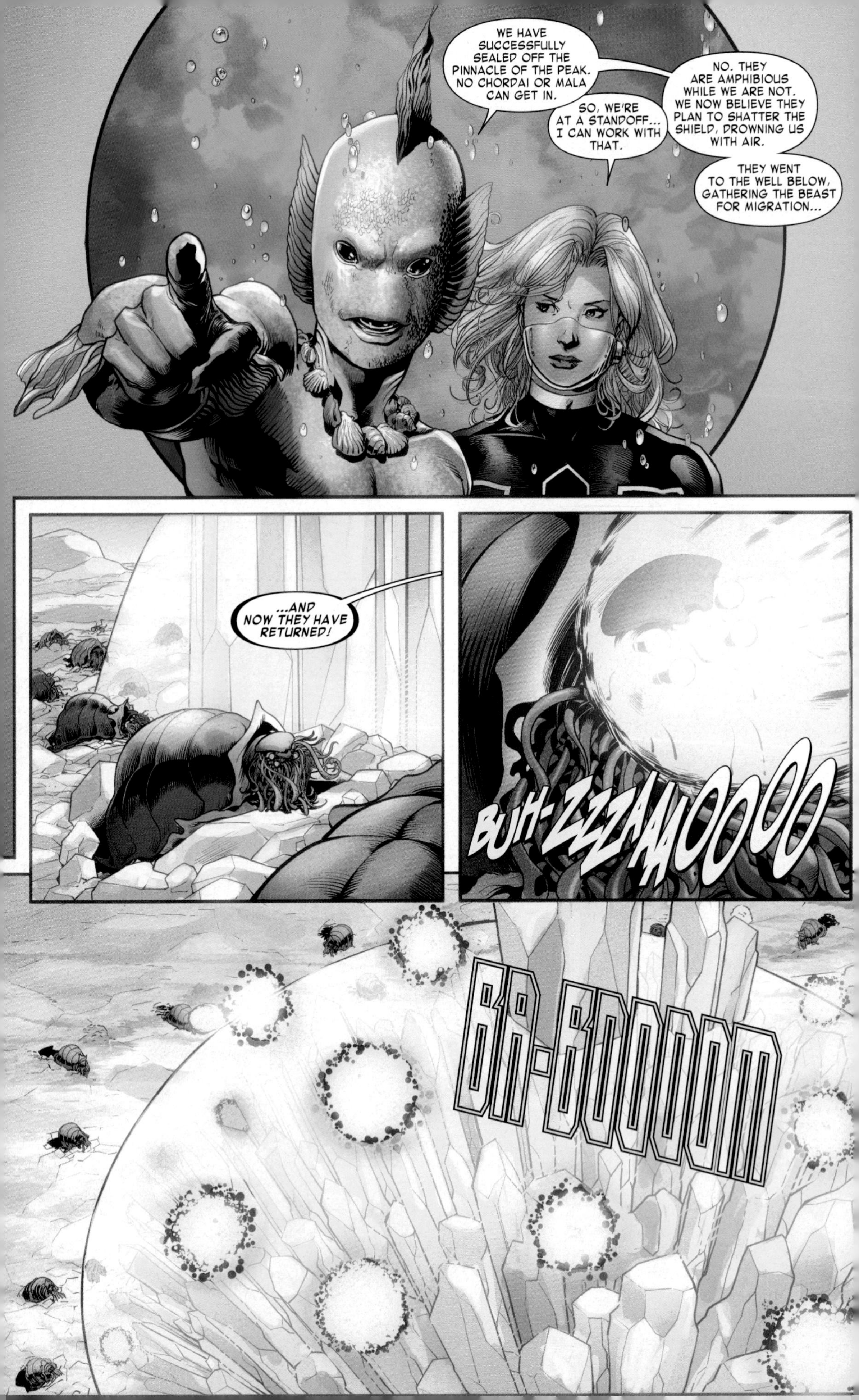
WE HAVE SUCCESSFULLY SEALED OFF THE PINNACLE OF THE PEAK. NO CHORDAI OR MALA CAN GET IN.
SO, WE'RE AT A STANDOFF... I CAN WORK WITH THAT.
NO. THEY ARE AMPHIBIOUS WHILE WE ARE NOT. WE NOW BELIEVE THEY PLAN TO SHATTER THE SHIELD, DROWNING US WITH AIR.
THEY WENT TO THE WELL BELOW, GATHERING THE BEAST FOR MIGRATION...
...AND NOW THEY HAVE RETURNED!
BUH-ZZZAAAOOOOO
BR-BOOOOOM

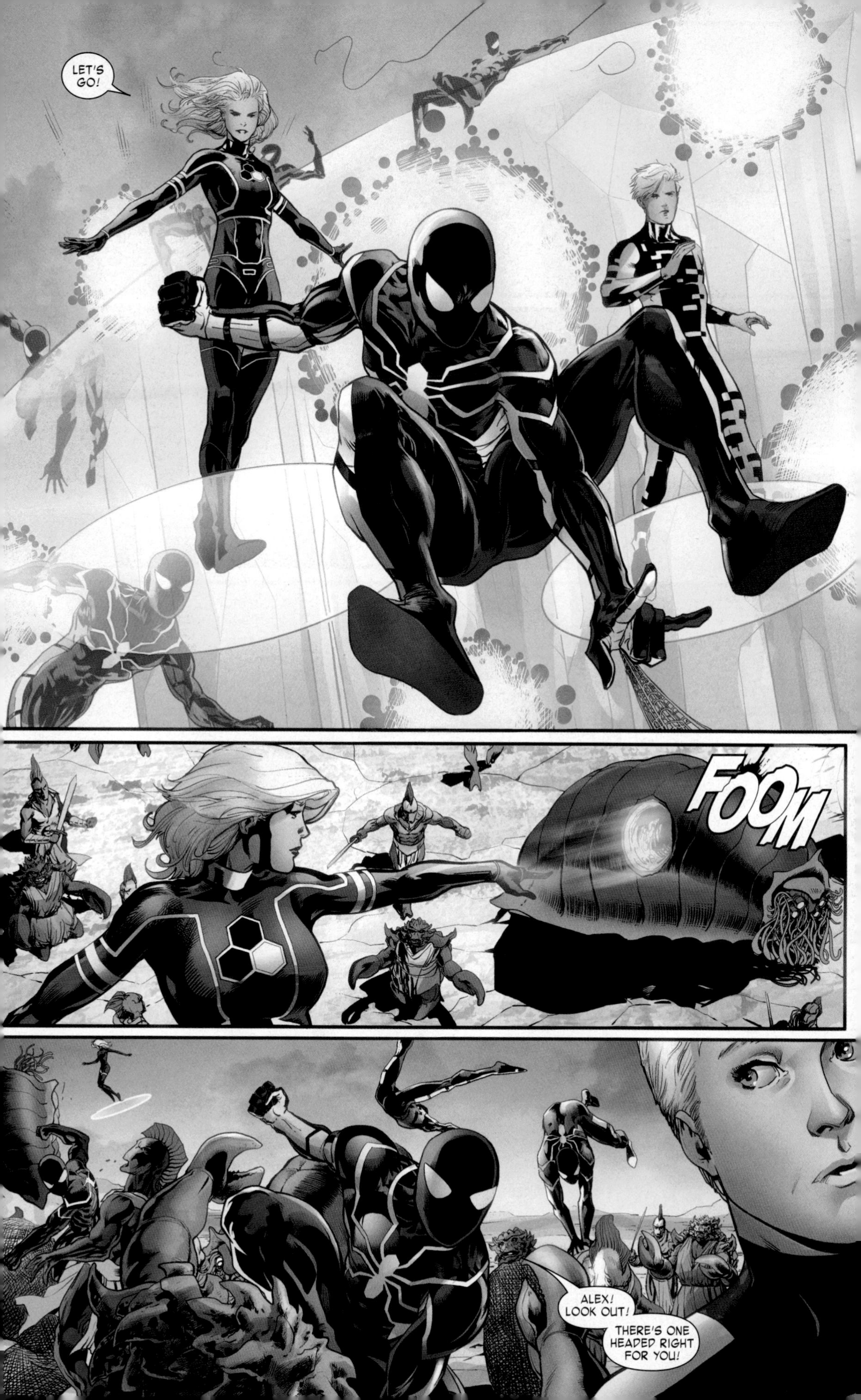
LET'S GO!
FOOM
ALEX! LOOK OUT!
THERE'S ONE HEADED RIGHT FOR YOU!

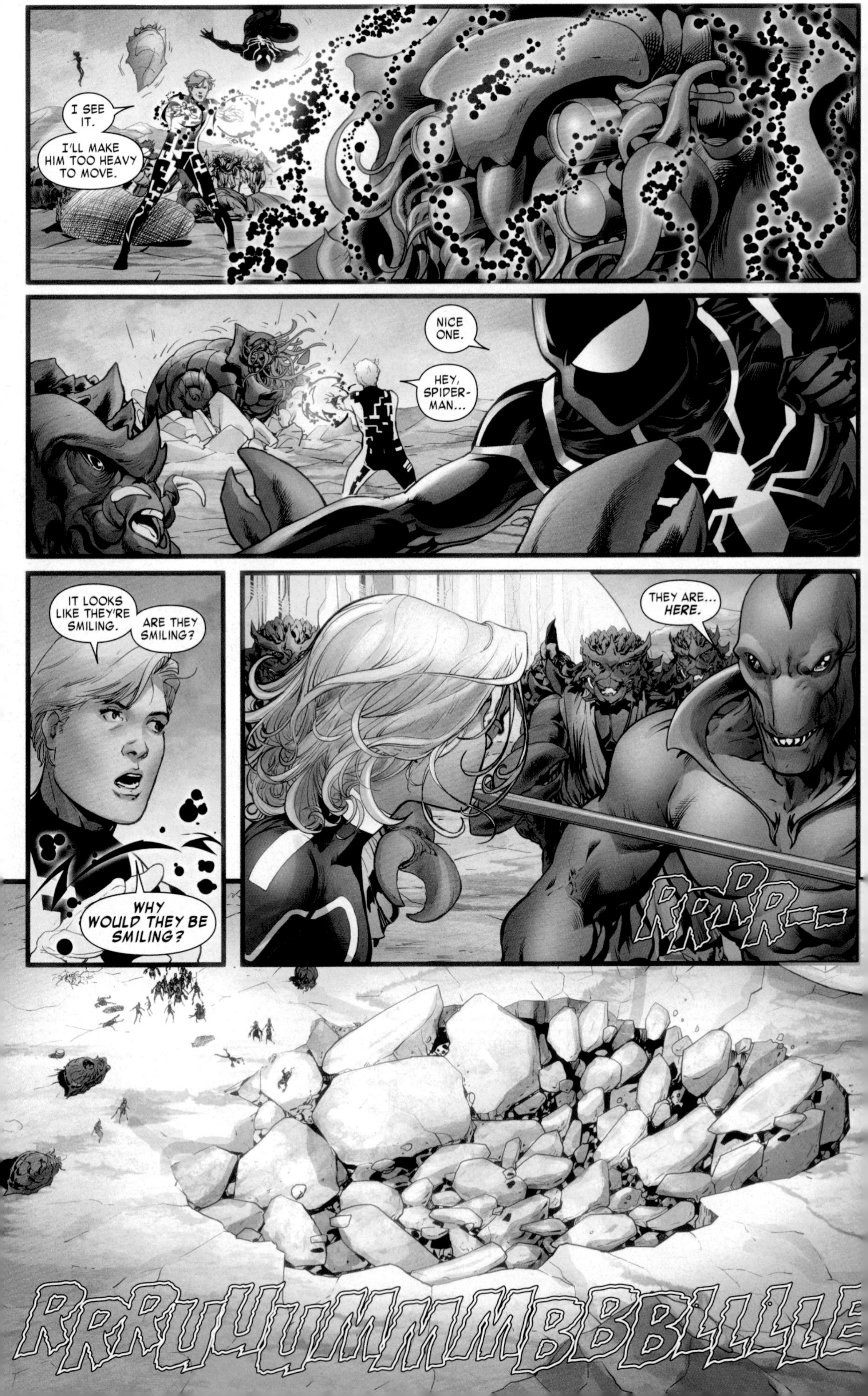
I SEE IT.
I'LL MAKE HIM TOO HEAVY TO MOVE.
NICE ONE.
HEY, SPIDER-MAN...
IT LOOKS LIKE THEY'RE SMILING.
ARE THEY SMILING?
WHY WOULD THEY BE SMILING?
THEY ARE... HERE.
RRRR--
RRRUUUMMMMBBBLLLE

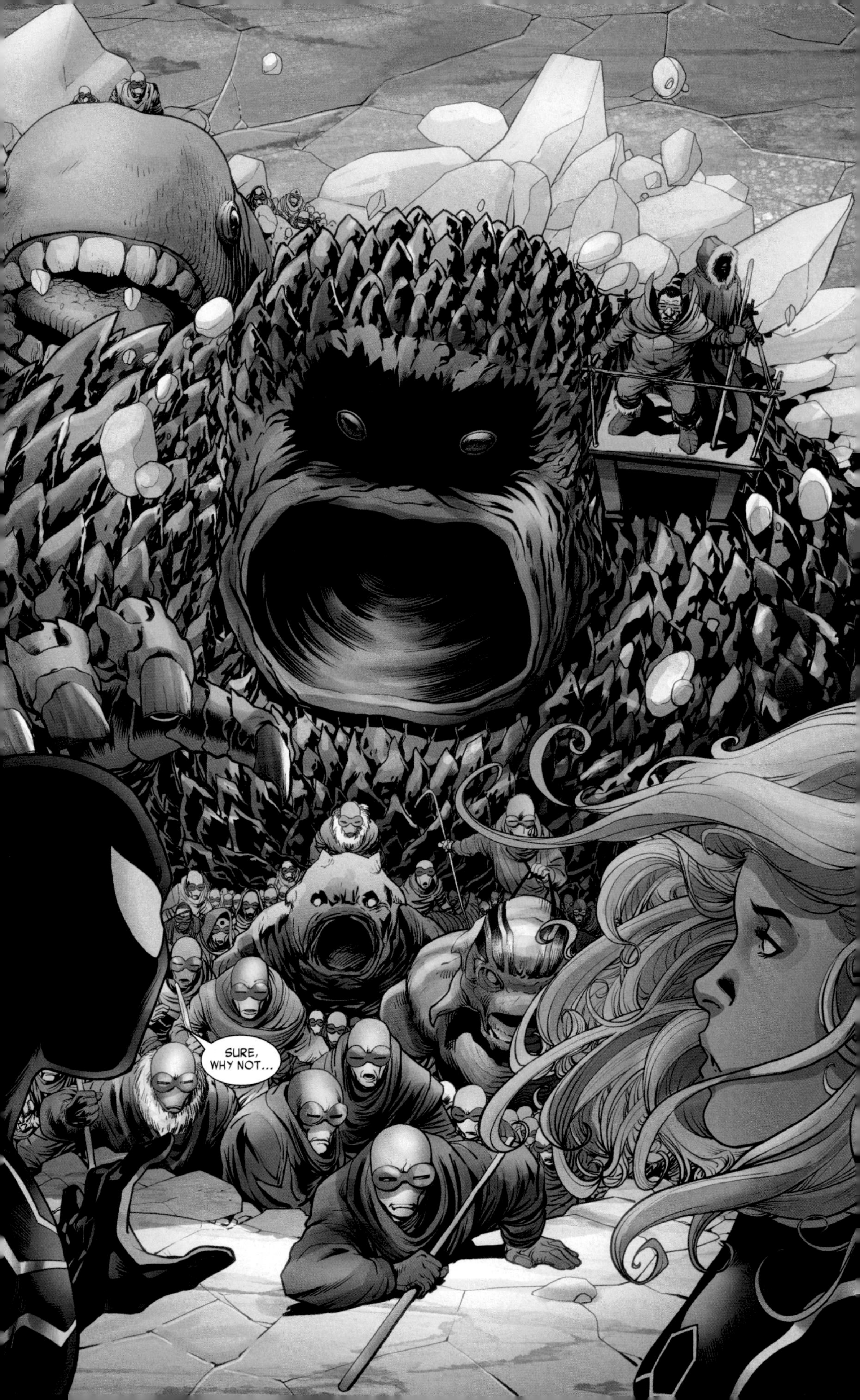
SURE, WHY NOT...

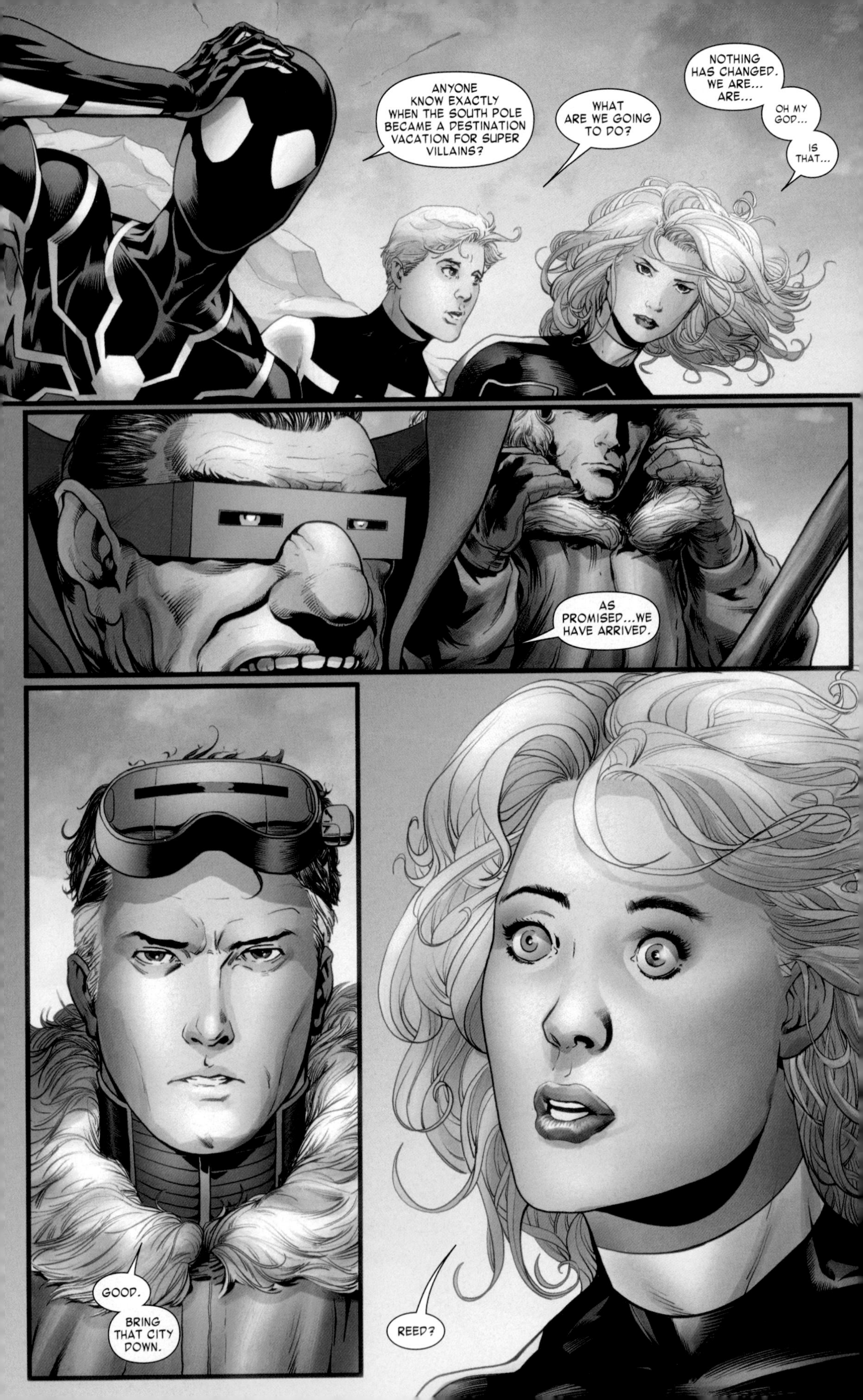
ANYONE KNOW EXACTLY WHEN THE SOUTH POLE BECAME A DESTINATION VACATION FOR SUPER VILLAINS?
WHAT ARE WE GOING TO DO?
NOTHING HAS CHANGED. WE ARE... ARE...
OH MY GOD...
IS THAT...
AS PROMISED...WE HAVE ARRIVED.
GOOD.
BRING THAT CITY DOWN.
REED?

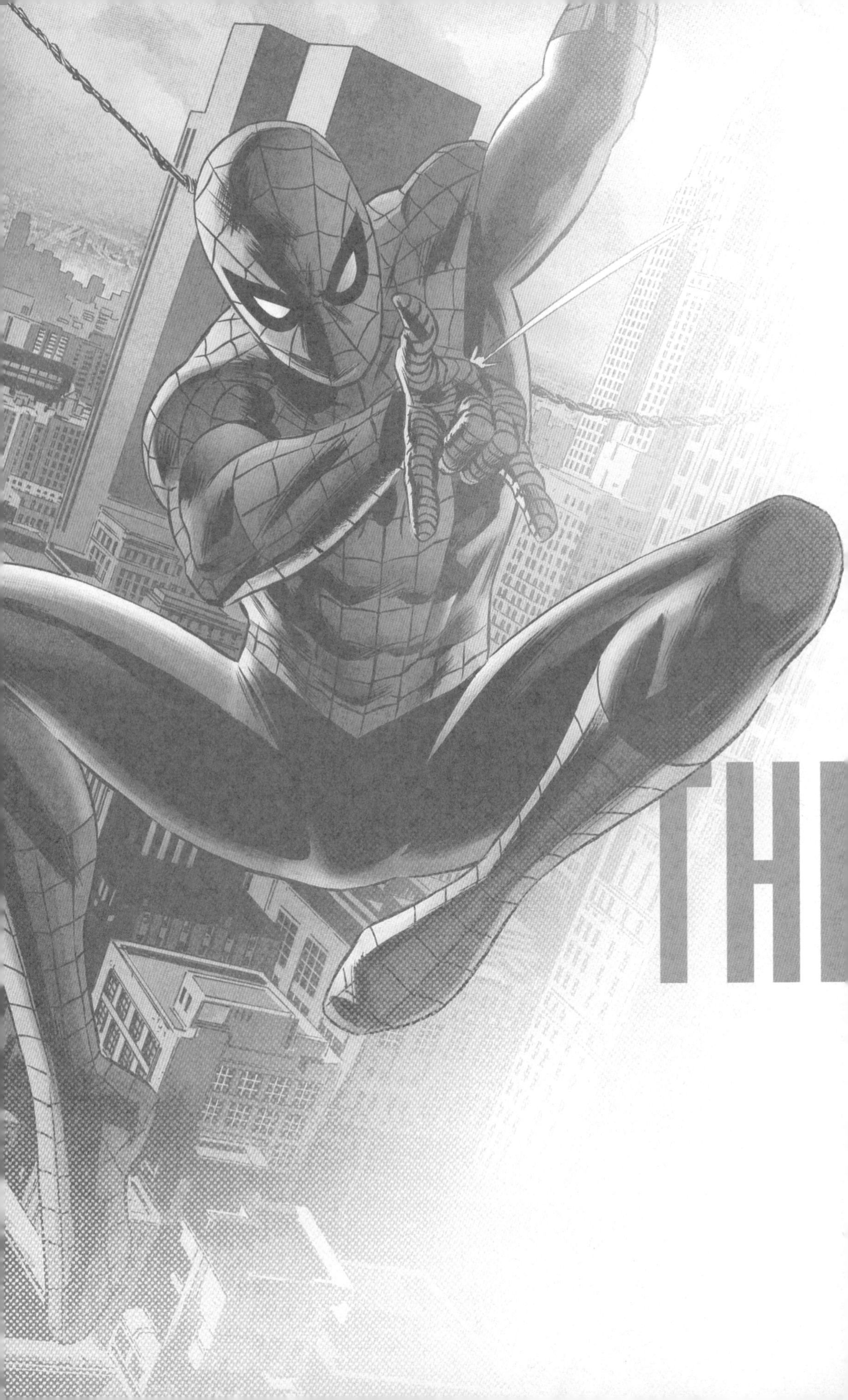
TH

SOUND OF
WAR

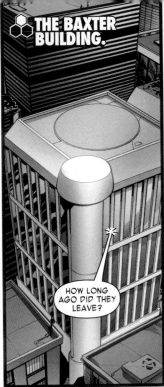

THE BAXTER BUILDING.

HOW LONG AGO DID THEY LEAVE?

TWO HOURS AGO, DOCTOR RICHARDS.

SHE ASKED US NOT TO BOTHER YOU, BUT WHEN THE SPIRAL STOPPED SINGING, THE DRAGON FELT YOU NEEDED TO KNOW.

THANK YOU, WU. YOU DID THE RIGHT THING.

I'M PRETTY SURE THIS DEVICE RELIES ON SPATIAL RESONANCE...

WE SHOULD BE ABLE TO FORCE A CONNECTION.

EASY, BOYS...

WE DON'T WANT A RUCKUS.

SOMETHING I CAN HELP YOU WITH, MISTER?

HMMM.

ANY LUCK, SON?

ONE MORE CONNECTION AND WE SHOULD GET...

SOMETHING.

I'LL TRY AND CLEAN UP THE SIGNAL, AND...OH!

IT'S... IT'S GONE...

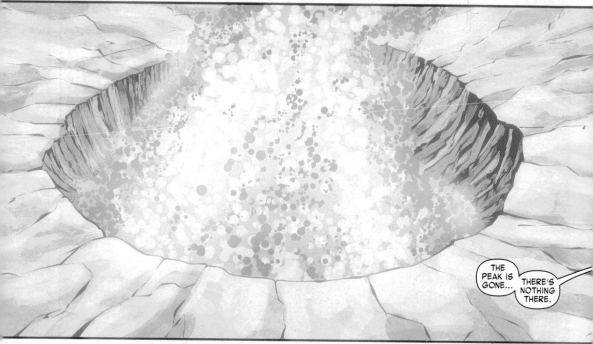

THE PEAK IS GONE... THERE'S NOTHING THERE.

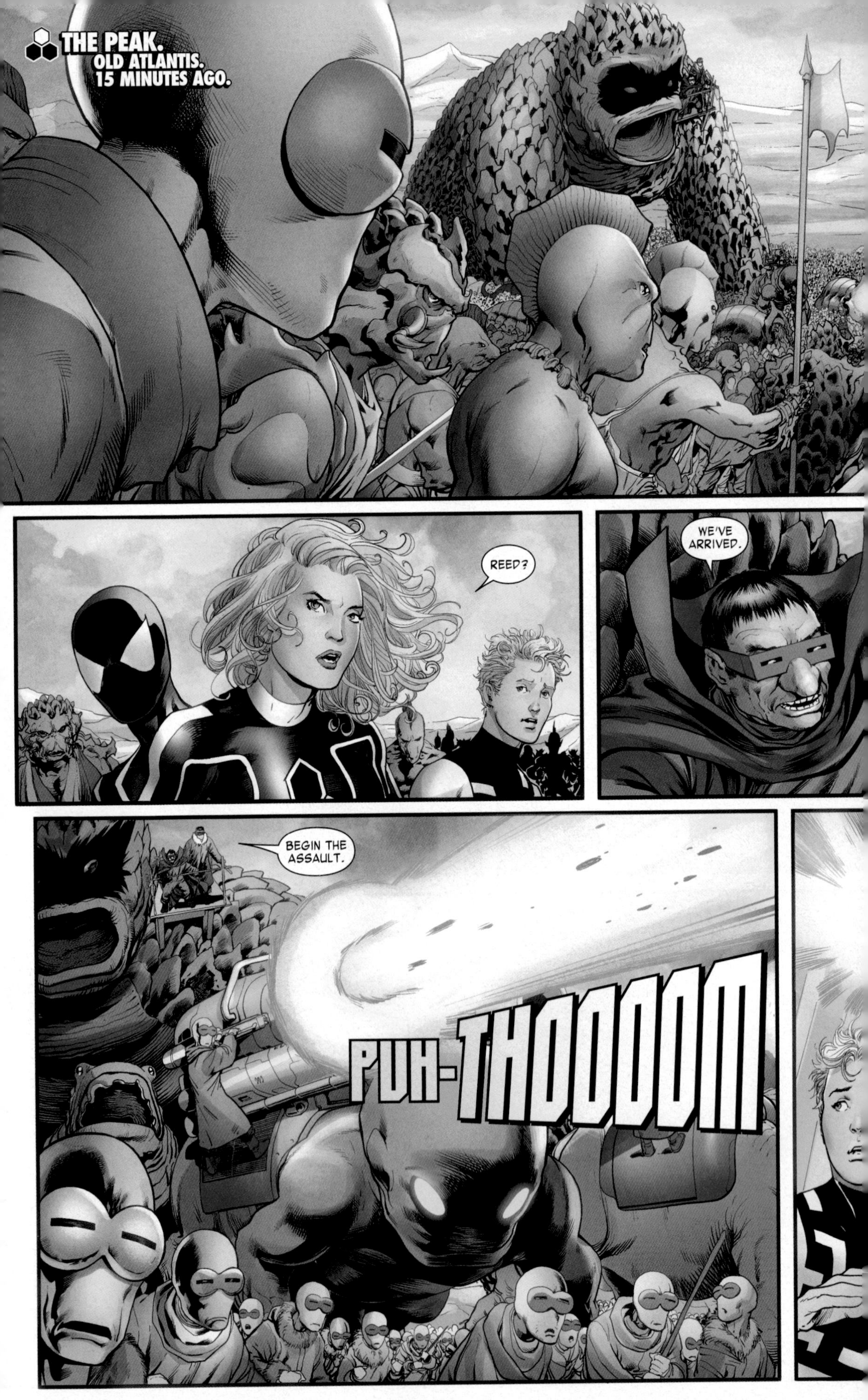
THE PEAK.
OLD ATLANTIS.
15 MINUTES AGO.
REED?
WE'VE ARRIVED.
BEGIN THE ASSAULT.
PUH-THOOOOM

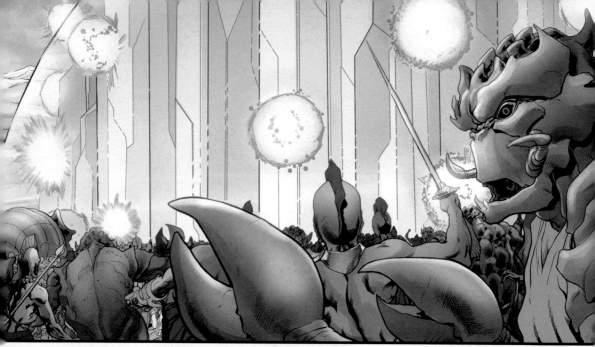

HAVE YOUR SLAVES ASSEMBLE THE MACHINES, MOLE MAN. I'LL PROVIDE A DISTRACTION.

THERE! STRIKE ON THE SOUTH SIDE. THERE'S A WEAKNESS IN THE SHIELD.

UH...WHY IS REED HELPING THEM ATTACK THE CITY?

YOU TWO STAY HERE.

WHERE ARE YOU GOING?

TO FIND OUT WHAT'S GOING ON.

HELLO, HARVEY. GET LOST AND SUDDENLY FIND YOURSELF IN A COLD AND UNINVITING PLACE?

AKKK! RICHARDS! WHAT ARE YOU DOING HERE?

I'M MORE INTERESTED IN WHAT YOU'VE ROPED MY HUSBAND INTO.

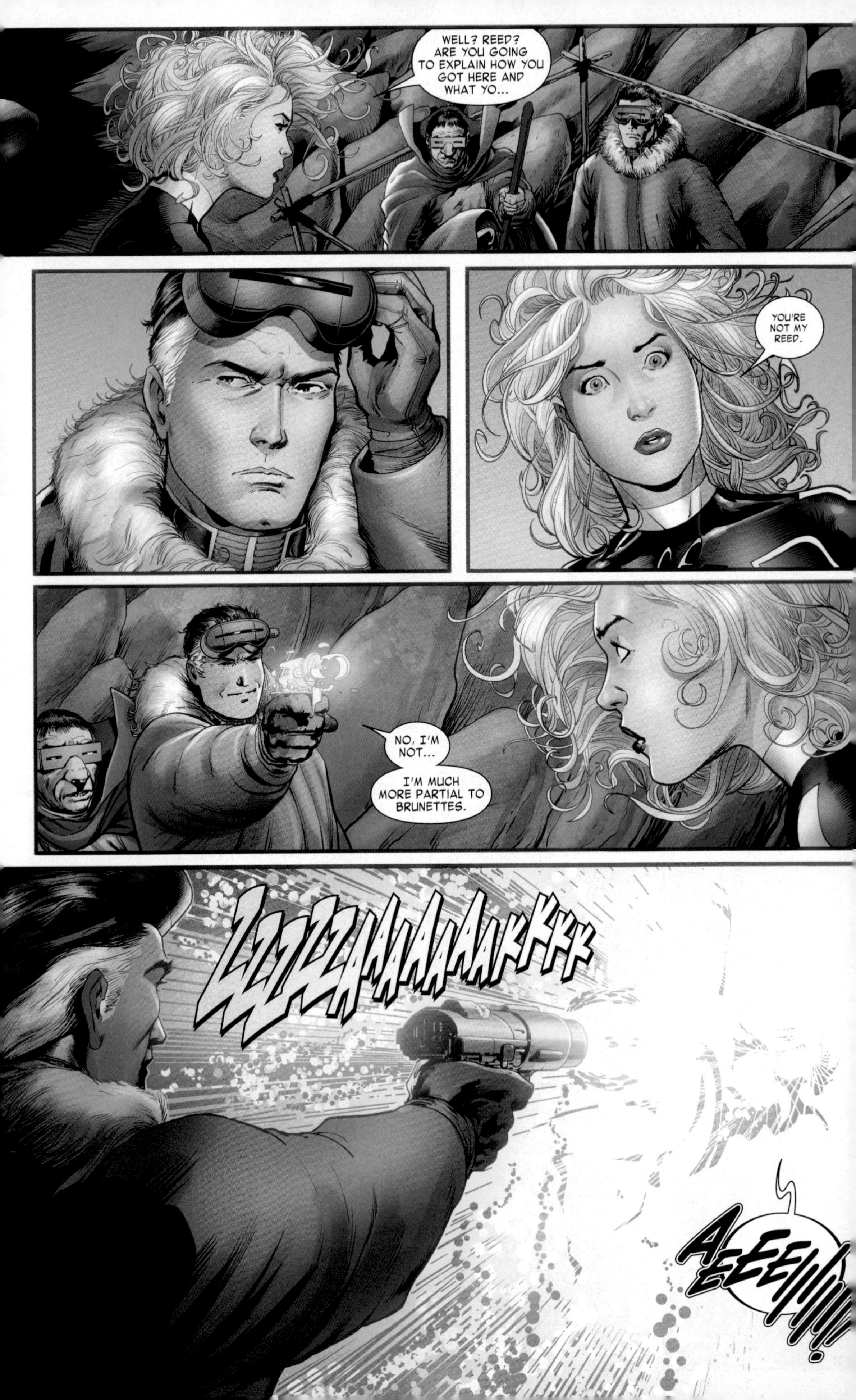
WELL? REED? ARE YOU GOING TO EXPLAIN HOW YOU GOT HERE AND WHAT YO...
YOU'RE NOT MY REED.
NO, I'M NOT...
I'M MUCH MORE PARTIAL TO BRUNETTES.
ZZZZZAAAAAAAAKKKK
AEEE!!!!!!

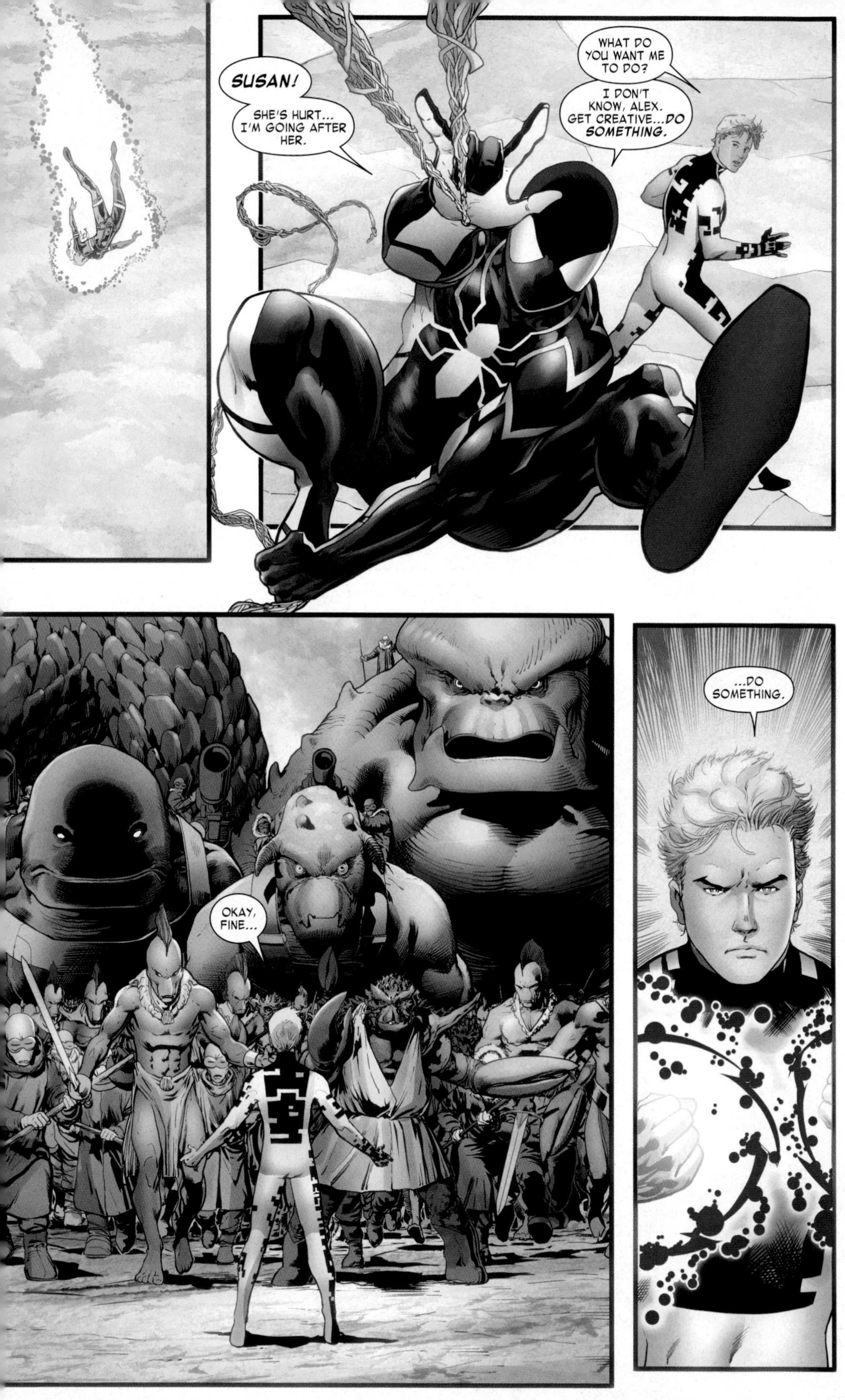
SUSAN!
SHE'S HURT... I'M GOING AFTER HER.
WHAT DO YOU WANT ME TO DO?
I DON'T KNOW, ALEX. GET CREATIVE...DO SOMETHING.
OKAY, FINE...
...DO SOMETHING.

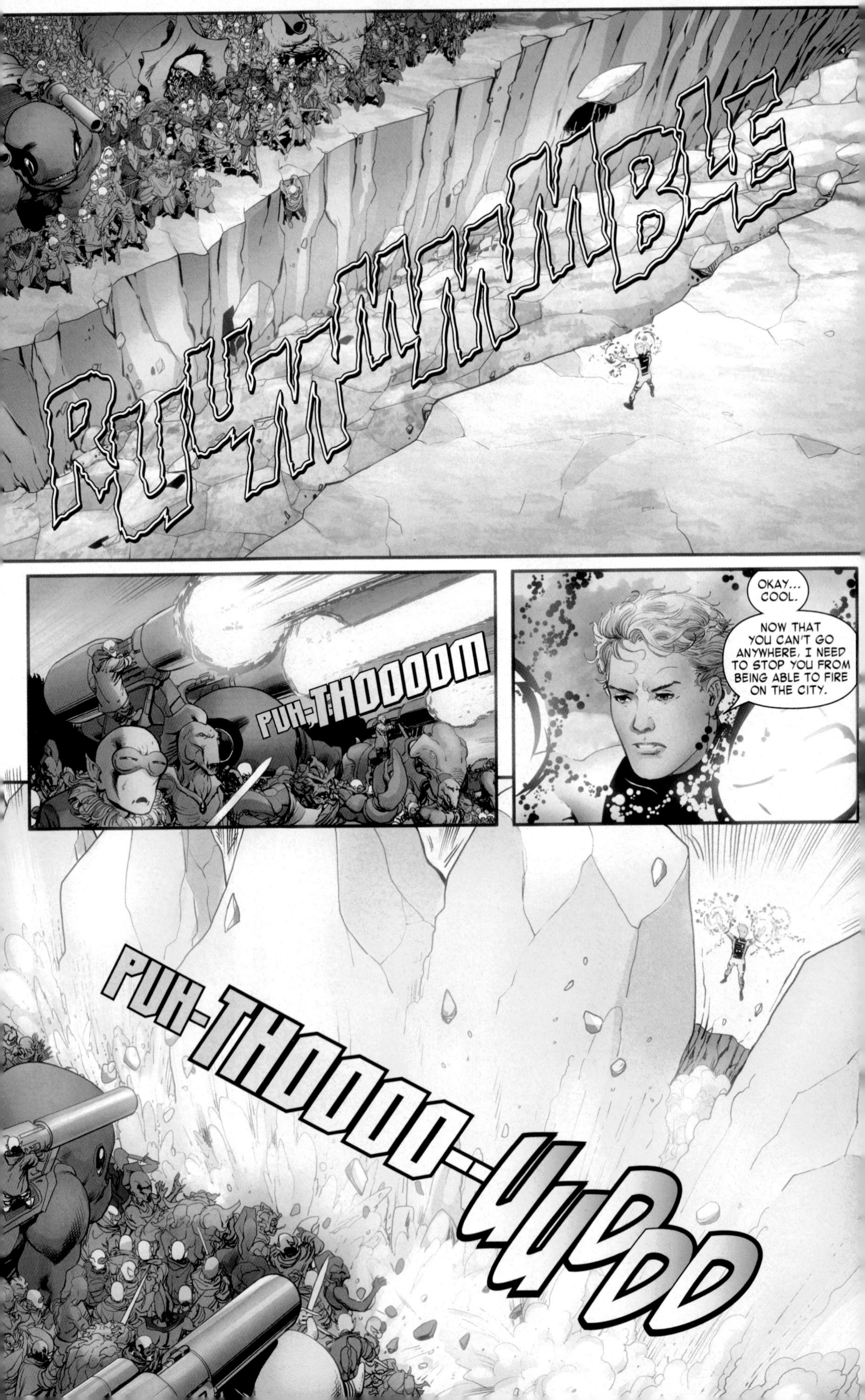
RUMMMMMBLE
PUH-THOOOOM
OKAY... COOL.
NOW THAT YOU CAN'T GO ANYWHERE, I NEED TO STOP YOU FROM BEING ABLE TO FIRE ON THE CITY.
PUH-THOOOO-UDDD

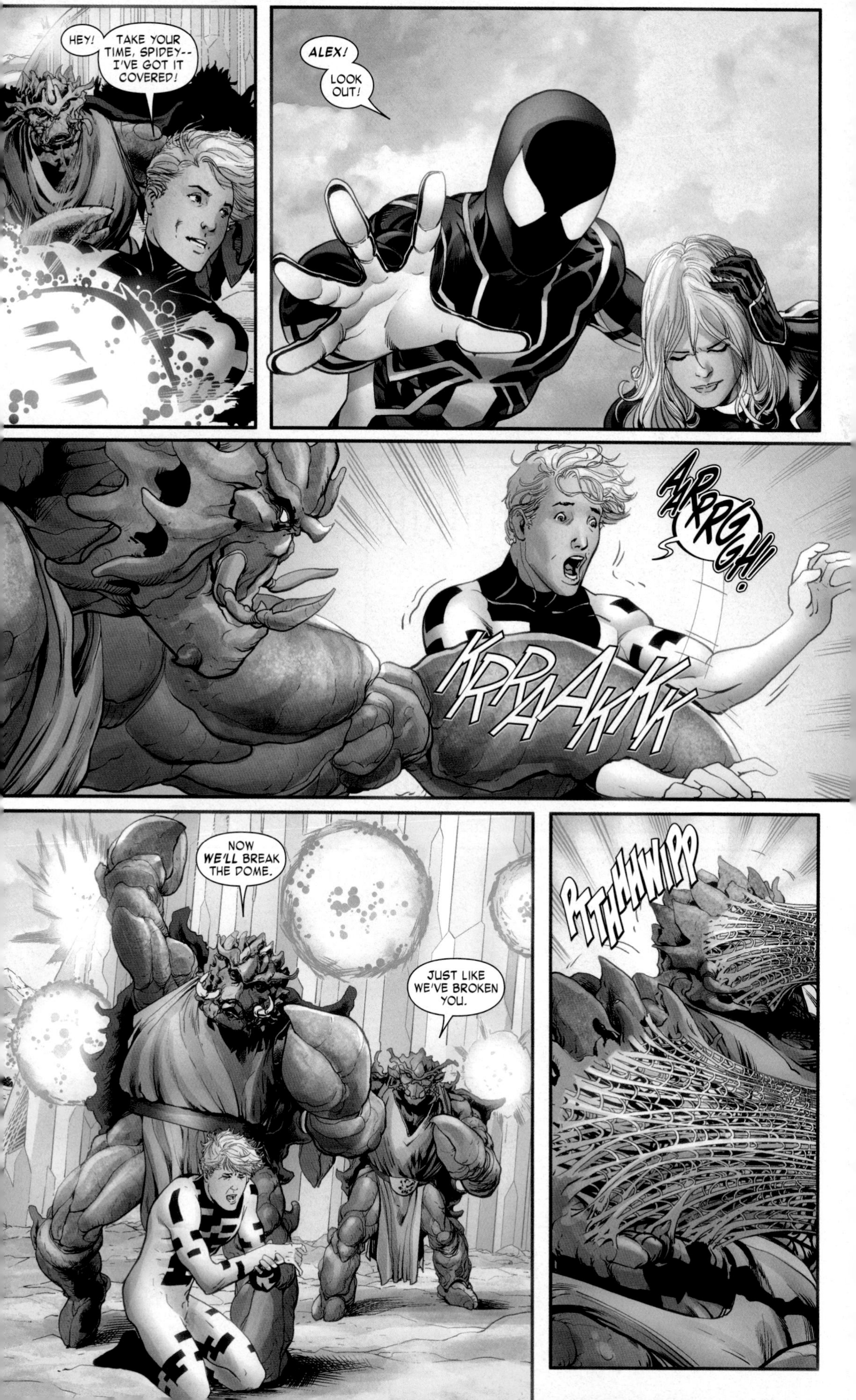
HEY!
TAKE YOUR TIME, SPIDEY-- I'VE GOT IT COVERED!
ALEX!
LOOK OUT!
ARRRGH!
KRRAAKKK
NOW WE'LL BREAK THE DOME.
JUST LIKE WE'VE BROKEN YOU.
PTTHHWIPP

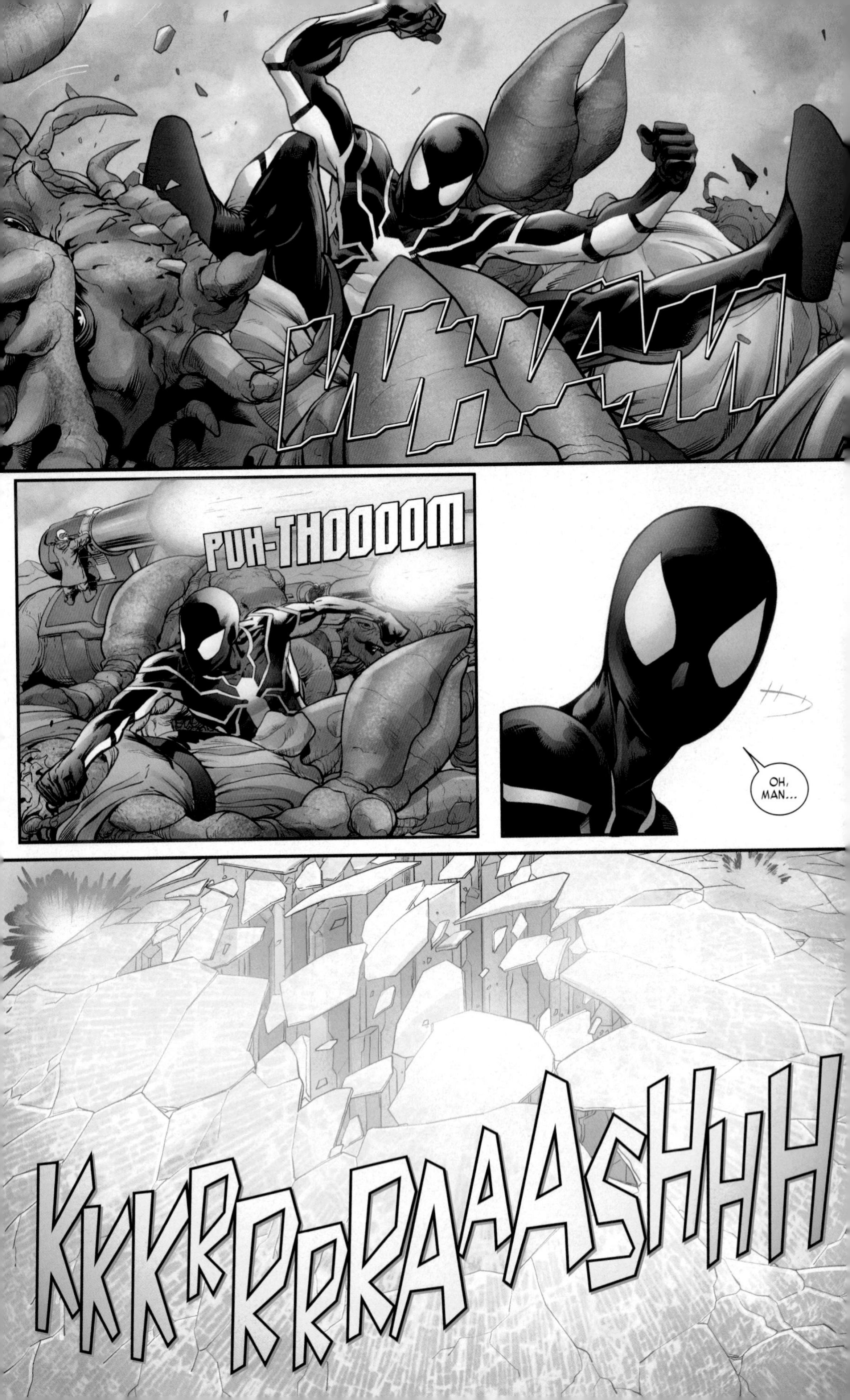
WHAM
PUH-THOOOOM
OH, MAN...
KKKRRRRAAASHHH

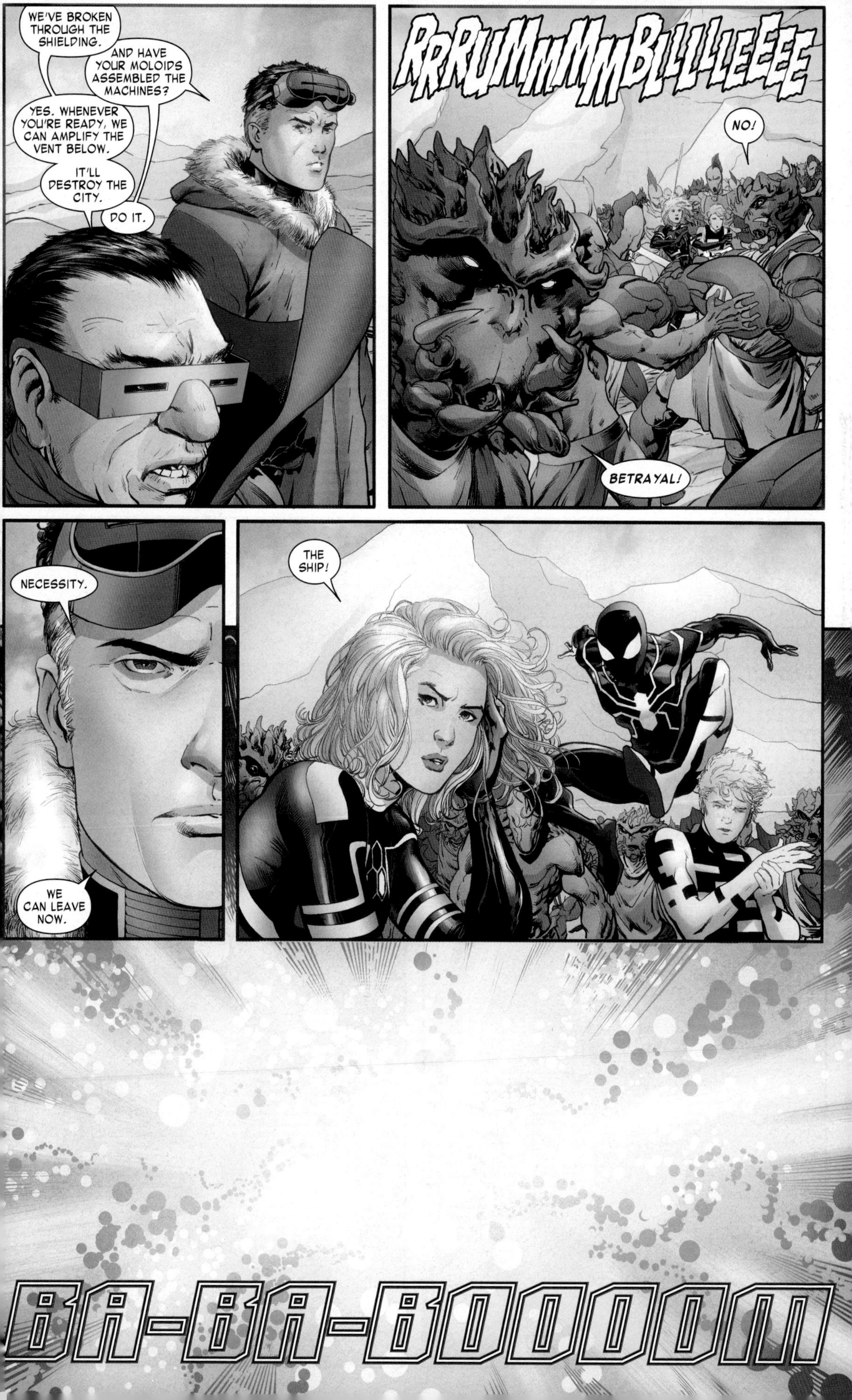
WE'VE BROKEN THROUGH THE SHIELDING.
AND HAVE YOUR MOLOIDS ASSEMBLED THE MACHINES?
YES. WHENEVER YOU'RE READY, WE CAN AMPLIFY THE VENT BELOW.
IT'LL DESTROY THE CITY.
DO IT.
RRRUMMMMMBLLLLEEEE
NO!
BETRAYAL!
NECESSITY.
WE CAN LEAVE NOW.
THE SHIP!
BA-BA-BOOOOOM

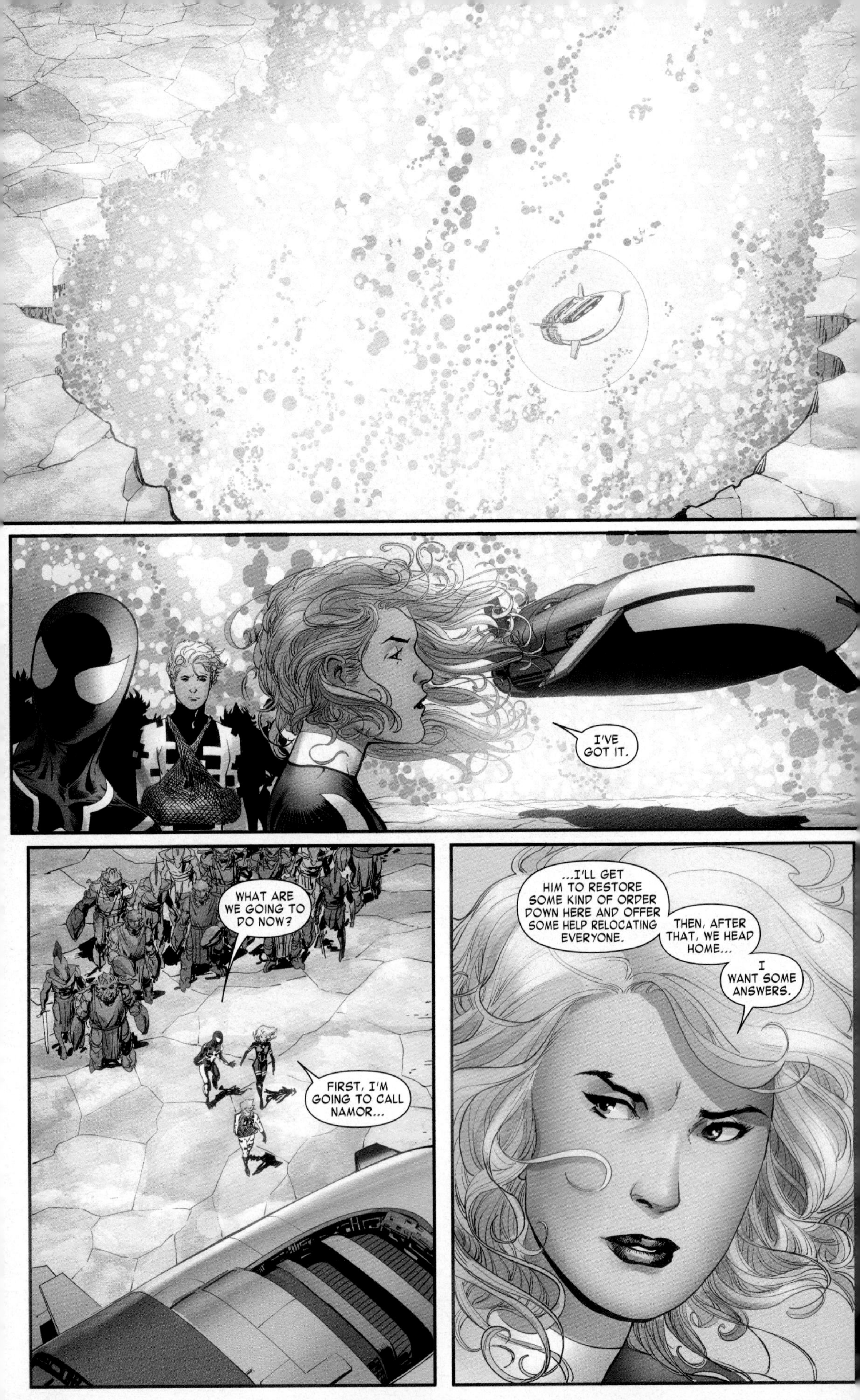
I'VE GOT IT.
WHAT ARE WE GOING TO DO NOW?
FIRST, I'M GOING TO CALL NAMOR...
...I'LL GET HIM TO RESTORE SOME KIND OF ORDER DOWN HERE AND OFFER SOME HELP RELOCATING EVERYONE.
THEN, AFTER THAT, WE HEAD HOME...
I WANT SOME ANSWERS.

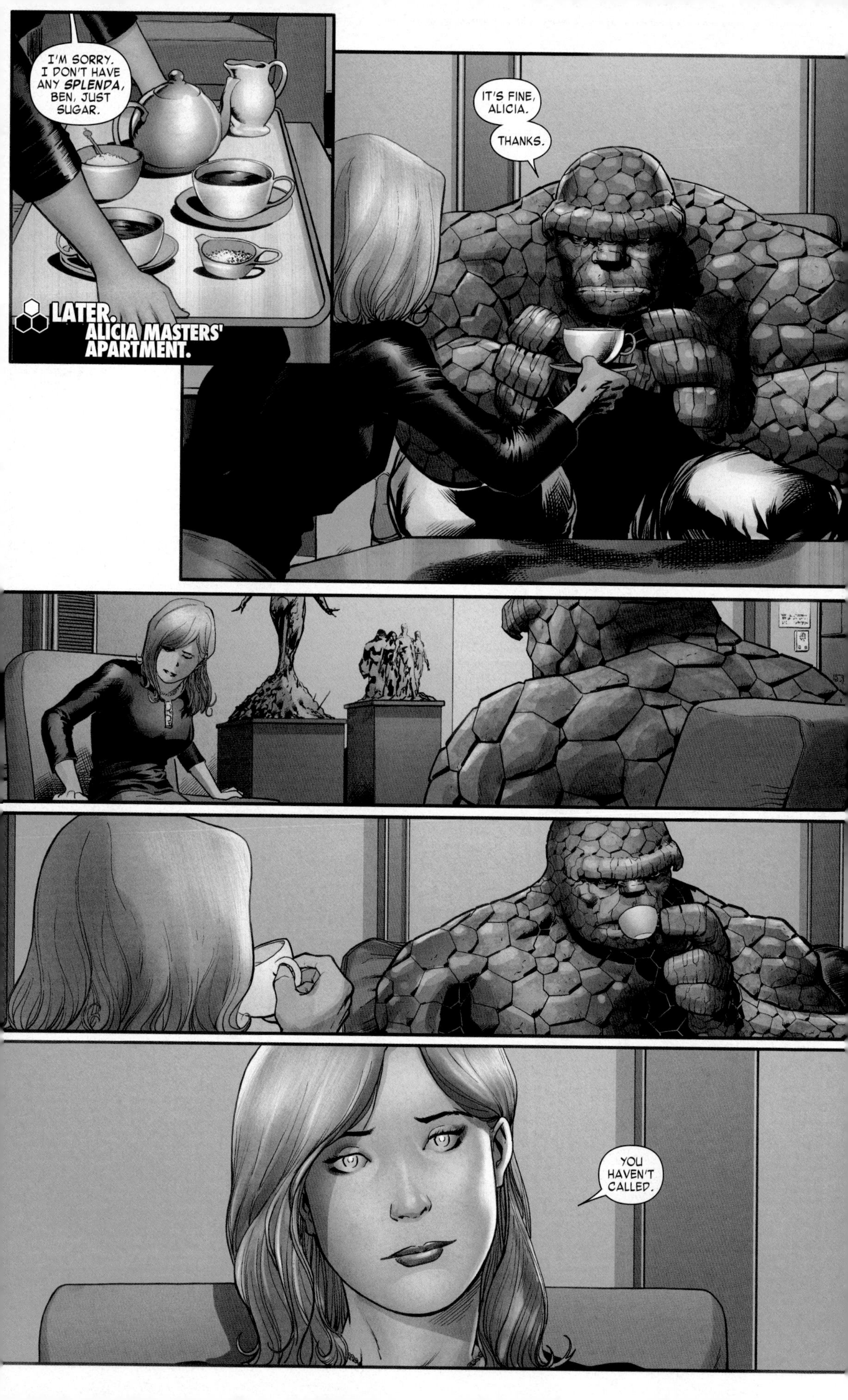
I'M SORRY. I DON'T HAVE ANY *SPLENDA*, BEN, JUST SUGAR.
LATER. ALICIA MASTERS' APARTMENT.
IT'S FINE, ALICIA.
THANKS.
YOU HAVEN'T CALLED.

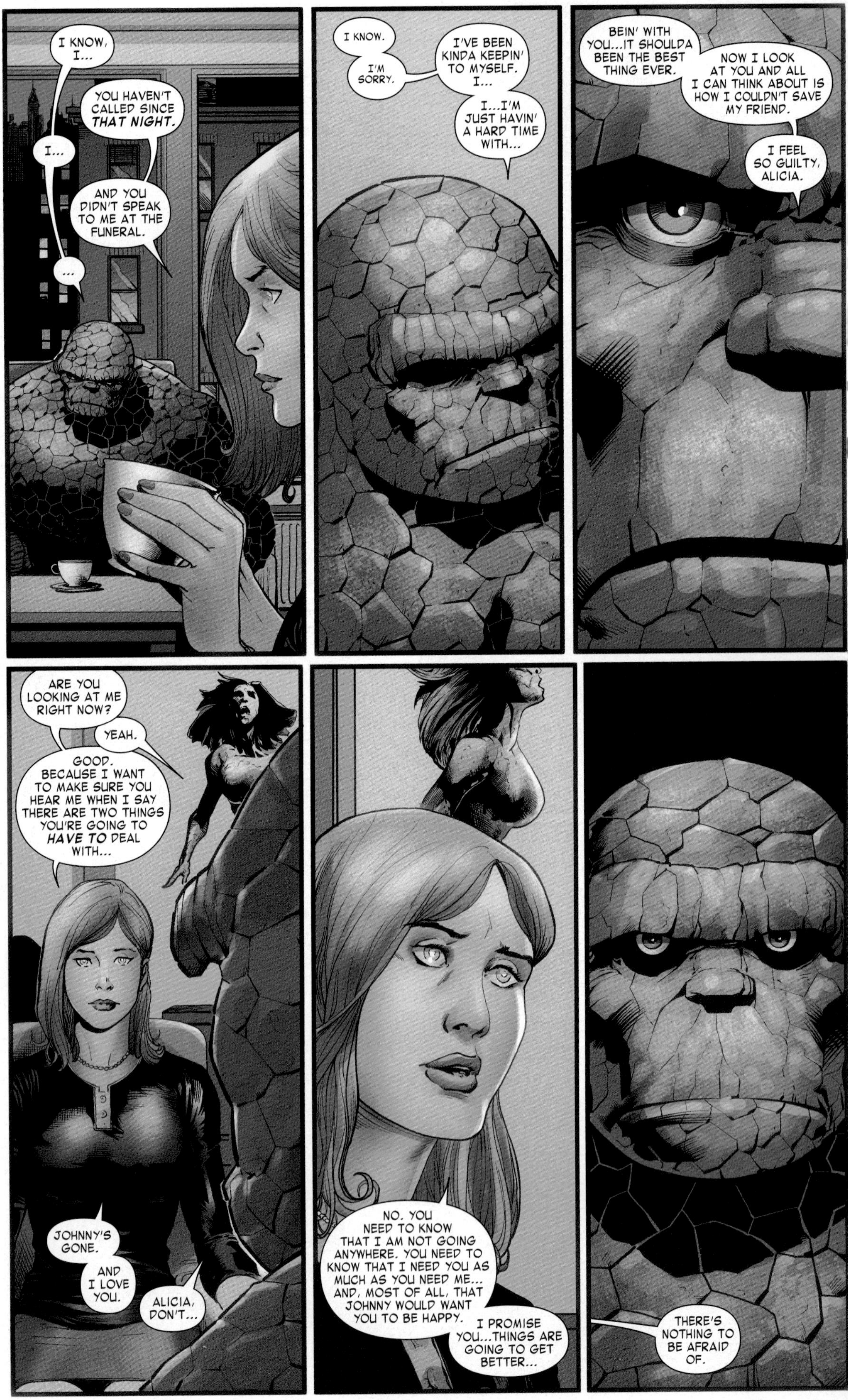
I KNOW, I...
YOU HAVEN'T CALLED SINCE *THAT NIGHT.*
I...
AND YOU DIDN'T SPEAK TO ME AT THE FUNERAL.
...
I KNOW.
I'M SORRY.
I'VE BEEN KINDA KEEPIN' TO MYSELF. I...
I...I'M JUST HAVIN' A HARD TIME WITH...
BEIN' WITH YOU...IT SHOULDA BEEN THE BEST THING EVER.
NOW I LOOK AT YOU AND ALL I CAN THINK ABOUT IS HOW I COULDN'T SAVE MY FRIEND.
I FEEL SO GUILTY, ALICIA.
ARE YOU LOOKING AT ME RIGHT NOW?
YEAH.
GOOD. BECAUSE I WANT TO MAKE SURE YOU HEAR ME WHEN I SAY THERE ARE TWO THINGS YOU'RE GOING TO *HAVE TO* DEAL WITH...
JOHNNY'S GONE.
AND I LOVE YOU.
ALICIA, DON'T...
NO. YOU NEED TO KNOW THAT I AM NOT GOING ANYWHERE. YOU NEED TO KNOW THAT I NEED YOU AS MUCH AS YOU NEED ME... AND, MOST OF ALL, THAT JOHNNY WOULD WANT YOU TO BE HAPPY.
I PROMISE YOU...THINGS ARE GOING TO GET BETTER...
THERE'S NOTHING TO BE AFRAID OF.

YOU FRACTURED YOUR ULNA IN THREE PLACES, ALEX.

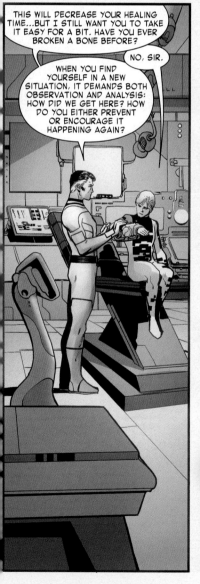

THIS WILL DECREASE YOUR HEALING TIME...BUT I STILL WANT YOU TO TAKE IT EASY FOR A BIT. HAVE YOU EVER BROKEN A BONE BEFORE?

NO, SIR.

WHEN YOU FIND YOURSELF IN A NEW SITUATION, IT DEMANDS BOTH OBSERVATION AND ANALYSIS: HOW DID WE GET HERE? HOW DO YOU EITHER PREVENT OR ENCOURAGE IT HAPPENING AGAIN?

SO NEXT TIME I SHOULD WATCH MY BACK.

HEH. YES, BUT DON'T BE TOO CRITICAL... SPIDER-MAN TOLD ME YOU WERE PRETTY FANTASTIC OUT THERE.

I'M PROUD OF YOU, ALEX. GO GET SOME REST.

YES, SIR.

NOW... LET'S HAVE A LOOK AT YOU.

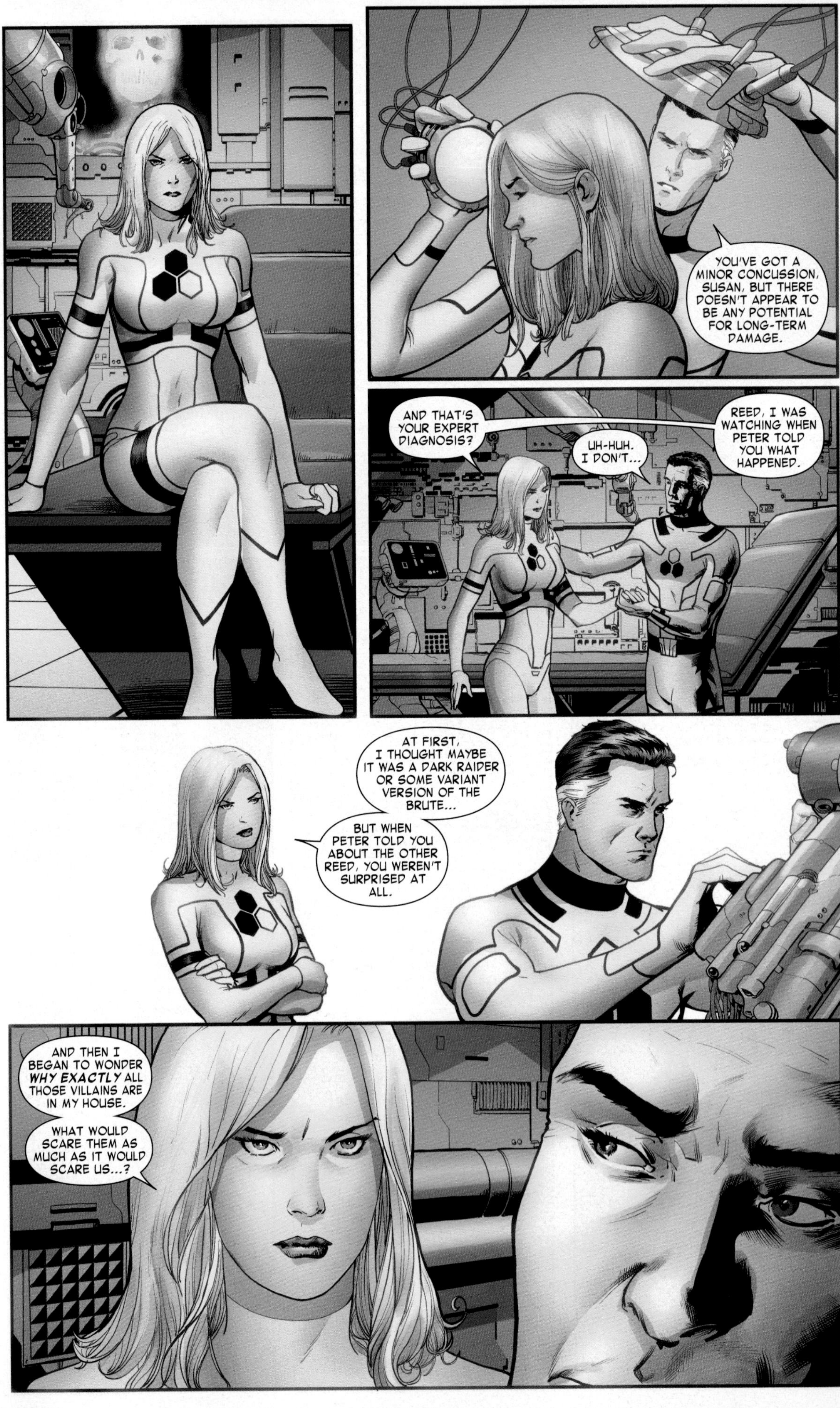
YOU'VE GOT A MINOR CONCUSSION, SUSAN, BUT THERE DOESN'T APPEAR TO BE ANY POTENTIAL FOR LONG-TERM DAMAGE.
AND THAT'S YOUR EXPERT DIAGNOSIS?
UH-HUH. I DON'T...
REED, I WAS WATCHING WHEN PETER TOLD YOU WHAT HAPPENED.
AT FIRST, I THOUGHT MAYBE IT WAS A DARK RAIDER OR SOME VARIANT VERSION OF THE BRUTE...
BUT WHEN PETER TOLD YOU ABOUT THE OTHER REED, YOU WEREN'T SURPRISED AT ALL.
AND THEN I BEGAN TO WONDER WHY EXACTLY ALL THOSE VILLAINS ARE IN MY HOUSE.
WHAT WOULD SCARE THEM AS MUCH AS IT WOULD SCARE US...?

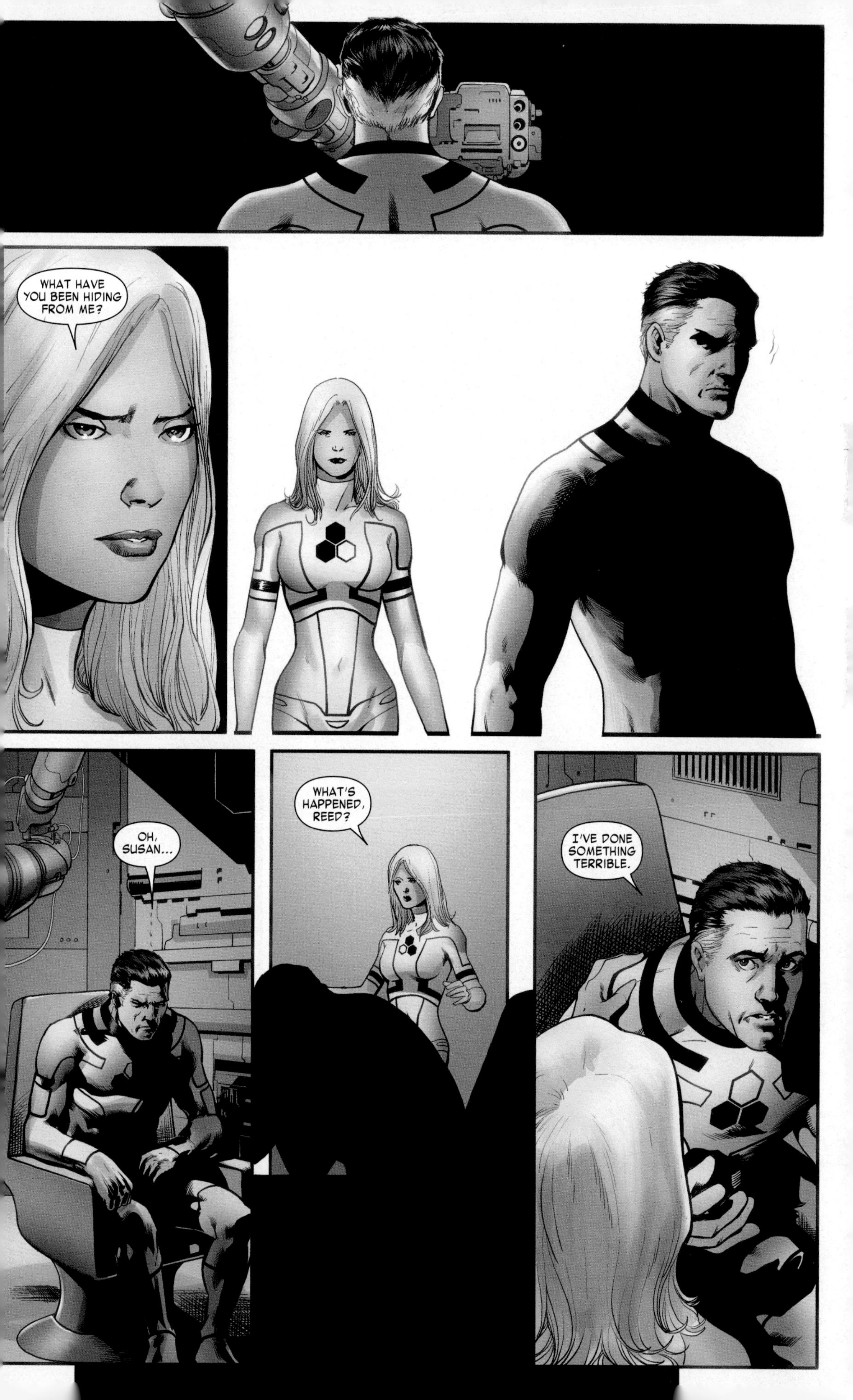
WHAT HAVE YOU BEEN HIDING FROM ME?
OH, SUSAN...
WHAT'S HAPPENED, REED?
I'VE DONE SOMETHING TERRIBLE.

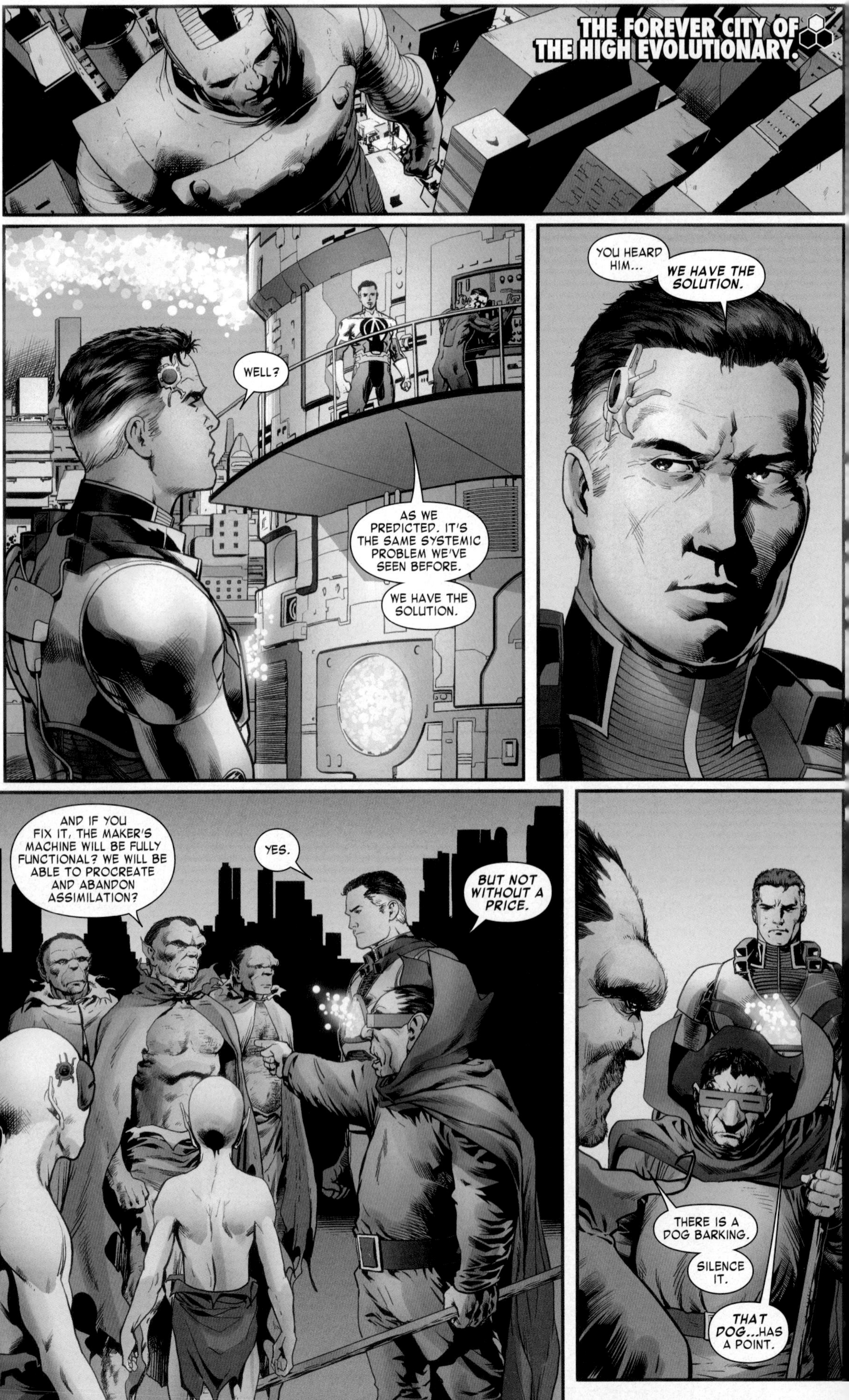
THE FOREVER CITY OF THE HIGH EVOLUTIONARY.
WELL?
AS WE PREDICTED. IT'S THE SAME SYSTEMIC PROBLEM WE'VE SEEN BEFORE.
WE HAVE THE SOLUTION.
YOU HEARD HIM...
WE HAVE THE SOLUTION.
AND IF YOU FIX IT, THE MAKER'S MACHINE WILL BE FULLY FUNCTIONAL? WE WILL BE ABLE TO PROCREATE AND ABANDON ASSIMILATION?
YES.
BUT NOT WITHOUT A PRICE.
THERE IS A DOG BARKING.
SILENCE IT.
THAT DOG...HAS A POINT.

VERY WELL.

REST EASY, ELDER.

THIS WAS A SIMPLE DECISION TO MAKE. AS YOU CAN SEE, OUR TECHNOLOGY HAS MADE US IMMUNE TO THE EFFECTS OF THE ASCENSION ENGINE'S RADIATION. WE *UNDERSTAND* THIS DEVICE.

NOW, MAKE YOUR PEACE.

WE WILL ABIDE BY WHAT WAS AGREED.

SAY THE WORDS.

⸸SIGH⸸-- IN RETURN FOR THE ENGINE BEING MADE WHOLE, WE WILL NO LONGER ACCEPT ANY REFUGEES FROM YOUR PEOPLE INTO OUR BODY.

THE DOORS TO THE CITY WILL REMAIN CLOSED.

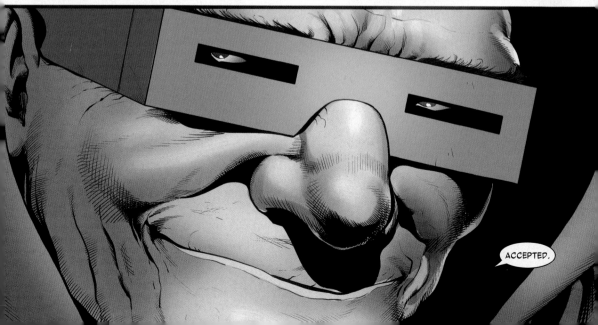

ACCEPTED.

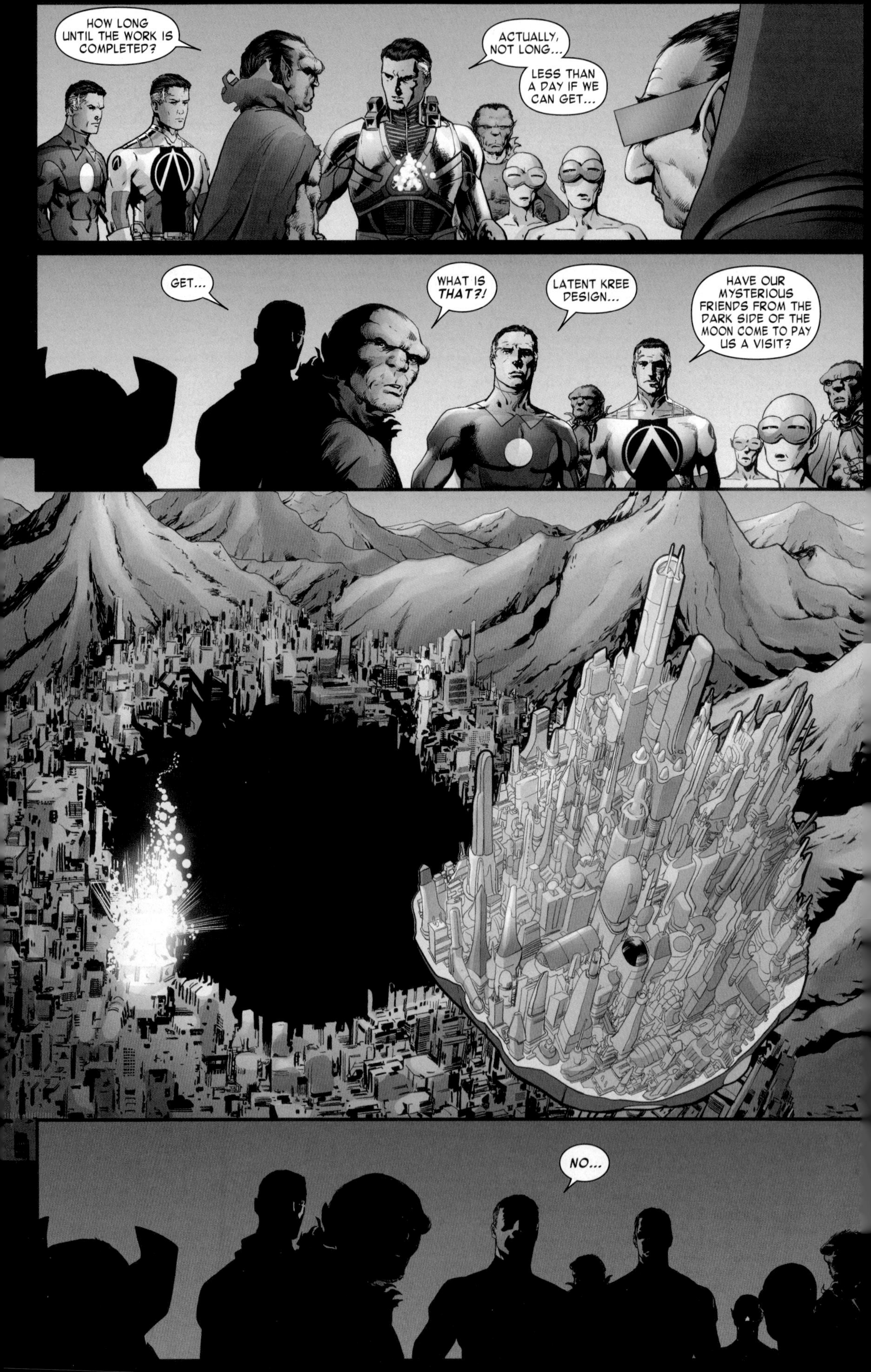
HOW LONG UNTIL THE WORK IS COMPLETED?
ACTUALLY, NOT LONG...
LESS THAN A DAY IF WE CAN GET...
GET...
WHAT IS THAT?!
LATENT KREE DESIGN...
HAVE OUR MYSTERIOUS FRIENDS FROM THE DARK SIDE OF THE MOON COME TO PAY US A VISIT?
NO...

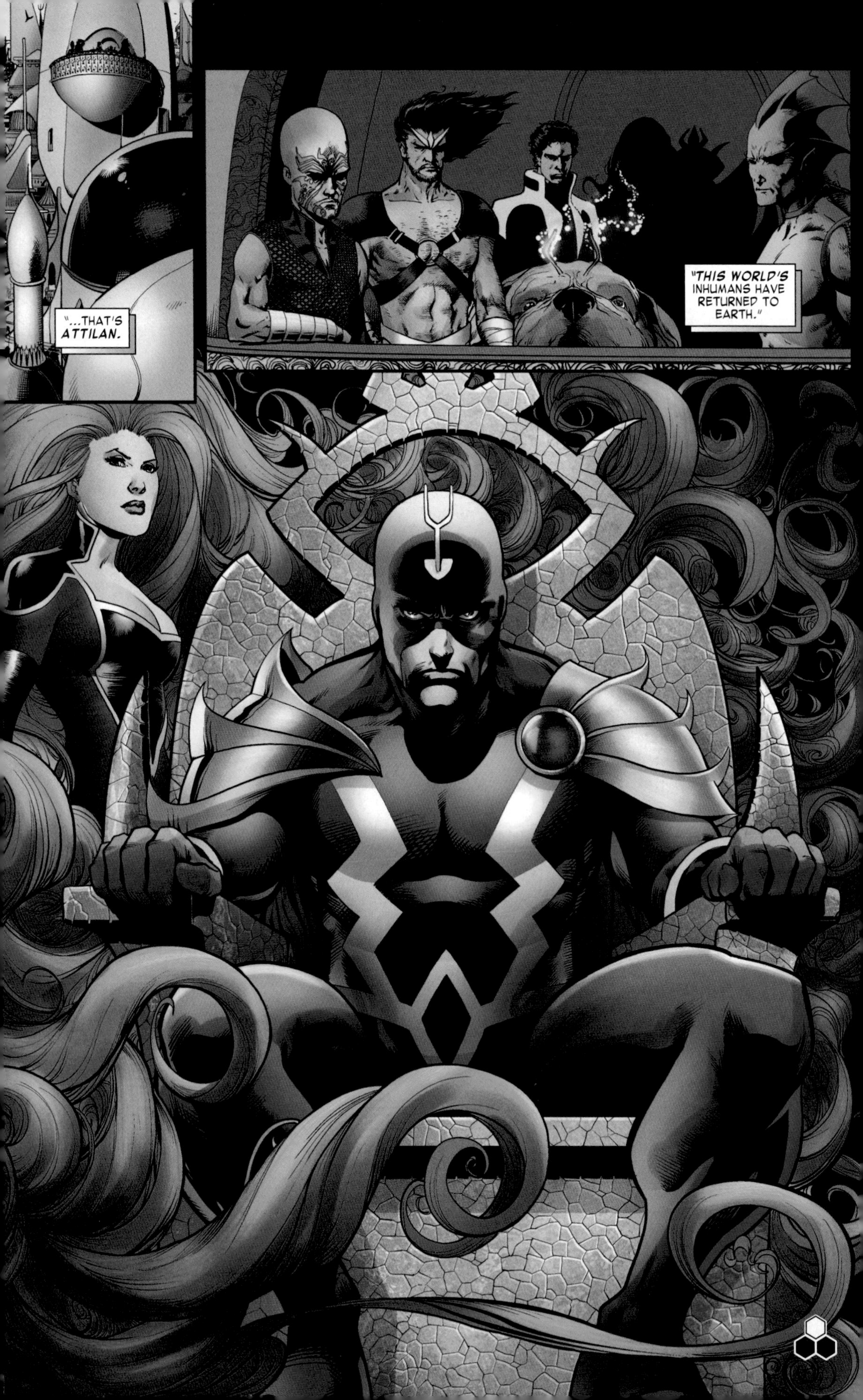
"...THAT'S ATTILAN.
"THIS WORLD'S INHUMANS HAVE RETURNED TO EARTH."

#1 COVER: STEVE EPTING

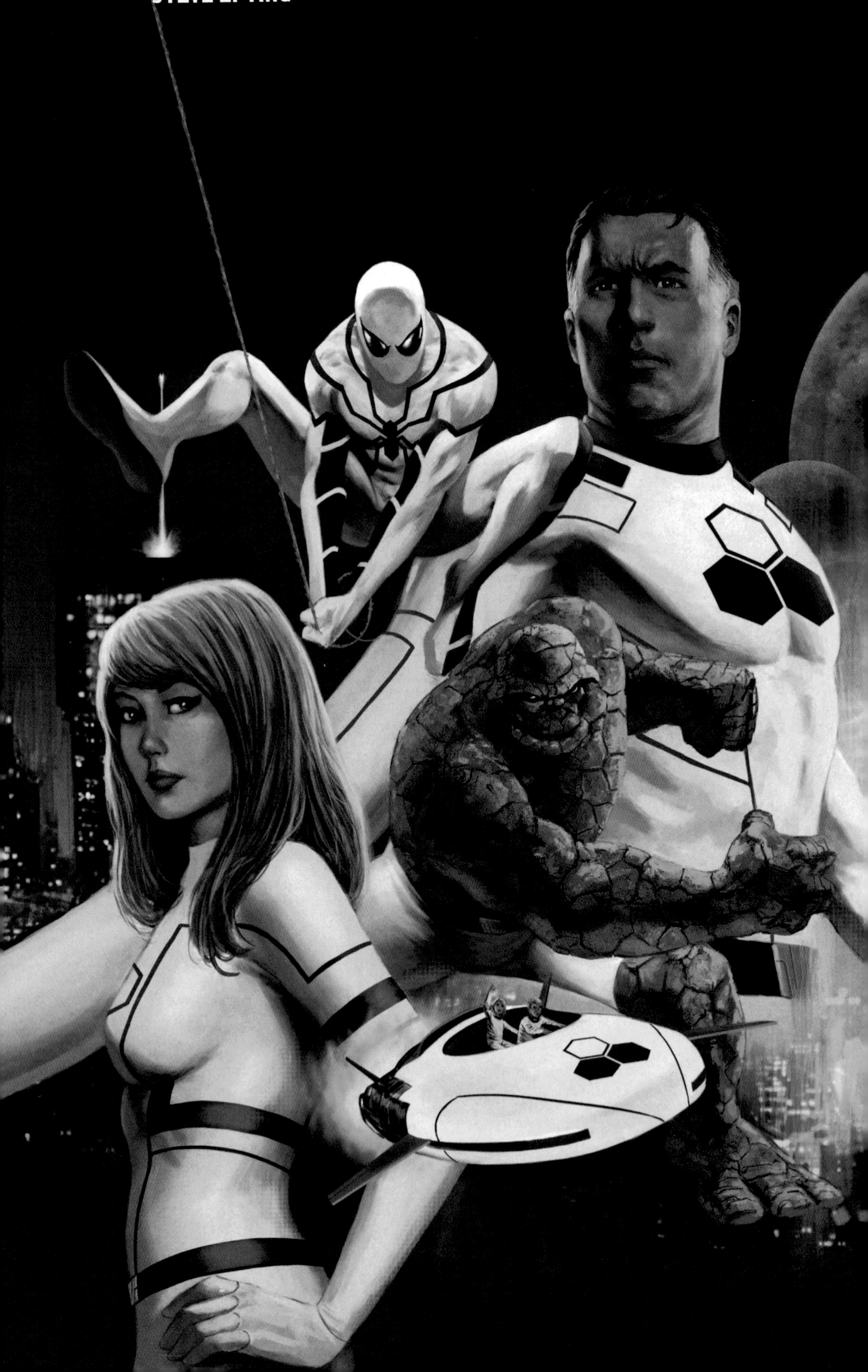

#2 COVER: **DANIEL ACUÑA**

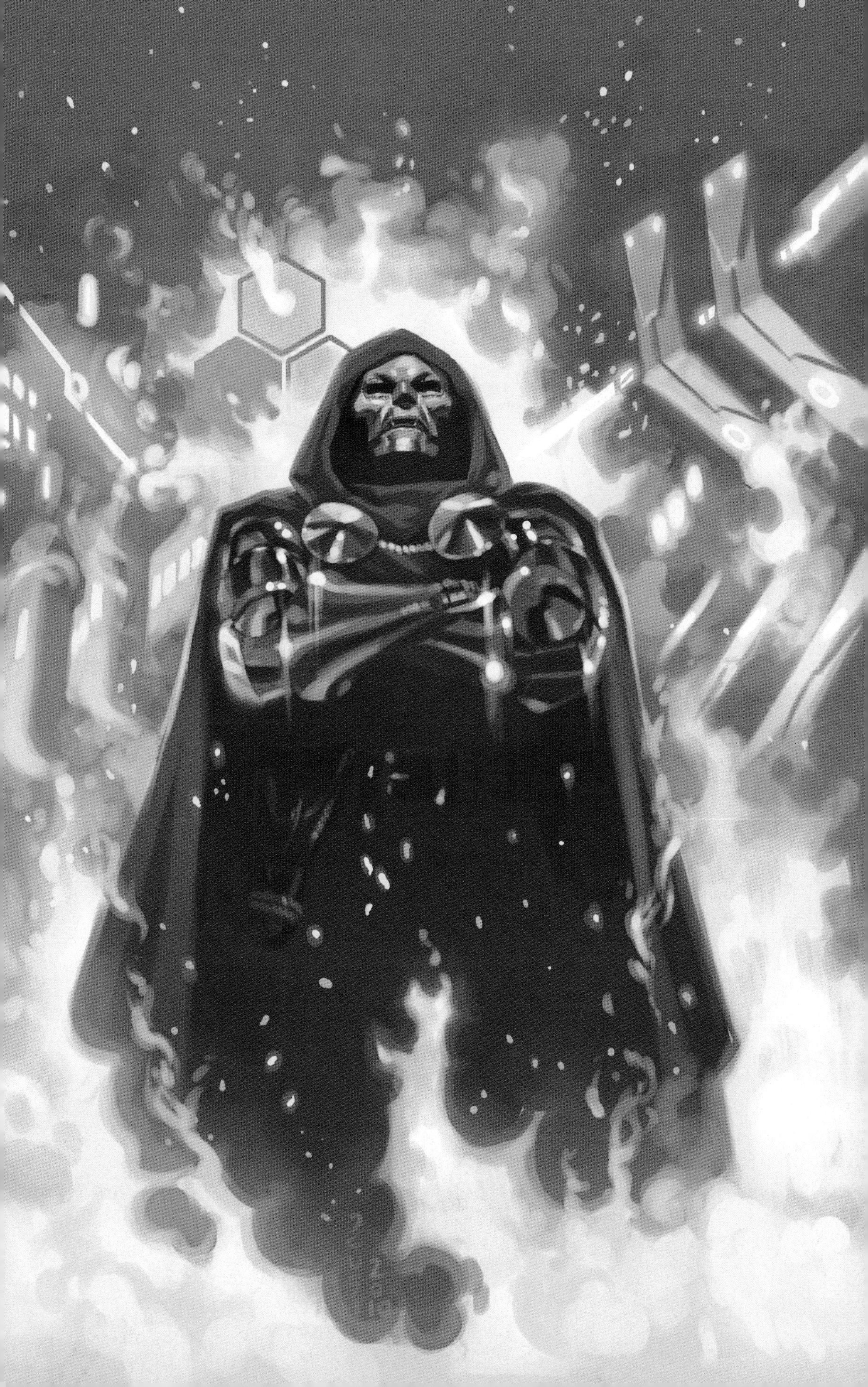

#3 COVER: **DANIEL ACUÑA**

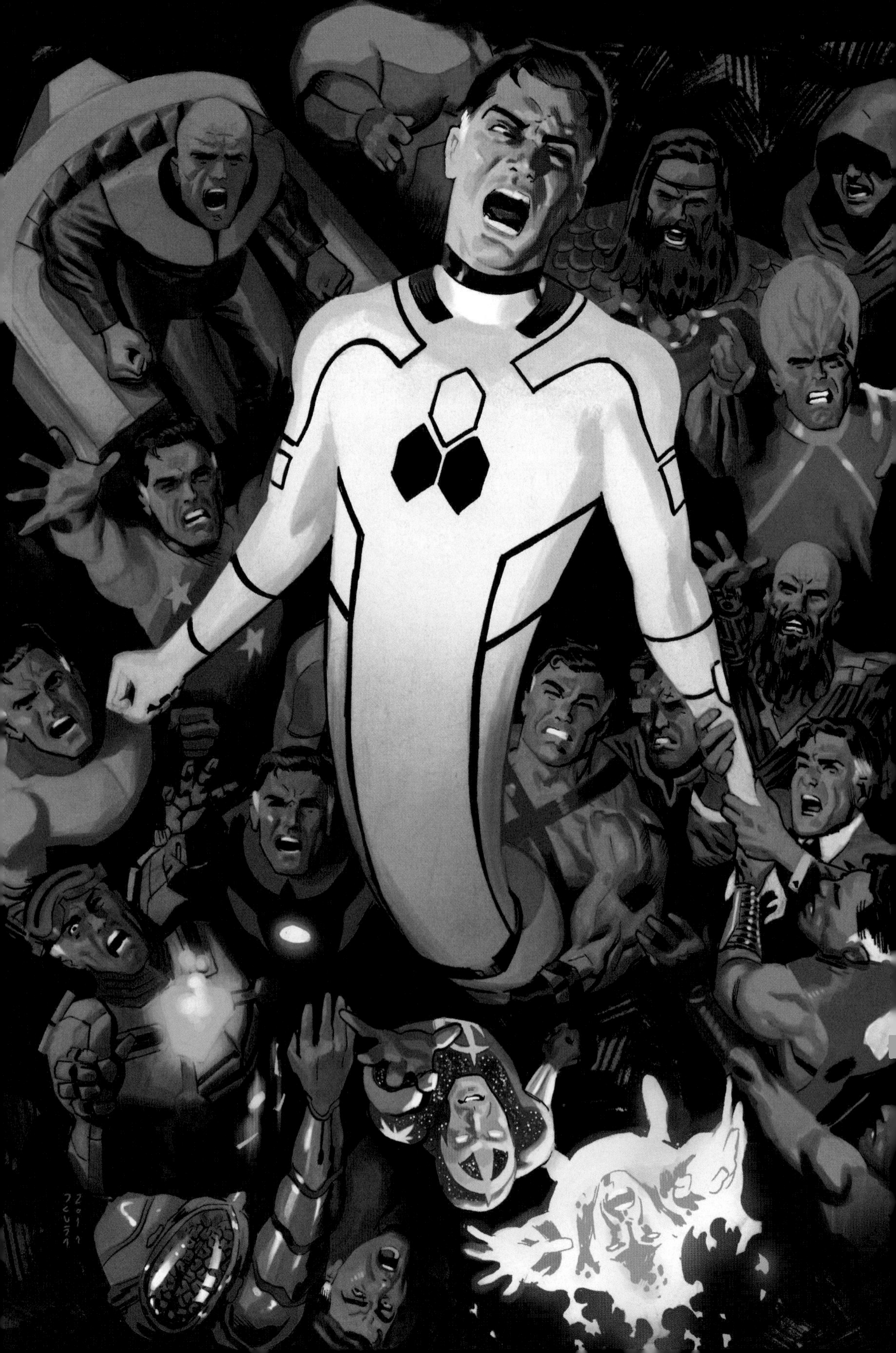

#4 COVER: **DANIEL ACUÑA**

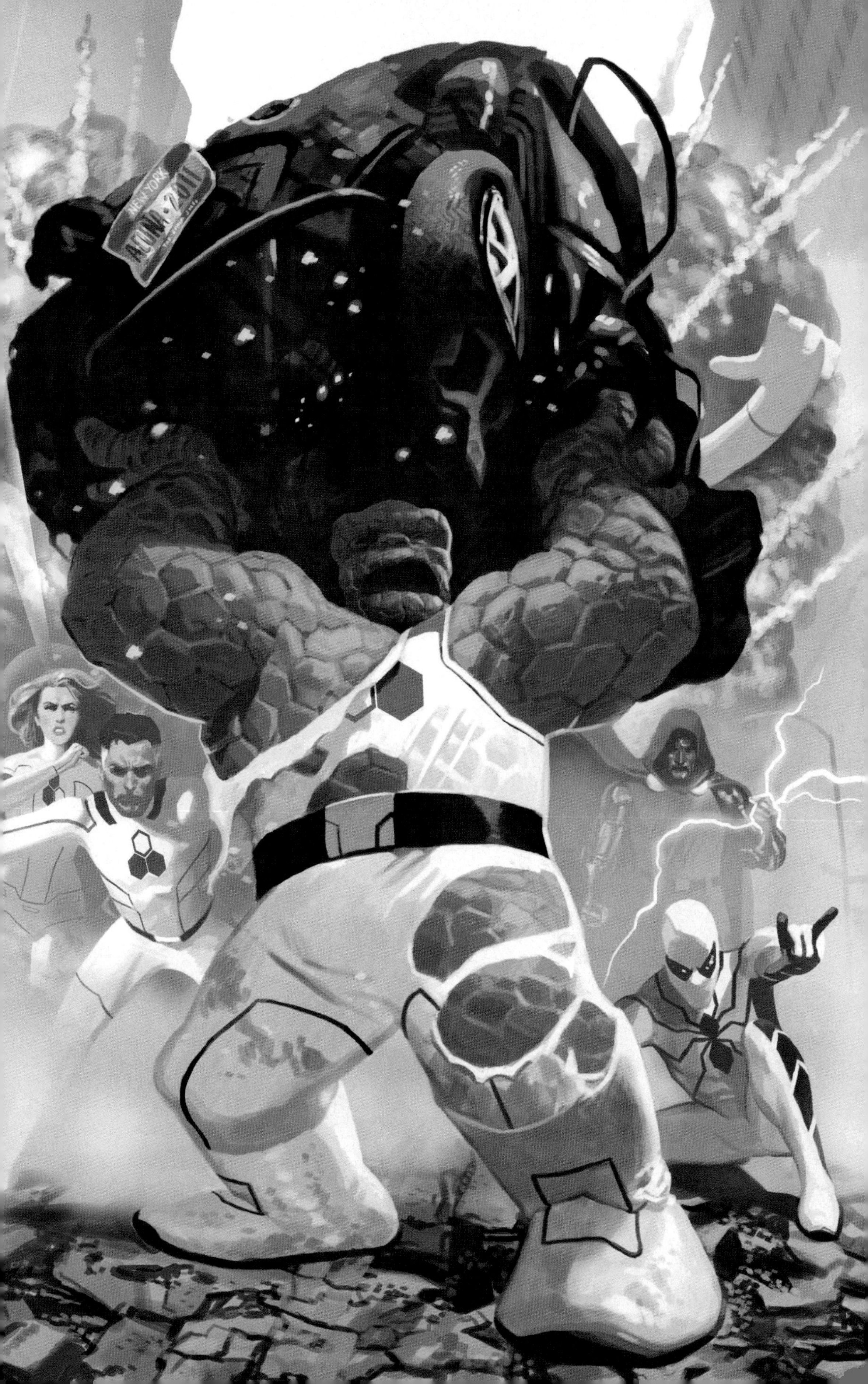
NEW YORK

#5 COVER: **MARK BAGLEY, ANDY LANNING & PAUL MOUNTS**

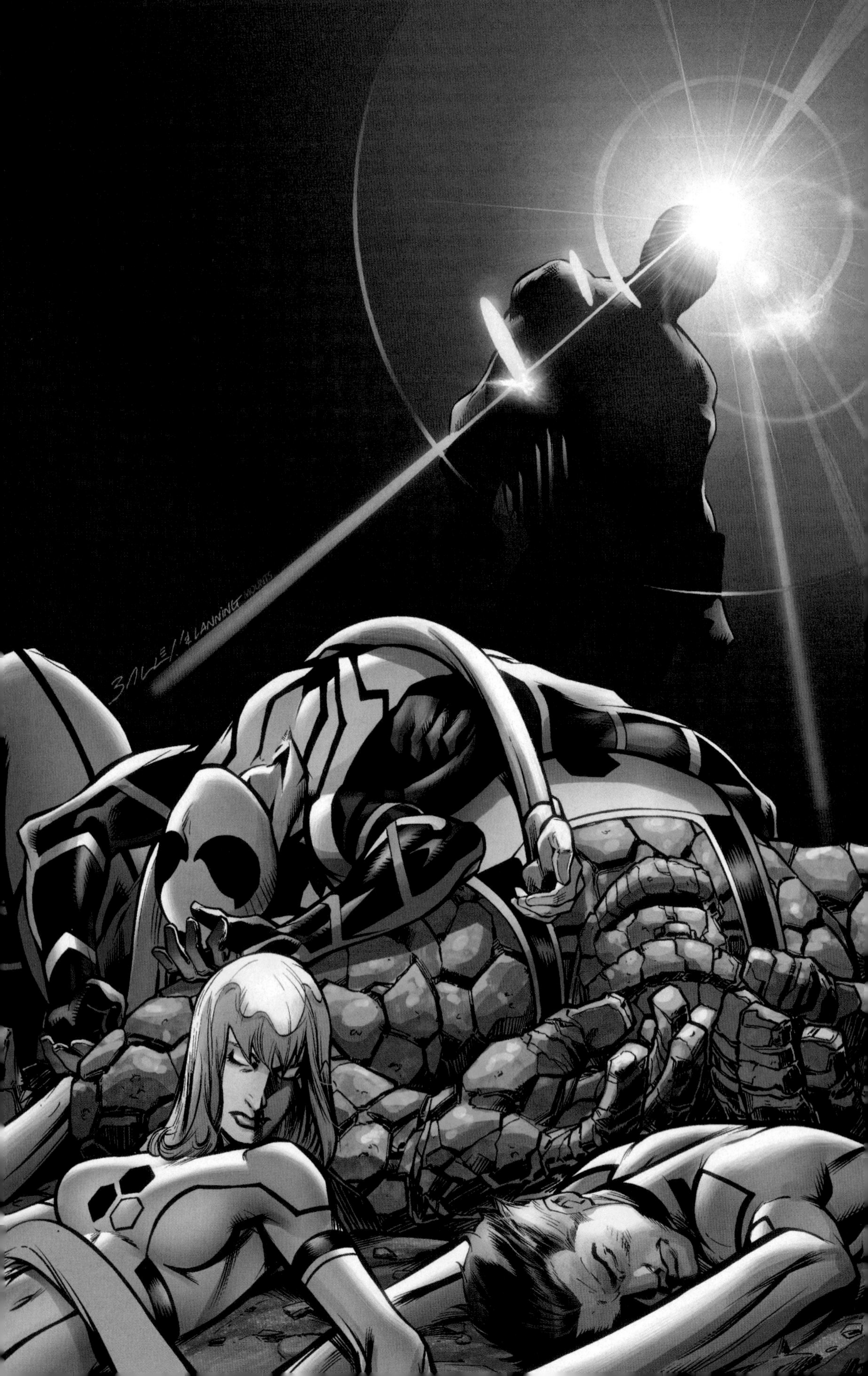

#1 VARIANT COVER: DANIEL ACUÑA

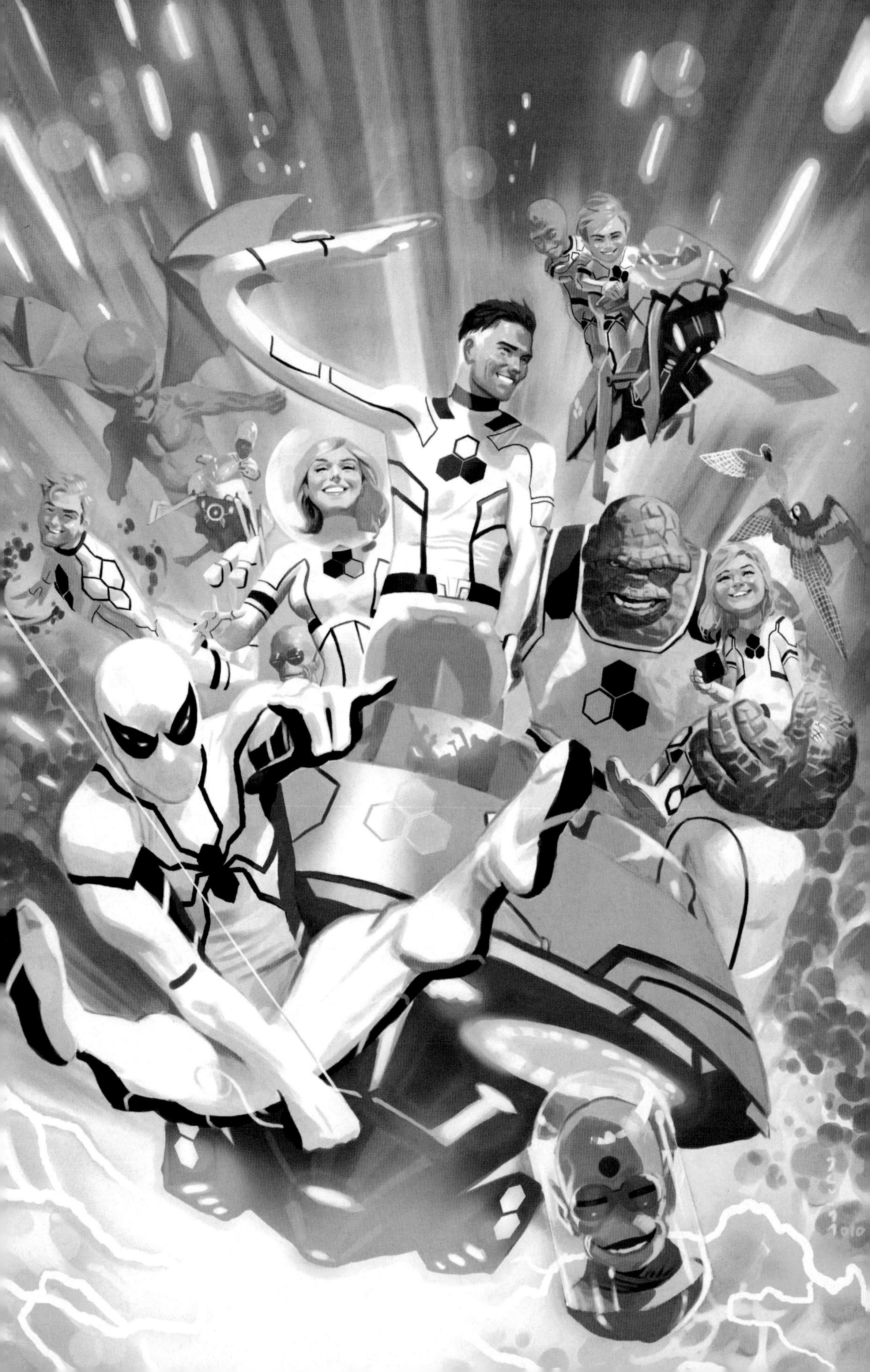

#1 VARIANT COVER: STAN GOLDBERG, JOE SINNOTT & VAL STAPLES

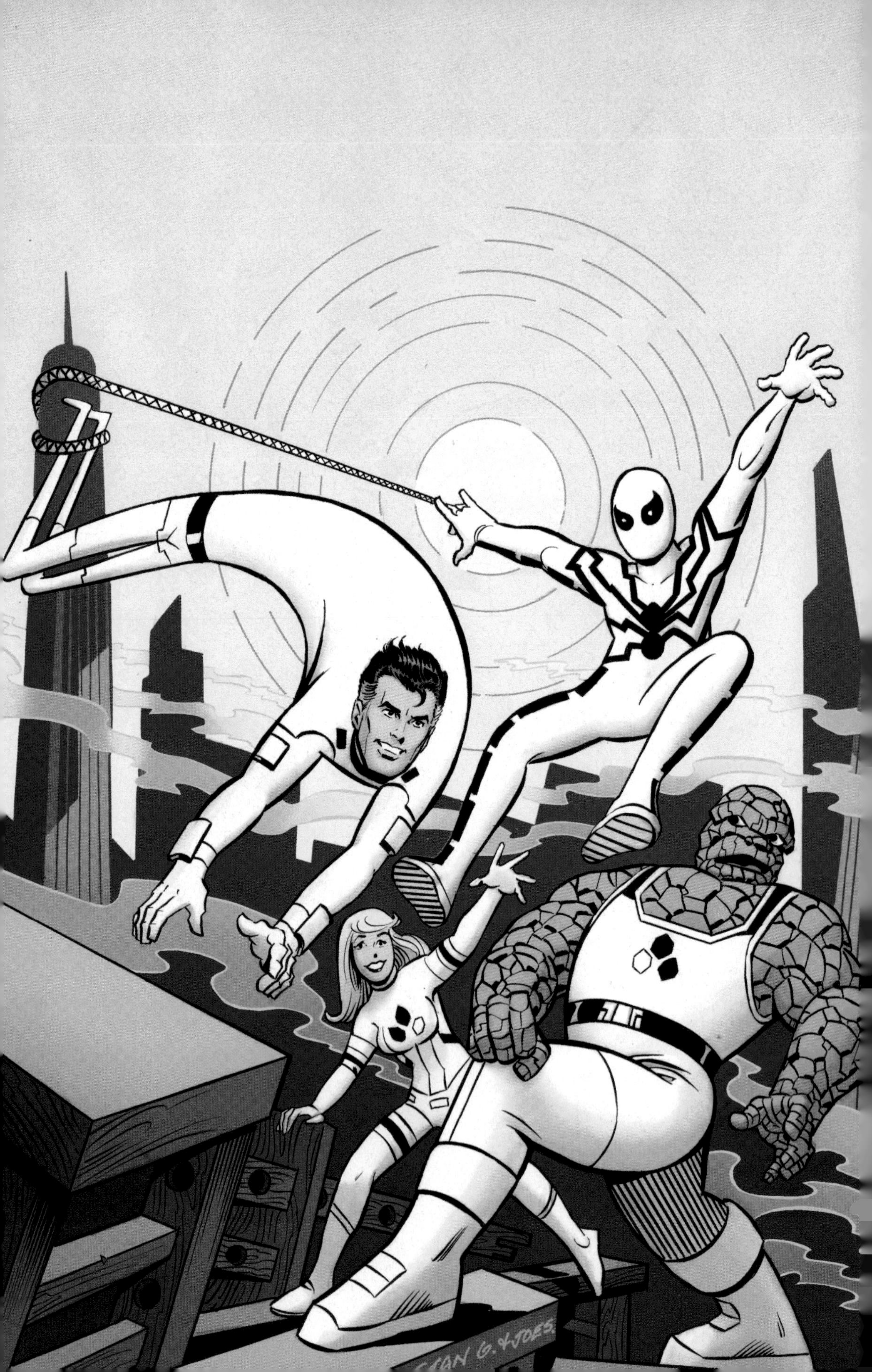

#1 50TH ANNIVERSARY VARIANT COVER: GERALD PAREL

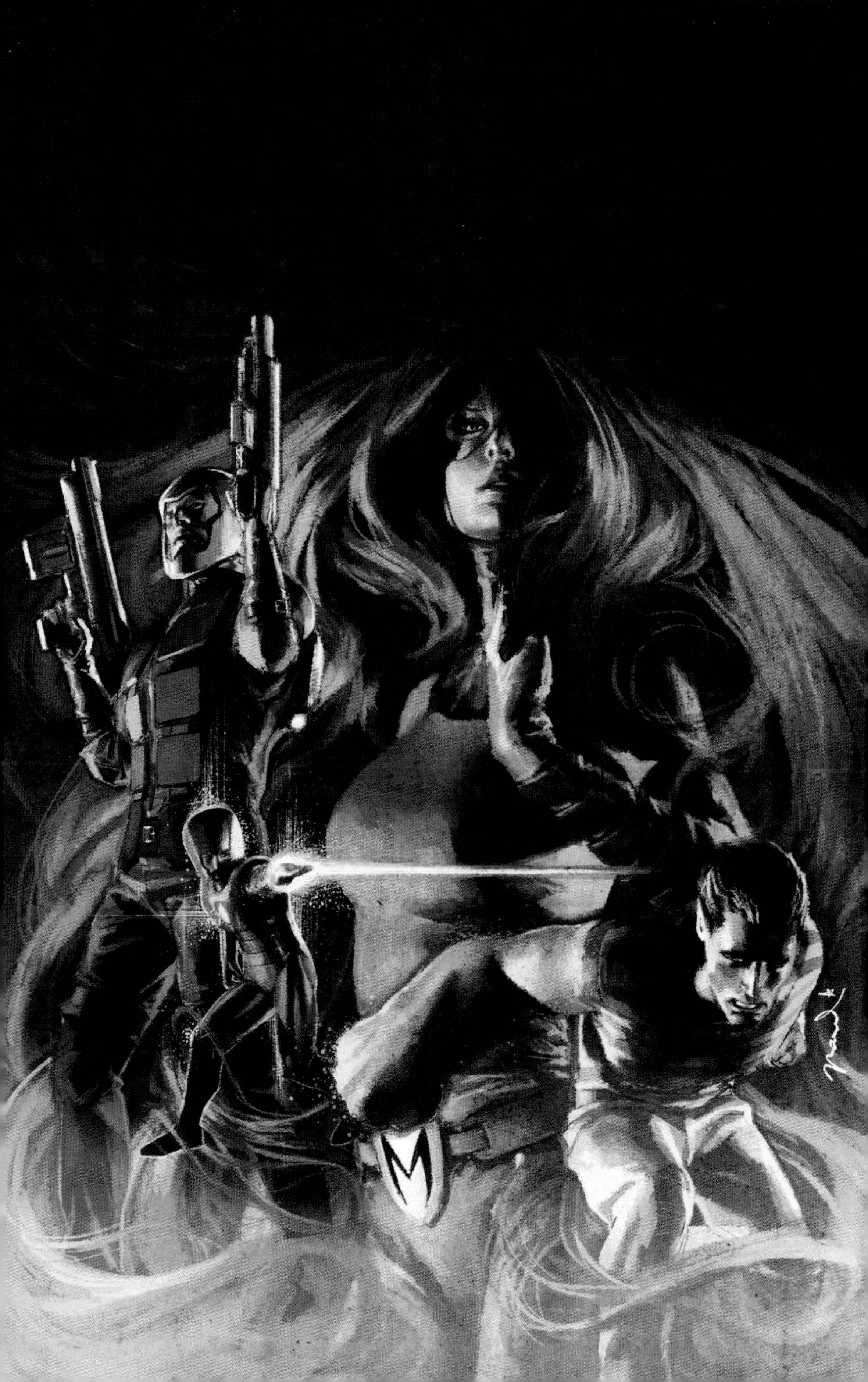

#1 2ND PRINTING VARIANT COVER: ED MCGUINNESS & CHRIS SOTOMAYOR

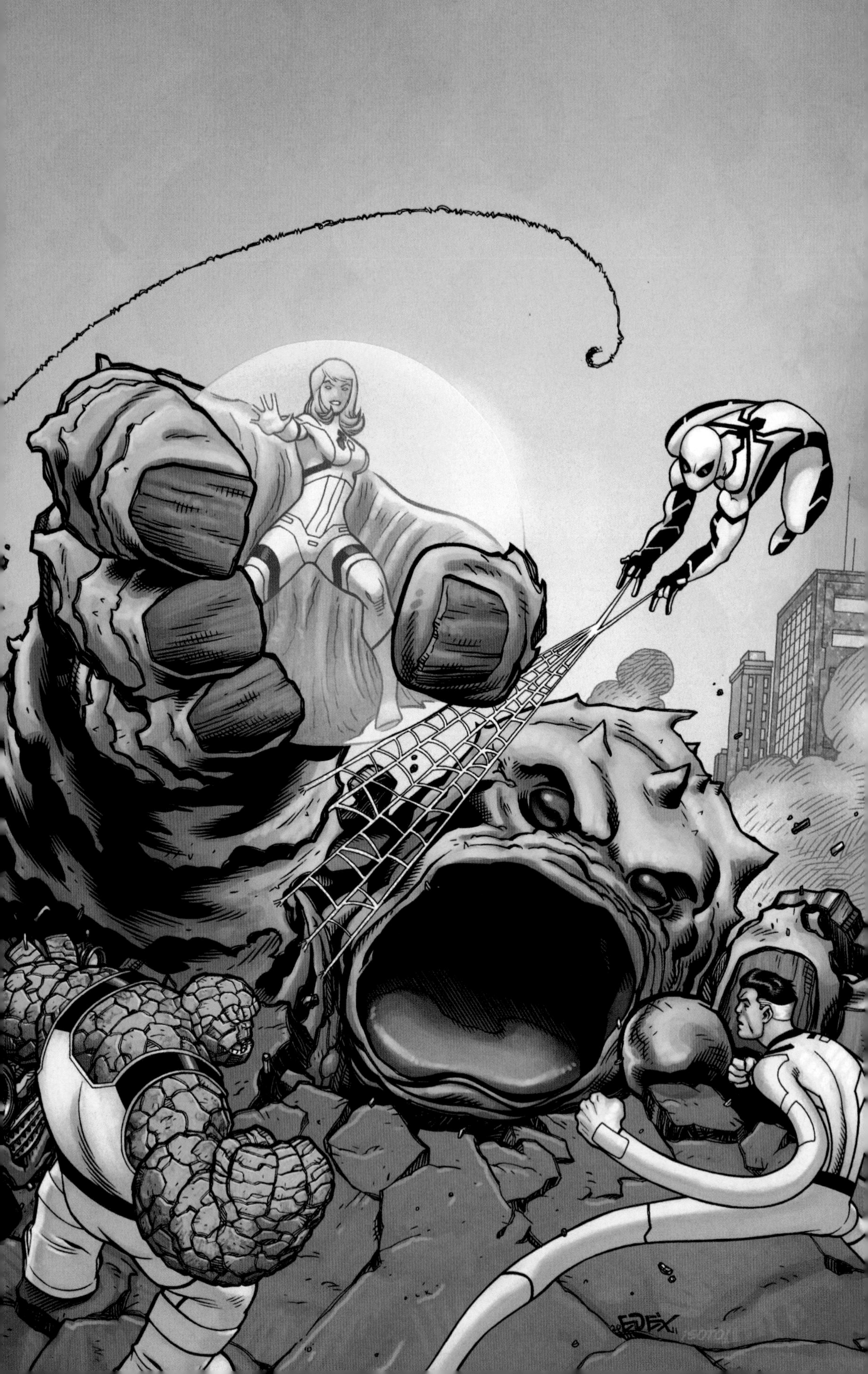

#1 CHARACTER VARIANT COVER: **MARKO DJURDJEVIC**

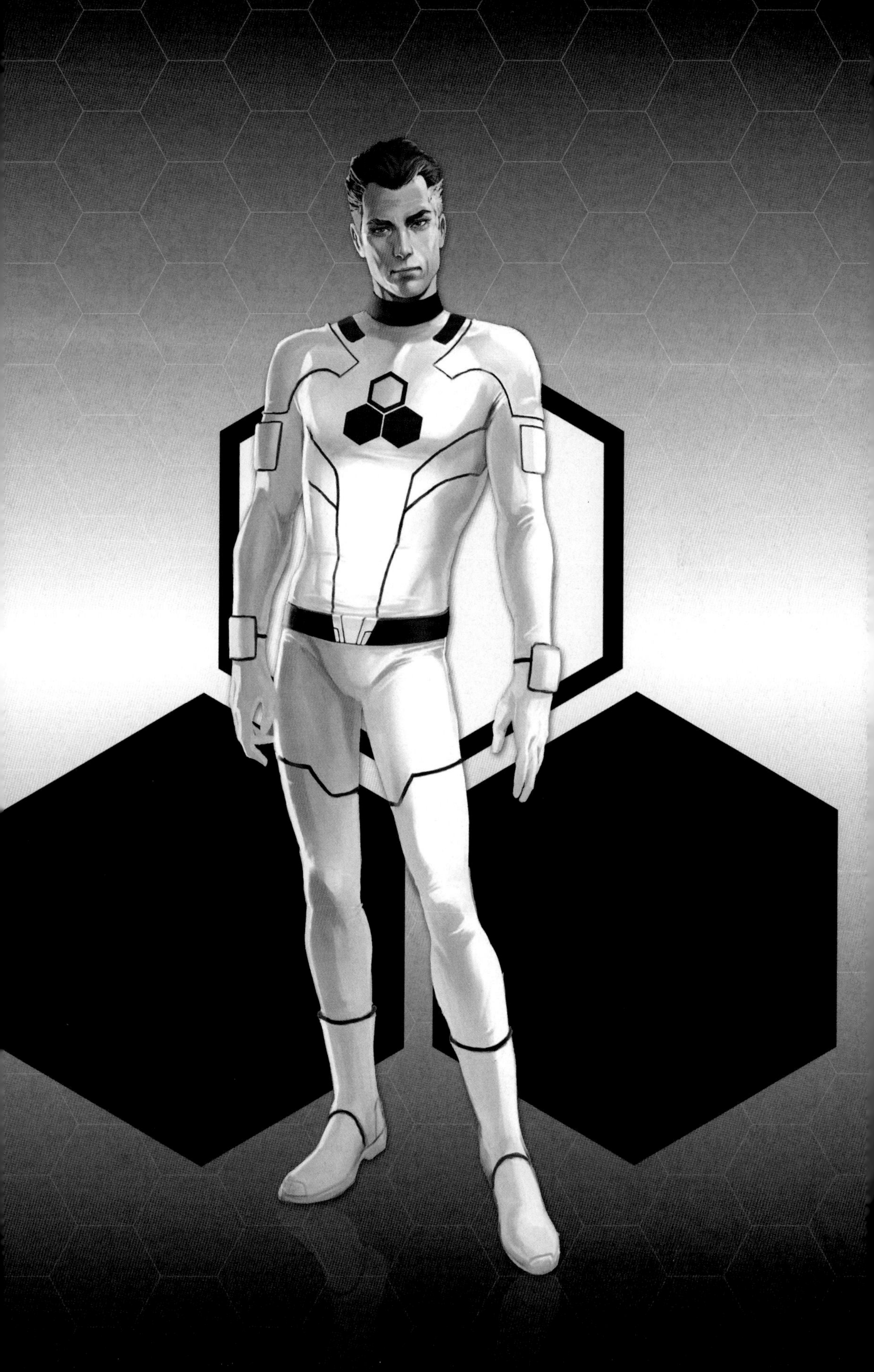

#2 CHARACTER VARIANT COVER: **MARKO DJURDJEVIC**

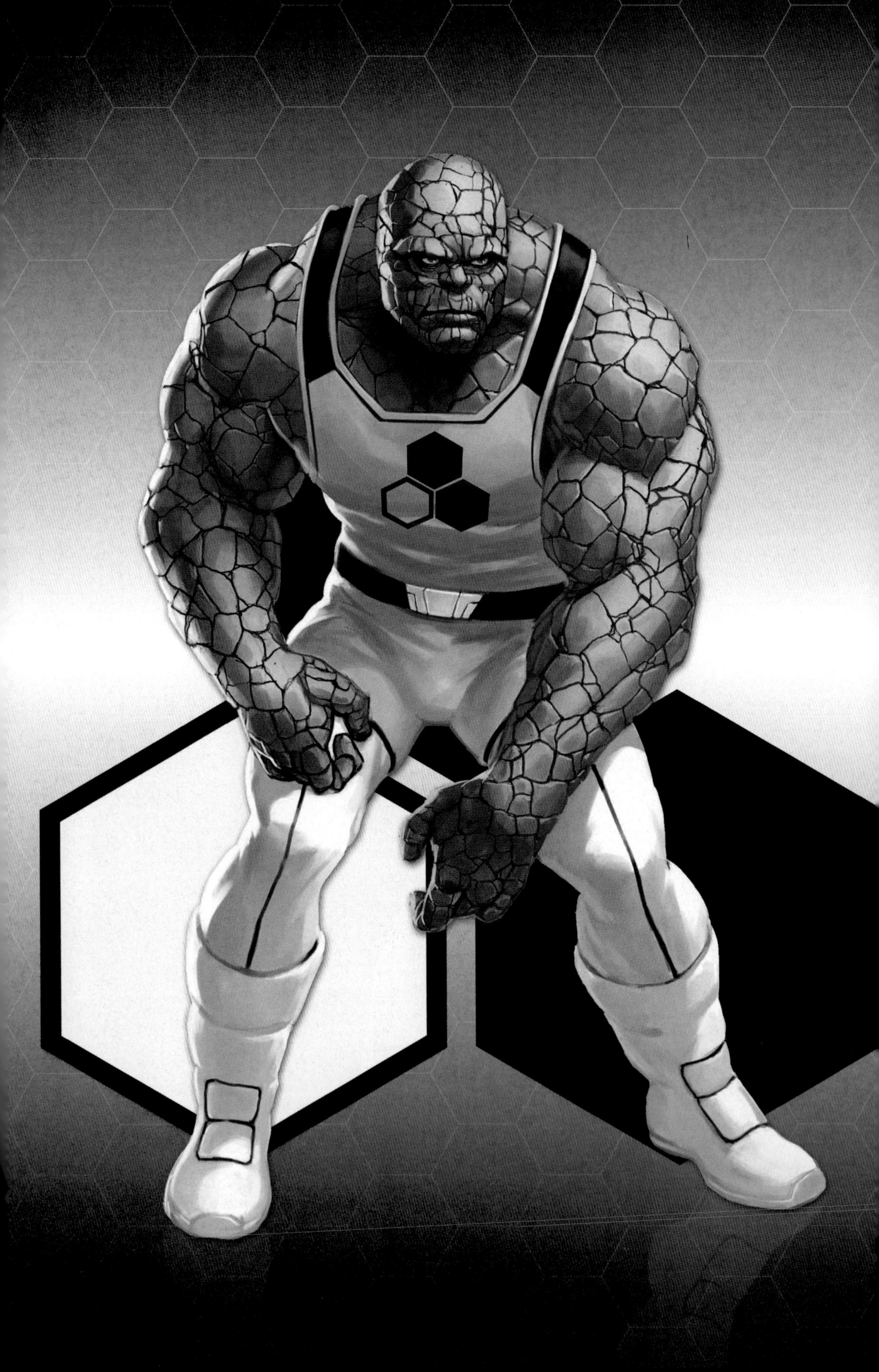

#3 CHARACTER VARIANT COVER: **MARKO DJURDJEVIC**

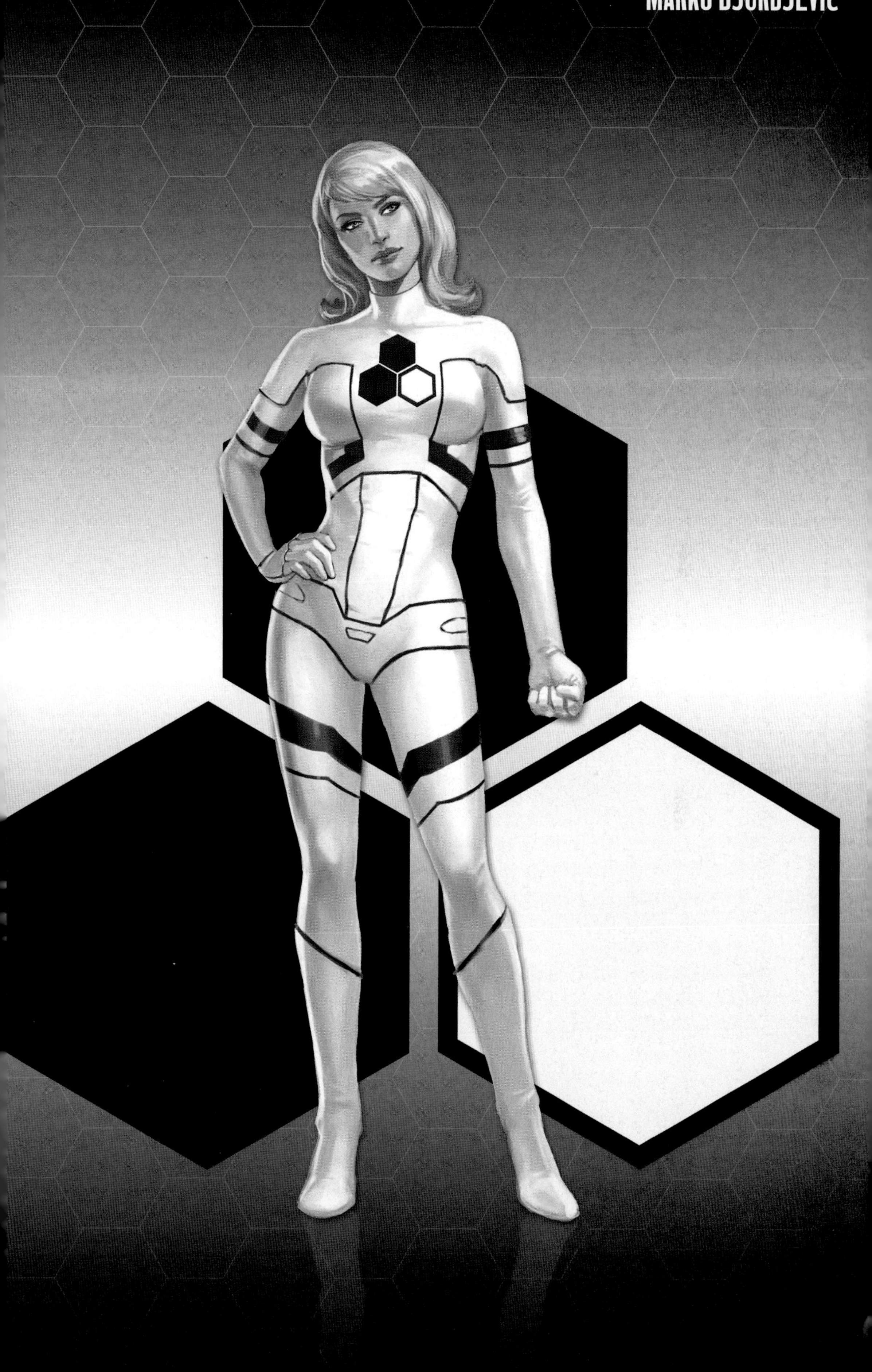

#4 CHARACTER VARIANT COVER: **MARKO DJURDJEVIC**

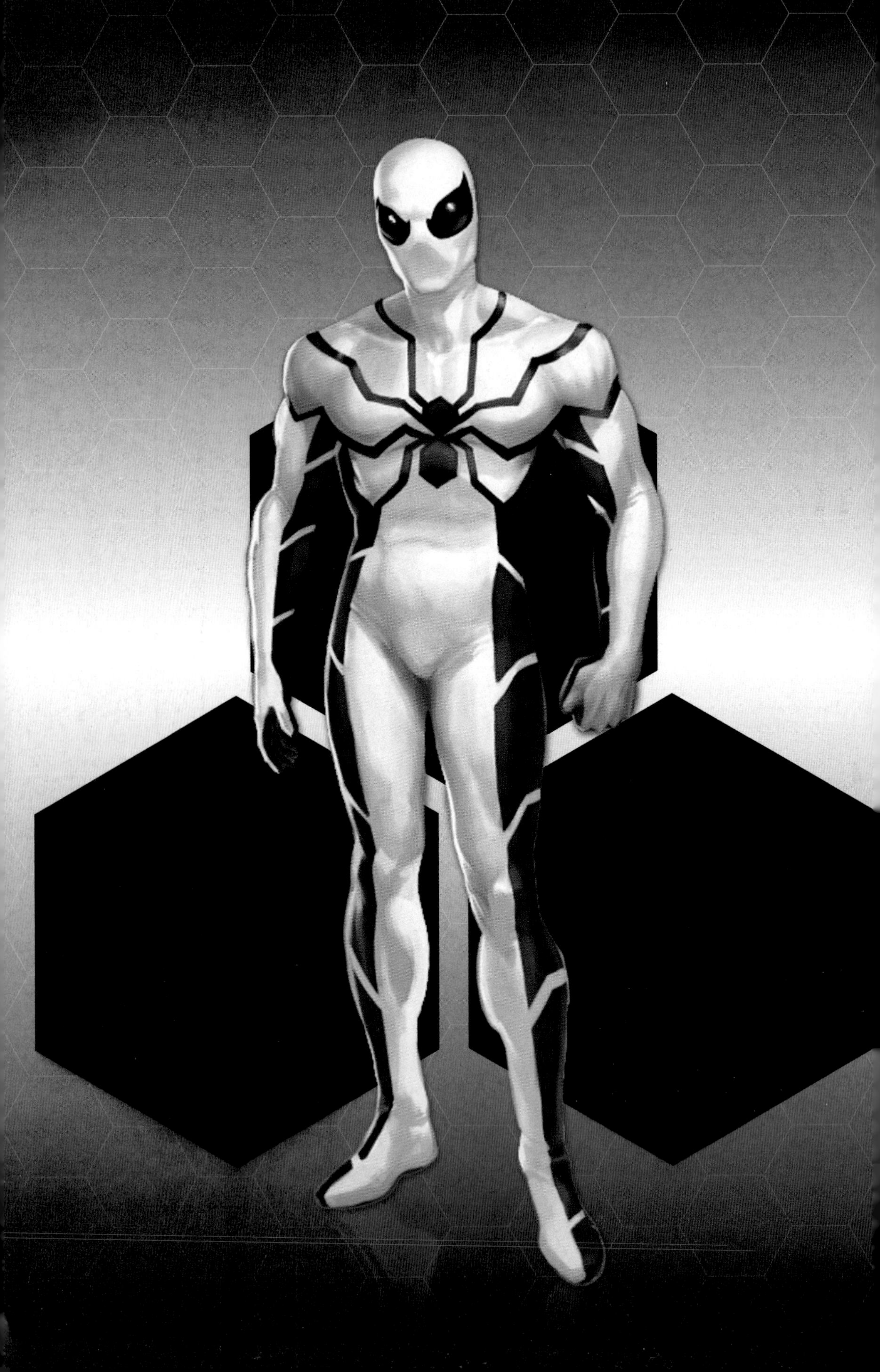